See My Body, See Me

"In the wake of ongoing church abuse scandal and the reality of sexual trauma in our society, Pamela Engelbert provides a comprehensive pastoral resource for church leaders. Academically researched, biblically grounded, and thoroughly Pentecostal, *See My Body, See Me* is at once sober, practical, and hopeful. It's both a vindication of local church efforts to address trauma in community and a call to wield Pentecostal practices to facilitate and deepen the work of healing."

—JOSEPH LEAR, pastor of preaching and theology,
Resurrection Assembly of God

"This is a must-read for Pentecostals! Sexual violence has too long been swept under the rug in our tradition. Pamela Engelbert's book does not shy away from the trauma experienced by women but offers a path forward toward healing. This is a book for survivors and their families, for counselors, and for pastors who wish to participate in Christ's healing ministry."

—MELISSA L. ARCHER, professor of biblical studies,
Southeastern University

"This book is a powerful call to attune to the lived experiences of Pentecostal survivors of sexual violence and to become those who can enter their unique journeys and companion them effectively through specific healing praxes. Pamela Engelbert skillfully weaves together theological, biblical, and psychological insights with the stories of survivor and counselor-participants. The result is a transformative and must-read resource for Pentecostal believers and their communities and for those providing care to them."

—HALEY R. FRENCH, LPC, assistant professor of professional
counseling, Oral Roberts University

"As we continue to discern how to navigate the reality of sexual violence in the church, Pamela Engelbert has written a masterful work that combines practical help for survivors of sexual violence and also a framework for those who lead in religious spaces to work to prevent sexual violence and to walk with survivors. I believe that Engelbert's work will bring healing to all who are impacted by the implications of sexual violence in our churches."

—JOY E. A. QUALLS, associate dean, Biola University

"Pamela Engelbert's book is a gem, bringing acute scholarship woven with her personal story and a cogent call for intentional awareness, grace, and healing. This book will be a welcome and needed resource for all those who have suffered such assault and for those in professional mental health and ministry roles—one that takes seriously her Christian and Pentecostal heritage. Get your copy of this book as soon as it is available!"

—GEORGE D. FESSLER, director of pastoral care,
SoCal Network Assemblies of God

See My Body, See Me

*A Pentecostal Perspective
on Healing from Sexual Violence*

PAMELA F. ENGELBERT

Foreword by
KIMBERLY ERVIN ALEXANDER

◆PICKWICK *Publications* · Eugene, Oregon

SEE MY BODY, SEE ME
A Pentecostal Perspective on Healing from Sexual Violence

Copyright © 2024 Pamela F. Engelbert. All rights reserved. Except for brief quotations in critical publications or reviews, no part of this book may be reproduced in any manner without prior written permission from the publisher. Write: Permissions, Wipf and Stock Publishers, 199 W. 8th Ave., Suite 3, Eugene, OR 97401.

Pickwick Publications
An Imprint of Wipf and Stock Publishers
199 W. 8th Ave., Suite 3
Eugene, OR 97401

www.wipfandstock.com

PAPERBACK ISBN: 979-8-3852-0479-3
HARDCOVER ISBN: 979-8-3852-0480-9
EBOOK ISBN: 979-8-3852-0481-6

Cataloguing-in-Publication data:

Names: Engelbert, Pamela F., author. | Alexander, Kimberly Ervin, foreword.

Title: See my body, see me : a pentecostal perspective on healing from sexual violence / Pamela F. Engelbert ; foreword by Kimberly Ervin Alexander.

Description: Eugene, OR : Pickwick Publications, 2024 | Includes bibliographical references.

Identifiers: ISBN 979-8-3852-0479-3 (paperback) | ISBN 979-8-3852-0480-9 (hardcover) | ISBN 979-8-3852-0481-6 (ebook)

Subjects: LCSH: Spiritual healing. | Pentecostalism. | Sex crimes—Moral and ethical aspects. | Sex crimes—Religious aspects—Pentecostalism. | Violence—Religious aspects—Christianity. | Sexual abuse victims—Rehabilitation. | Church work with victims of crimes—Pentecostalism. | Church and social problems.

Classification: BR1644 .E64 2024 (print) | BR1644 .E64 (ebook)

All Scripture quotations, unless otherwise indicated, are from the NET Bible® https://netbible.com copyright ©1996, 2019 used with permission from Biblical Studies Press, L.L.C. All rights reserved.

Scripture quotations marked MSG are taken from The Message, copyright © 1993, 2002, 2018 by Eugene H. Peterson. Used by permission of NavPress. All rights reserved. Represented by Tyndale House Publishers.

To survivor and counselor participants:

You have been my teachers.
Your willingness and courage to share your stories
has changed me.

Table of Contents

List of Illustrations xi
Foreword by Kimberly Ervin Alexander xiii
Preface xvii
Acknowledgments xix
List of Abbreviations xxii

PART ONE: How Pentecostals Heal from Sexual Violence

1. See, Hear, Believe the Story: The Introduction 3
2. The Body's Telling of the Story 25
3. Telling the Story as Healing 50
4. Telling the Unique Story 76
5. Telling the Story of False Gods 105

PART TWO: Providing a Safe Place for Survivors

6. Listen to My Story 137
7. Wait with Me in My Story 165
8. Learn from My Story 191
9. The Theory of Relational Trauma Training: The Conclusion 215

APPENDIX A: *The Process of Identifying, Collecting, and Coding Data* 227
APPENDIX B: *Interview Protocol for Survivors* 229
APPENDIX C: *Interview Protocol for Counselors* 232
Bibliography 235

List of Illustrations

Figure 1. Eight elements of the theory of Relational Trauma Training 216

Figure 2. Interconnection of the elements 218

Foreword

Kimberly Ervin Alexander

RECENTLY, AS YET ANOTHER scandal involving sexual assaults and cover-ups emerged out of a prominent and influential Charismatic ministry, I remembered a female student from years ago who excitedly shared of her acceptance as an intern there. I then recalled that when she returned from the experience, she was quite obviously disillusioned, though I didn't know why. A couple of weeks ago, feeling prompted by the Spirit, after a long period with little contact, I reached out to her and simply said, "I can't help but think of you and hope that disillusionment wasn't related to sexual abuse." Sadly, she affirmed that it was, and that it had taken years of therapy for her to deal with it; but also, that the latest news had been triggering her lingering trauma.

I wish I could write that her story was unique in my experience. But over the past forty years that I've been involved in the profession of teaching—with all of those years being spent in Pentecostal-Charismatic institutions, from middle and high schools to doctoral programs—girl after girl, and woman after woman have met with me and quietly and painfully shared their stories of sexual assault and the resulting trauma. In nearly all these cases, the abuse occurred in what should have been safe spaces: homes, schools, Pentecostal churches and universities, the military. In a few cases, as women in seminary classes—triggered by news of a prominent politician joking about inflicting sexual assault on women and the ensuing making of excuses by Christian leaders and ministers—tearfully shared their own stories of pain, men in the class, too, wept and were prompted to share the stories of witnessing the abuse of their mothers or the pain their wives had shared with them.

After all these years, what I *haven't* heard or read, is anywhere near a proportionate number of responses and acknowledgements from Pentecostal leaders; much less, public announcements of policy changes, implementation of training for ministers in the area of trauma counseling, or even publication of legal guidelines for reporting criminal activity.

It is incredibly ironic that a movement such as the Pentecostal-Charismatic one—that has been distinctive exactly because of its healing theology and practice, its emphasis on holiness of life, and its (at least on paper) endorsement of the Spirit's outpouring on daughters—would so obviously neglect to both call out the *sin* of sexual assault and intentionally pray for the healing of those who've been sinned against. As Engelbert points out in her introductory chapter, in a 2018 survey of ministers, only 24 percent of Pentecostal pastors surveyed reported that they were more inclined to preach on issues surrounding sexual and domestic violence, compared to pastors in other traditions where holiness and healing do not figure prominently in their theology or practice.

In the wake of the #MeToo movement and the accompanying silence from Pentecostal denominational leaders, in 2018, female scholars from the Society for Pentecostal Studies gathered to discuss a formal response. When over one hundred gathered at the 10:00 PM meeting—including quite a number of male scholars—woman after woman rose to share their own stories and the heartbreaking responses (or lack thereof) from their Pentecostal communities of faith. The result of that meeting was the crafting of a formal statement—titled "A Call to Redeem Our Bodies: Weeping in Sexual Brokenness, Walking in Sexual Holiness" that challenged Pentecostal institutions to act regarding education and training, legal responsibility, and resourcing. Additionally, the scholars called for ". . . Pentecostal and Charismatic churches to reclaim the legacy of holiness through which their prophetic witness flows by becoming *houses of healing and cities of refuge for the abused and traumatized instead of safe havens for violators who escape justice and their own restoration*" (italics added).[1] A further call emerging that night was for scholars to write and publish within their disciplines—biblical studies, historical and theological studies, and practical theology—in order to contribute to this reclamation. That call has been answered by a number of scholars since 2018, with the entire society responding when the 2020/21 program, under the

---

1. Pentecostal Sisters Too, "Call to Redeem Our Bodies," under sub-heading "A Call to Act."

leadership of Melissa Archer, focused on global violence against women. Engelbert's invaluable work is a direct response to that prophetic call.

As a historical theologian whose work has been at the intersection of recovering Pentecostal women's voices and reconstructing Pentecostal healing theology and practice, it has long been my passion to listen to what women tell us about their experiences of healing, deliverance, and transformation. I want to retrieve the words of their transformative and prophetic testimony and preaching. But what is all but impossible to retrieve and recover, are those stories of healing from sexual assault. Do they exist? I am sure they do—as I read between the lines of their stories. But, like women's stories for millennia, they have been—at best, suppressed and hidden; at worst, these women have been labeled as Jezebels, or, with the age-old way of writing off women: as hysterics or as unstable.

As a historical theologian, I know that for centuries, women have been both the recipient of the healing of their bodies—and *in* their bodies—and the agents of healing for others. As they've been relegated to spaces of nurture and healing, sitting with and listening to those who suffer, they've come to identify with the sufferers, and with the suffering Jesus.[2] I know that, as desert mothers listened and offered counsel, they became "lovers of souls," as Mary C. Earle has noted.[3] So, when Engelbert calls for listening to stories of trauma as a way to bring healing of traumatized minds, emotions, spirits, and bodies, it rings true.

As a Pentecostal who has her own stories of sexual harassment and assault, but who also has my own testimonies of healing, both instantaneous and over time, I am convinced that healing from sexual trauma is possible. Like Engelbert, I believe Pentecostal and Charismatic Christians are uniquely traditioned and positioned to bring healing to hurting women (as well as men). It is not a coincidence that our go-to biblical "shared experience" of healing prayer is the story of the woman whose hemorrhaging body was healed by touching Jesus, and who was restored as a *daughter* of a community that had shamed and shunned her.[4] We believe that divine healing is provided in the atoning work of Jesus—whose incarnation, death, and resurrection began the *process* of recovering all that was lost in Eden. Our commitments to testimony, tarrying prayer, waiting on the Lord, listening to the Spirit, and prayer for healing are all practices that situate us ideally for this time.

2. Alexander, "Healing in the History of Christianity."
3. Earle, *Desert Mothers*, 10.
4. Alexander, "'With Blessings They Cover the Bitterness,'" 46.

See, hear, and believe the stories of these women. See, hear, and believe the wise instruction of Pam Engelbert as she offers a real way forward for the Pentecostal (and other) communities of faith, where women are holding up half the sky, even in their pain. May we listen, learn, and pray to the God of all comfort, our Healer.

Preface

IF YOU ARE READING this preface, you possibly share my concern about the problem of sexual violence. Additionally, like me, you may be a pentecostal who wonders how pentecostals heal from said violence. This was my question, which came to the forefront of my mind in 2018 in the form of a call to conduct this research. As a survivor of sexual violence, I doubted in the beginning about the appropriateness of my researching this topic. However, the wise words of a former professor quieted my uncertainty: "God gives us questions through our experiences."

Yet, as you scan a few pages, you may be wondering if this book is only for survivors and/or licensed counselors. This book is actually for anyone who is interested in how pentecostals heal from sexual violence. More narrowly, it is geared to those who know a survivor and who desire to offer support. This implies it is for pastors, instructors, counselors, relatives, spouses, friends, survivors, etc. who may want to help other survivors.

You also may be questioning if this book is a how-to manual with specific steps on how pentecostals heal from sexual violence. I admit that as an American, I too appreciate prescribed points or specific stages. They create the illusion of control as we attempt to meet needs for efficiency, order, and empowerment. Such stages generate sameness and thereby add a layer of predictability and security. But in actuality, life is messy. Although there were many commonalities in the healing journeys reflected in this work, surprisingly, one of the first things I learned while completing this project was a paradoxical commonality of uniqueness.

Perhaps an analogy pertaining to the content of this book may be beneficial. The subject material in the following chapters is similar to a mosaic. It contains several variegated pieces being placed together in order to describe a few pentecostals' healing journeys from sexual violence.

These pieces include physical, relational, spiritual, cognitive, sexual, and emotional aspects of a human being—that is, the whole person. As each person is different, so each of these aspects is diverse from person to person. As in a mosaic, survivors' pieces are not identical in shape, color, and size as they vary for each survivor. Yet, also like a mosaic, beauty appears when the different pieces begin to come together as the survivor moves toward wholeness.

In many ways, the title *See My Body, See Me* intrinsically contains a dual call to see beauty. It first beckons pentecostals to see beyond the body of a person to seeing a person's entire being. It is a call for us as pentecostals to be increasingly identified as viewing persons, not as objects to be consumed or jettisoned, but as whole persons with many parts. In doing so, we simultaneously will be answering the second portion of the call. As pentecostals participate in Christ's healing ministry to survivors through our seeing them, the world will also see beyond the pentecostal church to seeing the Healer. In this light, *See My Body, See Me* becomes the following charge for us as pentecostals: May our healing response to survivors be so Christlike that the world sees not only the church, Christ's body, but Jesus himself. Therefore, may it be said of us that we see the beauty of whole persons in such a way that the world may see the healing beauty of Jesus Christ.

While this book is an invitation for the church to participate in Christ's ministry of healing to those who have experienced sexual violence, it is also my hope that it will foster healing movement in you, as the reader, through the stories you are about to hear. That is to say, I hope that this book may participate in Christ's healing ministry in you as it has in me.

In it together,
Pam Engelbert
Summer 2023

Acknowledgments

It may be exceedingly obvious to say that this project could not have been completed without the help of others. But that does not make it less true. Books are not written in isolation even though the writer spends oodles and oodles of time alone. Yes, it is accurate to say that writers regularly labor in solitude as they carefully craft sentences, rearrange words, and wade through synonyms (and then secretly break out in a dance when the ideal word is found). Yet, without others, whether they be conversation partners via other books, emails, phone calls, or face to face, this book could not have been written. There may be only one name listed as the author, but this author did not complete the task solo without having an unseen choir in a supportive role. The following are a few of the other unseen voices:

I am grateful for Wipf & Stock who saw the importance of this project by accepting my proposal, providing the necessary feedback, and publishing the manuscript.

I am very appreciative to Chris Jarosh and Robin Weaver for helping me with my images. I am so grateful that you were willing to use your skills and technological knowledge to assist me in tweaking and formatting the illustrations. Since my skills are quite limited in this regard, I simply could not have accomplished this without your help.

I am thankful for so many of you who helped by spreading the word about this qualitative research project when I needed participants. Many individuals posted and reposted on social media or personally contacted others to inform them about this opportunity. You were a vital part of this research as you made it easier for participants to hear about the project.

For Carla Dahl, thank you for taking the time to provide feedback and insight after I had constructed a proposal. You helped me to see that being a survivor myself did not disqualify me but qualified me to conduct this research. This nourished my confidence.

For Marcia Clarke and Susan Maros, I am exceedingly appreciative of your support for this project, which was exhibited each time you accepted my practical theological proposals to present papers at meetings for the Society for Pentecostal Studies (SPS). This offered me opportunities to introduce material from four of the chapters to other pentecostals.

I am very grateful for those of you who read portions (e.g., papers for SPS or chapters) or entire drafts of this book, offering feedback: Melissa Archer, Bill Bray, Bob Cook, Carla Dahl, Haley French, Annise Herbin, Susan Maros, Martin Mittelstadt, and Meg Robsahm.

I am thankful to Melissa Archer, George Fessler, Haley French, Joseph Lear, and Joy Qualls who believed in me and this project by personally endorsing this book.

For Bill, who was available when this work, not surprisingly, produced my own triggers. Thank you for listening and normalizing my experiences, enabling me to continue to listen to the stories. I also thank you for pointing me to some important resources that were used in various chapters, including books from your personal library.

For Friday night Journey Church, particularly Dave Ruckman, who repeatedly prayed for me to have insight, clarity, creativity, and inspiration and frequently asked, "How is the book coming?"

Thank you, Kim Alexander, for believing in me. I remember how encouraging you were when I first mentioned in 2019 at the SPS meeting in Lanham, Massachusetts about my plan to research how pentecostals heal from sexual violence. Your immediate response was: "This is so needed." I clung to those words when things particularly seemed to become bogged down (as we know they do while writing).

I am deeply, deeply grateful to the participants, both survivors and counselors, who demonstrated courage by contacting me, a stranger, and agreeing to tell your stories to someone who is unknown. This book would not have existed without your willingness and your courage. And I would not be the person I am today as your stories continue to change me.

To my husband Lincoln, the words of one small paragraph seem immensely inadequate for expressing my gratitude for your help during these years of my laboring over the writing of this book. You were the first person to pour over each word, sentence, and chapter. I am deeply indebted to your willingness to be committed to wade through each page, not only once but multiple times. Your encouragement in this regard granted me a sense of security and confidence. Your dedication to me, and thereby this project, tangibly illustrates that you are definitely my biggest fan.

To Father God, the Son Lord Jesus Christ, and the Comforter the Holy Spirit, this project would not have begun without your invitation to participate in your healing ministry in the world through this research. I am grateful for the privilege to conduct research and engage in writing about such an important topic. Words seem insufficient to communicate my thankfulness (and at times downright giddiness) of fulfilling a childhood dream to become a writer. You have taught me and changed me through this research, teaching me about your character and molding me to be more of a reflection of your image.

List of Abbreviations

CDC	Centers for Disease Control and Prevention
DBT	Dialectical Behavior Therapy
EMDR	Eye Movement Desensitization and Reprocessing
KJV	King James Version
NAMI	The National Alliance on Mental Illness
NET	New English Translation
NSVRC	National Sexual Violence Resource Center
NT	New Testament
PTSD	Post Traumatic Stress Disorder
RAINN	The Rape, Abuse & Incest National Network
SPS	Society for Pentecostal Studies
WHO	World Health Organization

PART ONE

How Pentecostals Heal from Sexual Violence

1

See, Hear, Believe the Story: The Introduction

God is what I have now. He knows. He sees. He hears. He believes. As a survivor, to be seen, to be heard, to be believed, those are super important in the life of a survivor.

—Elizabeth, a survivor-participant

Listen to some survivors and believe them when they talk about how long that journey has been, how difficult it's been, and how painful it's been.

—Jade, a survivor-participant

Sexual violence is real, as we all know, hopefully know.

—Dominique, a survivor-participant

I AM THE YOUNGEST of three children, having been born into a White, middle-class family of five. My upbringing had similarities to that of an only child since my sister and brother are eleven and seven years older than I, respectively.[1] I was an inquisitive, energetic, and congenial child, who preferred jeans and T-shirts to frills and lace.

I am a farmer's daughter.

---

1. For more on personality traits related to birth order, see Richardson, *Family Ties That Bind*, chapter 7.

I was raised on the farm on which my father was born. This means I am the product of a three-generational farming environment with a strong German work ethic. I learned early that farm work was not a nine-to-five job. Instead, it was an integral part of every walking, talking, healthy family member, from child to adult. Therefore, whether I was a child helping in the sheep barn, a school-age youth pulling weeds in the garden, or a teen driving large farm implements in the field, I was involved in the day-to-day operations of the farm.

I am part of a Classical Pentecostal family.[2]

Some may presume that my Midwestern, Christian upbringing was like a Noman Rockwell painting. My family gathered for devotions in the living room each evening, and my parents prayed together at breakfast each morning. On Sundays, we were dressed in our Sunday-best while scrambling to be at church on time (we rarely were) for both Sunday morning and Sunday evening services. In church, I heard stories from the Bible and memorized Bible verses in Sunday School, and I joined the saints praying at the altar after the conclusion of the evening sermon. I attended my first pentecostal kid's camp at eight years old, and two years later, I was baptized in the Holy Spirit while attending such a camp. During my teen years, I experienced the exuberance of pentecostal youth meetings and teen camp, and at some point, I sensed that God was calling me into full-time ministry. My mother's prayers had been answered.

I am a survivor of sexual violence.

Despite my family living on a farm thirty miles from town, I was not completely sheltered from childhood sexual abuse. As with a majority of survivors, I knew the perpetrator; he was a pentecostal, a family friend. I told no one about my experience. In time, it slipped away from my immediate awareness, but its impact did not go by unnoticed.

Residing in the country approximately twenty miles from school meant I had to ride a big yellow bus, one hour each way to and from school. My extended time on the school bus naturally translated into my forming a friendship with the bus driver. After school one afternoon, as the buses awaited their young passengers to board, I was sitting in the front seat with another girl when my bus driver asked why my personality had changed. According to him, I had become less talkative and increasingly sad. His question caught me off guard, so I mumbled an

---

2. I use small *p* pentecostal in this book, which refers to all classifications of pentecostals and Charismatics. Exceptions to this are my quoting other authors or my identifying others as Classical Pentecostals. For more clarification, see below.

evasive answer. I doubt at the time that I fully understood or remembered what had happened to me, but I was later to learn that he was not the only one to note my altered persona. After I was married, I informed my brother about the sexual violence. He told me a similar story of how he had observed a personality change in me, but he had said nothing.

My healing journey from said sexual violence began with remembering.

For approximately ten years, I was unaware of my deep, internal injury. As a child, I was emotionally incapable of healing the hidden wound within me, but I coped with it the best way I knew: I attempted to forget. I buried the sexually abused and shamed parts of me. I dissociated. Unbeknown to me, the wound was oozing out of me in a myriad of ways. It manifested most distinctively through self-protective strategies such as emotionally overreacting, people-pleasing, and/or being a perfectionist. These strategies served as my protectors[3] while simultaneously masking profound longings for connection, safety, and security—the parched needs within me. Eventually, the incident reappeared from the shadows, the murky recesses of my mind. When it emerged, it played frame by frame, like a movie in my mind. My adult part stared in shock and disbelief at the identity of that little girl: I was that girl.

I am a pentecostal, and I believe in divine healing.

My pursuit of healing began shortly after remembering. Amidst my shock, I approached a trusted pentecostal for help. After telling the person my story, I was led through a technique of healing of the memories, which involved imagining the sexual abuse while Christ was present with me. Despite this therapeutic session, doubts plagued my mind about being healed; however, the person insisted, "You are healed. Do not let Satan bring this back into your life." Since these words implied I was to blame if the impact of the sexual abuse reappeared, I felt pressure to believe that I was healed.

A few years later, I was in a wedding gown and being escorted down the aisle by my parents to say "I do" to my soon-to-be husband. At that time, I remained naïve about what awaited me. Little did I know that being married would intensify the uncertainty of my being totally healed

---

3. This is employing Internal Family Systems (IFS), which describes protectors (internal parts of self) that emerge to guard us from the pain of the wound (the exile). See Riemersma, *Altogether You*. Jennifer Baldwin also notes that being a people-pleaser or a perfectionist are some of the socially acceptable ways by which the effects of trauma emerge. See Baldwin, *Trauma-Sensitive Theology*, loc. 560–61.

from sexual violence. In the end, I pursued counseling from a licensed psychologist, who was a pentecostal. After undergoing several months of therapy, which produced noticeable changes, the psychologist informed me: "You are healed." As I departed from therapy, I was confident that I was a changed woman. I self-assuredly stated, "I am completely healed from sexual violence." I unquestioningly believed it could not haunt me anymore.

My husband and I eventually answered God's call to minister overseas.[4] While we knew this ministry was in a patriarchal context, we were ignorant of its high rates of incest, domestic violence, and publicly posted pornography. Unfortunately, the unfamiliar environment heightened my lack of control and awakened the sexual trauma within my body. I felt intense shame as I became haunted by images and bodily sensations of sexual dirtiness, causing me to withdraw intimately from my husband. My shame mounted as I concluded I had lost my healing. I believed I was to blame for the sensations that were involuntarily plaguing my whole being.

Ultimately, I pursued help from another pentecostal, a licensed counselor who taught me about ongoing triggers. This new information was in direct contrast to my expectation of complete healing. I was surprised to learn how survivors usually re-visit the trauma throughout their lives when they experience triggers, such as major life events (e.g., marriage) or innocuous smells, sights, touch, or noises. These triggers are frequently unexpected, and they are beyond the survivor's control. Therefore, rather than my fearing the loss of healing, I now acknowledge that triggers will remain a part of my ongoing healing journey—they are the body's attempts to tell my story. And it is this story, my experience of healing from sexual violence, that has generated this inquiry on how other pentecostals heal from physical sexual violence and how pentecostals may provide a haven for said survivors.

See me. Hear me. Believe me.

SEEING, HEARING, AND BELIEVING IN A PROBLEM

Sadly, my story is not an isolated case. The reality of the statistics is grim. The World Health Organization (WHO) collected and analyzed data

---

4. During the application process, my previous psychologist had to assure the missionary sending board that I was completely healed from my experience of sexual violence.

(from 2000 to 2018) from "161 countries and areas" and discovered that "nearly 1 in 3, or 30%, of women have been subjected to physical and/or sexual violence by an intimate partner or non-partner or both" in their lives.[5] According to the Centers for Disease Control and Prevention (CDC), "Over half of women and almost 1 in 3 men have experienced sexual violence involving physical contact during their lifetimes. One in 4 women and about 1 in 26 men have experienced completed or attempted rape."[6] Regrettably, only a portion of all acts of sexual violence are reported. The Rape, Abuse & Incest National Network (RAINN) explains, "Only 310 out of every 1,000 sexual assaults are reported to police. That means more than 2 out of 3 go unreported."[7] In this light, it could be said that sexual violence is a silent epidemic. Even if sexual violence is discovered, it may be denied. Sigmund Freud, for example, altered his theory about the cause of hysteria in his female clients because he could not accept that sexual abuse was so rampant among households during the Victorian era.[8] The church, too, has been complicit. As Jennifer Erin

---

5. WHO, "Violence against Women," heading "Scope of the problem." In an online survey of approximately 1000 men and 1000 women commissioned by Stop Street Harassment and reported in February of 2018, "1 in 2 women (51%) and 1 in 6 men (17%) were sexually touched in an unwelcome way." Kearl, *Facts Behind the #MeToo Movement*, 7.

6. CDC, "Fast Facts: Preventing Sexual Violence," heading "How big is the problem?"

7. RAINN, "Criminal Justice System: Statistics," heading "The Majority of Sexual Assaults Are Not Reported to the Police." Using findings from a survey, Anna Brown reports, "Overall, relatively few Americans say that false reporting of incidents of sexual harassment or assault in the workplace are common, but close to half (46 percent) say it's extremely or very common for those who have had these types of experiences at work to *not* report them" (italics in original). Brown, "More Than Twice as Many Americans," 5. Courtney Ahrens in her qualitative study of survivors of rape learned that silence came as a result "of negative reactions including blaming, ineffective, insensitive, and inappropriate responses." Ahrens, "Being Silenced," 270. Judith Alpert, in writing about the silent transmission of intergenerational trauma, points out how persons are willing to talk about various other horrors committed during genocide but tend to remain silent on the reality of sexual violence inflicted on women. She calls rape "one of the most silenced atrocities committed during genocide." Alpert, "Enduring Mothers, Enduring Knowledge," 296–311.

8. Herman notes that when Freud published *The Aetiology of Hysteria*, he theorized that in each case of hysteria, premature childhood sexual experiences had occurred. However, Herman writes, "Within a year, Freud had privately repudiated the traumatic theory of the origins of hysteria. His correspondence makes clear that he was increasingly troubled by the radical social implications of his hypothesis. Hysteria was so common among women that if his patients' stories were true, . . . he would be forced to conclude that what he called 'perverted acts against children' were endemic, not only among the proletariat of Paris, where he had first studied hysteria, but also among the

Beste notes, the church has historically resisted believing the women and children who have reported sexual violence; it has downplayed the effects of the violence, or it has found fault with the victims.[9]

Fortunately, the problem of sexual violence is being seen, heard, and believed to a greater extent in recent years. The utilization of hashtags is one avenue that has brought sexual violence to the fore in Western culture. Hashtags are common on social media, with some hashtags challenging and changing culture more than others. They have the prospect of constructing an alternative, and perhaps more accurate, reality. The #MeToo Movement is one of those, bringing to light the stories of sexual violence, spawning similar hashtags of #ChurchToo and #pentecostalsisterstoo. In October of 2017, multiple women stepped forward with stories of sexual violence that were perpetrated by film producer Harvey Weinstein. In the middle of that same month, actress Alyssa Milano asked on social media for individuals to type #MeToo to demonstrate the extensive nature of sexual violence.[10] *The Facts behind the #MeToo Movement* reports that 45 percent of Facebook users in the United States "had at least one friend who had posted #MeToo on their timeline."[11] Such stories have now appeared in all sectors of life from Hollywood to the Olympics, from politics to religion, from universities to seminaries, and among pentecostals.

A month after the sexual assault stories surfaced about Weinstein, Hannah Paasch and Emily Joy gave rise to the #ChurchToo Movement, which centered on sexual violence that was perpetrated "by religious leaders, in religious communities and/or upheld by purported religious values."[12] Joy commented that the morning after she and Paasch typed #ChurchToo, thousands of individuals from around the world had tweeted about the hashtag, and their message box was overflowing.[13] In March of 2018, in response to the #MeToo Movement, stories were heard at the first gathering of #pentecostalsisterstoo at a meeting of SPS. This

---

respectable bourgeois families of Vienna, where he had established his practice. This idea was simply unacceptable. It was beyond credibility." Herman, *Trauma and Recovery*, 23–24.

9. Beste, *God and the Victim*, 115.

10. The #MeToo Movement's history is documented by Kearl, *Facts Behind the #MeToo Movement*, 9.

11. Kearl, *Facts Behind the #MeToo Movement*, 9.

12. Colwell and Johnson, "#MeToo and #ChurchToo," 185–86.

13. Joy, "#ChurchToo," paras. 1–2.

movement recognized that sexual violence was a part of pentecostal history as in the public story of Recy Taylor, a young black woman who was walking home from a pentecostal church service when she was raped by a group of local white teenagers in 1944.[14] At that first meeting of #pentecostalsisterstoo, numerous women and some men indicated that they had been sexually violated. Some women spoke of how such violations continued in actions and innuendos as well as through the lack of respect by their male counterparts.[15] The flood of stories that are being told is now an outcry against the refusal of both the culture and the church to see, hear, and believe survivors, and it seems this outcry is being heard. At the five-year anniversary of the #MeToo Movement, it was reported that "six-in-ten" Americans perceive "that those who report harassment or assault at work are now *more likely* to be believed" (italics in original).[16]

Now Is the Time for Healing Stories

Amidst this inundation of stories of sexual violence, Tarana Burke, the original founder of "'Me Too' movement" in 2007, stated in an interview that she wants to "move beyond the stories of trauma to stories of healing.[17] This conveys that now is the time for stories that speak of survivors' courage to heal from violent sexual acts. I believe pentecostals are ideally positioned to be inherently helpful because of their theology and practices.

It is no secret that pentecostals are known for their belief in divine healing. Pentecostal revivals frequently include miraculous physical healings. Nancy Hardesty asserts that the Azusa Street Revival, for instance, began with an incident of divine healing.[18] Some researchers argue that the common trait among pentecostals is not speaking in tongues but the belief in divine healing. Contributors to *Global Pentecostal and Charismatic Healing* maintain that in some regions, healing is the focal point of

---

14. Chan, "Recy Taylor, Who Fought for Justice after a 1944 Rape, Dies at 97," paras. 1, 10.

15. To read more about this meeting, see the article by Ambrose and Alexander, "Pentecostal Studies Face the #MeToo Movement," 1–7.

16. Brown, "More Than Twice as Many Americans," 4.

17. Harris, "She Founded Me Too. Now She Wants to Move Past the Trauma," paras. 1, 5, 10.

18. Hardesty, *Faith Cure*, 101.

pentecostalism and is the reason for pentecostalism's growth.[19] The Pew Forum concludes in a survey of pentecostals in ten countries: "In all 10 countries surveyed, large majorities of pentecostals (ranging from 56% in South Korea to 87% in Kenya) say that they have personally experienced or witnessed the divine healing of an illness or injury."[20]

Not only are pentecostals known for their emphasis on healing, but they are also known to be people of stories. Pentecostals have traditionally sought to place themselves in God's story by proclaiming through testimonies that what occurs in Acts occurs in the church today. As scholar Robert Menzies writes, "We Pentecostals have always read the narrative of Acts, and particularly the account of the Pentecostal outpouring of the Holy Spirit (Acts 2), as a model for our lives. The stories of Acts are *our* stories" (italics in original).[21] This indicates that the healings by the apostles in Acts have become a paradigm of healing for contemporary pentecostals. Some pentecostals have even begun to relate their stories of healing from sexual violence. Amy Farley, an Assemblies of God missionary, was brutally raped in her home in Senegal in 2014. After spending time in daily counseling for eight months, she traveled to Vietnam to be with missionary friends and is now serving there. She states, "I'm not the person I was before the attack, even through all the grief and pain. I like much better who I am now. My love for the Father is so much deeper, my love for people is so much greater, and my faith is so much stronger."[22] One participant from my previous study told me his story of his experience with *theophastic prayer*, in which he received a powerful experience of healing as he envisioned Jesus being present during the abuse that he experienced as a child.[23]

Yet, healing from sexual violence may not occur in a straightforward matter. Pentecostal Jeanette Salguero, who is an associate senior pastor and chief operating officer at Calvario City Church in Orlando, speaks of her ongoing healing: "As a Pentecostal pastor, I know about the laying on of hands and the sprinkling and the handkerchiefs and all that good stuff. But it's a lot more than that . . . We cannot link hands and say, 'Woman you are healed go.' 'Man you are healed, go on your merry way.' This is a process." About her own healing process she says, "I'm not denying the

---

19. Brown, *Global Pentecostal and Charismatic Healing*.
20. Lugo et al., *Spirit and Power*, 6.
21. Menzies, *Pentecost*, loc. 289–91.
22. Kennedy, "SAGU Alumna Receives AG Young Influencer Award," paras. 4–9, 20.
23. Engelbert, *Who Is Present in Absence?*, 112–13.

SEE, HEAR, BELIEVE THE STORY: THE INTRODUCTION 11

power of the Holy Spirit, but I do know, as a thriving victim, that therapy is a must."[24] Salguero indicates that trauma's power is not isolated to a solitary incident, but it has persistent repercussions. This is also substantiated in the upcoming pages through the stories of thirteen participants consisting of both survivors and counselors. Hence, pentecostals who are survivors of sexual violence or those who walk alongside survivors are potentially theologically challenged because the story of sexual trauma often fails to have a satisfactory ending in this life. It was my experience of being challenged in my beliefs about healing from sexual violence that motivated me to hear the healing stories of other pentecostal survivors.

SEEING, HEARING, AND BELIEVING PARTICIPANTS

Healing begins with seeing, hearing, and believing the stories that are told. Classical Pentecostal Lauren Raley underscores how the reaction of the initial person to hear the survivor's story of sexual violence particularly shapes the healing journey of that survivor. She goes on to emphasize the importance of this individual to see, hear, and believe the survivors and for survivors to be in a community of "embrace and trust for their ultimate well-being."[25] Unfortunately, not all believers are willing to see, hear, and believe. In interviewing counselors for this book (see below), a counselor-participant, who is referred to as Joel, told me about the resistance of some pentecostal colleagues, who were taking courses in a pentecostal seminary, to see and hear about sexual trauma. Joel watched colleagues place "their hands over their ears and close their eyes" during classes on trauma "because they didn't want to be exposed to that reality."[26] He also has borne witness to how, in a pentecostal environment, people have refused to see, hear, and believe by being "dismissive" and couching it "in holiness and in moral authority." This is very hurtful as survivors may be "shamed again" or "re-traumatized." Joel defines re-traumatization in the church as occurring when survivors are "not accepted" or when the

---

24. Lee, "Max Lucado Reveals Past Sexual Abuse at Evangelical #MeToo Summit," paras. 20–26.

25. Raley, "Toward a Pentecostal Ecclesiology," 216.

26. I have edited the quotes by removing immaterial words such as fillers (e.g., uh, um, that, you know), stammers, or the repeated words when a participant starts and restarts a sentence. This has been done to eliminate distractions from the thrust and power of a participant's message.

sexual violence is not discussed or addressed.[27] When also interviewing survivors for this study (see below), a survivor-participant, who I call Elizabeth, implied this type of dismissiveness when she mentioned minimization: "I think the minimization from people who have not experienced it has been the part that has been the hardest for me. Yes, these things [sexual violence] can happen within the church, and yes, they can happen without you asking for them." If churches fail to allow survivors to tell their stories within its walls, it can exacerbate their pain by communicating that survivors are to remain silent.

I acknowledge that seeing, hearing, and believing the stories demands from us courage and the willingness to take risks. It is a risk that we will be transformed. As Beste writes, "To listen to and believe survivors' accounts of subjection to such severe interpersonal harm and its devastating effects can be excruciating, for it conflicts with our most comforting assumptions about the world and God. To embark on this journey with survivors involves a willingness to disrupt our sense of well-being, comfort, and security, and to be challenged in our view of ourselves, our world, and God."[28] The stories contained in the forthcoming chapters are drawn from real experiences of other pentecostals in order to seek answers on how pentecostals heal from sexual violence and to contribute to a pentecostal theological praxis of healing from sexual violence. As a practical theologian, I intersected these experiences with Scripture, theology, psychology, and culture.[29] I conducted a qualitative study over quantitative because pentecostals underscore stories and experiences to inform their theology and because stories teach and transform both the storyteller and the storylistener (see chapters 3 and 7).

The fundamental purpose of this book is to center on how pentecostals heal from sexual violence. Thus, a reader may notice in the upcoming chapters that minute details about the survivor-participants' experiences of sexual violence will not be the focus of the stories. This does not imply that all the content on these pages will be devoid of hard-to-read subject matter. But it does mean that when elements of sexual violence are presented, they are for educational purposes, pointing toward the

---

27. This was also noted by Raley who comments that when a community is unwilling to see, hear, and believe survivors, they "are forced to remain silent" and subjected to "'secondary trauma.'" Raley, "Toward a Pentecostal Ecclesiology," 216.

28. Beste, *God and Victim*, 126.

29. I discuss my definition of practical theology and how it differs from applied theology in *Who Is Present in Absence?*, 18–22.

characteristics and complexities of the healing journey. They are not for the sake of cheap curiosity—that is, voyeurism. In the retelling of the stories that you are about to read, I have attempted to maintain integrity by adhering closely to the context of the data. The names of people and places along with some identifying characteristics have been changed in order to uphold confidentiality; however, I also acknowledge that complete anonymity is impossible since a reader, who is personally acquainted with a participant, may recognize some details of a story.

By way of introduction, this chapter provides a broad overview of a few of the characteristics of the participants. These pages contain two kinds of pentecostal participants: eight survivors and five licensed counselors, none of whom were considered my personal friends at the time of the interviews (see appendix A for more details on the process of collecting data). The participants are citizens of either Canada or the United States. Of the survivors, six identify as female and two as male, and of the counselors two identify as male and three as female. Only one survivor informed me of experiencing sexual violence as an adult while the others are survivors of childhood sexual abuse.[30] As a side note, three of the five counselors voluntarily mentioned that they, too, were survivors. Each survivor-participant was over the age of forty and has been on a healing journey for five years or more at the time of the interview. This latter component is significant when one considers the pentecostal responses to the survivors. The responses, which appear throughout this book, are unvarying, which means pentecostals have altered very little over the years in how they respond to survivors. Concerning the general traits of the counselors, three of the five had not planned to become counselors as they were in other professions. All the counselors had a sense that God was ordering their steps, experiencing personal direction by the Holy Spirit to pursue counseling with an emphasis on healing from sexual violence.

---

30. A reference for the church on the subject of childhood sexual abuse is Heggen's *Sexual Abuse in Christian Homes and Churches*. Heggen seeks to help prevent abuse and develop a healthy sexuality in the church. She is drawing from her years of experience in counseling adult survivors as well as her previous research endeavors. She includes topics such as issues resulting from sexual abuse; theories concerning perpetrators; the issue of forgiveness and reconciliation; and congregational responses to abuse.

THE PURPOSE OF SEEING, HEARING, AND BELIEVING THESE STORIES

The evidence collected from research concerning sexual violence and the church seems to be mixed in relation to the church's potential response to said violence. In 2019, LifeWay Research conducted an online survey of 1,815 Americans in which Protestants were asked to present their impressions and acquaintance with sexual misconduct and the church. Forty-four percent stated they had experienced one or more of the following: "unwanted sexual joking, unsolicited sexual messages, unwanted compliments, and inappropriate glances," with 12 percent of these experiencing sexual misconduct at church.[31] At the same time, 72 percent believed their church was "at least somewhat prepared to help someone who has experienced sexual assault," and 93 percent held that their congregation was "a safe place where adults are actively protected from sexual assault in the church." As far as being a place of healing, 90 percent believed the church that they attended was a healing place for adult survivors, and 89 percent perceived that their church was healing for a youth who was a survivor of sexual abuse.[32] Both statistics are in contrast to evidence put forth by Joshua Pease who, in drawing heavily from accounts of survivors such as Rachael Denhollander, describes how the message to survivors of sexual abuse within the evangelical church is: remain silent as the church does not believe survivors.[33] But there is another voice that tends to be silent: the church. John Wigger notes that while "the gospel" is to "challenge abuse of power, protect the vulnerable, and give voice to survivors," it is in contrast to the "silence" of pentecostals in regard to sexual violence, which "denies mercy and justice" for survivors.[34]

Evidence additionally indicates that some clergy and churches may not be prepared to help survivors of sexual violence. Elil Yuvarajan and Matthew S. Stanford discovered in their mixed methods research that clergy increasingly blamed survivors the more that the perpetrator was familiar with the survivors (except for rape within a marriage).[35] They go on to note that the "more control" a victim appeared to have, the more that clergy blamed the victim; thus, the authors surmise that "the

31. Earls, "Churchgoers Split," under heading "Room for improvement."
32. Earls, "Churchgoers Split," under heading "Church preparation and optimism."
33. Pease, "Sin of Silence."
34. Wigger, "Jessica Hahn and Pentecostal Silence on Sexual Abuse," 30.
35. Yuvarajan and Stanford, "Clergy Perceptions of Sexual Assault Victimization," 588, 596–97.

judgments that clergy make about sexual assaults varies [sic] more according to victim characteristics and actions rather than perpetrator factors."[36] Their study also revealed that it was not necessarily the clergy's religious beliefs but their "hostile sexism," which "strongly correlated" with the clergy placing blame on survivors.[37] This is in contrast to the perceptions of surveyed churchgoers who stated that "their church would respond to someone who had experienced sexual abuse, sexual assault or rape with respect (73%), sympathy (70%), privacy (63%) and protection (60%). Few believe their church would ignore the person who shared their experience (2%), see them as an attention-seeker (2%) or as partly to blame (2%)."[38]

LifeWay Research conducted a phone survey of 1,000 Protestant pastors in 2018. While 85 percent had "heard of #MeToo Movement," only 16 percent of pastors had heard of #ChurchToo (and probably even a smaller percentage would have heard of #pentecostalsisterstoo).[39] Of those who had heard of the #MeToo Movement, 41 percent "of Protestant senior pastors" were "more inclined to preach about sexual and domestic violence in response to the movement." The survey found that only 24 percent of pentecostal pastors were more inclined to respond by preaching on these topics in comparison to 57 percent of Methodists and 52 percent of Presbyterian/Reformed pastors. Half of the pastors who responded to the survey stated they did not "have sufficient training to address sexual or domestic abuse," and "only about half (55 percent) of the pastors" surveyed were "familiar or very familiar with domestic violence resources in their community."[40]

When considering the above studies, it is significant that more than one participant in my research underscored the importance for the church and its leaders to acknowledge the prevalence of sexual violence. Survivor-participant Sutton mentioned being surprised as he was

---

36. Yuvarajan and Stanford, "Clergy Perceptions of Sexual Assault Victimization," 601.

37. Yuvarajan and Stanford, "Clergy Perceptions of Sexual Assault Victimization," 601.

38. Earls, "Churchgoers Split," under heading "Church preparation and optimism."

39. Smietana, "Pastors More Likely to Address Domestic Violence," under heading "Most aware of #MeToo."

40. Smietana, "Pastors More Likely to Address Domestic Violence," under heading "#MeToo Leads to Action, Confusion." This supports the qualitative study of Houston-Kolnik et al. in which religious leaders desired training concerning intimate partner violence. Houston-Kolnik et al., "Overcoming the 'Holy Hush,'" 135–52.

becoming more and more aware "of how widespread sexual abuse in the church really is." Counselor-participants Joel and Kiley sought to remind pentecostal clergy that they have survivors sitting in their church pews right now. Joel asked, "What are you doing with that?"[41] Unfortunately, 46 percent of ministers of various traditions, who fail to preach on sexual and/or domestic violence, believe it is not a problem in their church, and 19 percent assert it is not a problem in their local area.[42] Similarly, counselor-participant Dayton wondered about the incongruity between the prevalence of sexual violence and how little is offered in terms of care within churches. In his experience, churches do not believe in discussing it. This book seeks to contribute to the pentecostal understanding of healing from sexual violence while offering our pentecostal churches theological healing acts of ministry for survivors.[43]

WHAT YOU WILL SEE AND HEAR

Broadly speaking, the upcoming chapters highlight seeing, hearing, and believing stories of survivors of sexual violence. This book is divided into

---

41. This is an important question in light of a study conducted by Houston-Kolnik and Todd in which they studied the programs available in congregations for female survivors of violence from 1998 to 2012. While congregations have the potentiality to empower women, few churches reached this potential. Evangelical congregations, which included pentecostal congregations, offered very few programs for survivors of both domestic and sexual violence. Houston-Kolnik and Todd, "Examining the Presence of Congregational Programs," 459–72.

42. Smietana, "Pastors More Likely to Address Domestic Violence," under heading "Domestic abuse less taboo." The same paragraph also states that of those pastors who do not speak about sexual/domestic violence, 29 percent think that "other topics are more important"; 19 percent declare that "they don't know the issue well enough," and 16 percent believe "it is not appropriate to address domestic or sexual violence publicly."

43. Academic pentecostals have also approached the subject of sexual violence. *Pneuma: The Journal of the Society for Pentecostal Studies* published articles in which pentecostals interacted with the #MeToo Movement. The SPS meeting in 2020 (which was postponed) and 2021 centered on the theme "'This is My Body': Addressing Global Violence against Women" in which multiple papers concentrated on sexual violence. Several members of SPS collaborated in the publication *Sisters, Mothers, Daughters* in which the authors emphasize the Holy Spirit and perceive how responding to the problem of violence against women as an issue to be addressed by the entire church. Several of these articles were papers presented at SPS 2021. While many of these articles, papers, and chapters discuss sexual violence from perspectives of pentecostal history, theology, philosophy, biblical interpretation, and practical theology, none of them systematically and analytically interviewed pentecostal survivors who were healing from sexual violence to develop a pentecostal theological praxis of healing.

two parts with chapters 1 through 5 centering on the experiences of healing from sexual violence, as described by the participants, and chapters 6 through 8 underscoring three praxes that are historically pentecostal and foster healing, which is followed by a concluding chapter. With that being said, the reader is to note that the distinctions between parts one and two may not appear as stringent as stated here. The first part concentrates on elements of the healing journey while including some aspects of appropriate healing responses by the church. The second part is explicitly dedicated to studying healing praxes. Each of these chapters begins with a praxis and seeks to expand the church's understanding of that praxis by drawing from science (e.g., psychology, communication, education), culture, pentecostal history, theology, and/or Scripture. Since I believe that the Spirit is moving throughout the earth in a variety of ways, the chapters from both parts draw not only from the participants' stories and pentecostal theology and/or Scripture (specifically 1 Corinthians) but also culture and/or the sciences. Rather than compartmentalizing and separating the sciences from theology, the employment of other disciplines informs my understanding of how the Spirit is moving and illuminates how pentecostals may participate in Christ's healing ministry in the world.

Chapter 2 centers on the complexities of sexual violence and healing from it. It draws from both the experiences of the participants and trauma theory to convey how the body tells the story of trauma—that is, trauma is embodied. By examining 1 Corinthians 11, this chapter underscores the story of Christ's trauma that is embodied in the partaking of the Lord's Supper. Chapter 3 highlights how each survivor-participant informed someone about his/her experience of sexual violence; thus, it researches how stories may foster healing, particularly since pentecostals are traditionally known for telling stories and for their emphasis on healing. Once again, it employs 1 Corinthians 11 and the words "you proclaim the Lord's death until he comes," recognizing how the story of Christ's trauma is told again and again through the partaking of a meal. This chapter considers the type of atonement story told during the Eucharist, and it invites persons to implement the story of Christ's shame on the cross as a way to foster healing for survivors. Chapter 4 looks at the commonality of the uniqueness of each participant's healing journey. Using the work of Alan Wolfelt, it highlights nine characteristics that signal the uniqueness of the journey. This is followed by an exploration of unity and diversity as seen in 1 Corinthians 12. The final chapter of part one emphasizes the change in the survivor's experiential-theological understanding of God. I discovered an implicit and explicit shift in the survivors in which the survivors experienced healing in relation to their understanding of spiritual authority and/or how they related to God. Some changes were more gradual due to repeated study or developmental growth, and other changes emerged in part due to mystical experiences with God. I underscore in this chapter how pentecostalism has been connected to Christian mysticism in that God enters our nothingness, our impossibility, and heals it. Bearing this in mind, I then explore 1 Corinthians 12 and 14.

Having accentuated the healing journeys of the survivor-participants, I turn towards specific ways the church may cultivate a safe, healing place for survivors in part two. In each of these chapters, I again draw from the emphases presented by the participants. Chapter 6 focuses on the praxis of embodied listening. I point out how historically pentecostals have been a listening people as they listen for God, who is Holy Other, both privately and communally. Using the work of Lisbeth Lipari, a professor of communication, I emphasize how listening is not simply a function of the ear, but it is embodied, involving a self-emptying. I draw from Michael Gorman's emphasis on cruciformity in 1 Corinthians and assert that the church in Corinth is being called to listen to each other, or to empty themselves through listening. This self-emptying is what it means to be spiritual. Chapter 7 develops the praxis of embodied waiting that is based on the unpredictability and the lifelong journey of healing from sexual violence. Embodied waiting is in opposition to Western culture's emphases on linearity and instantaneity. Unfortunately, pentecostals are not immune to the influence of Western culture's narrative of time with the pentecostal expectation of instantaneous healing. However, pentecostalism has traditionally embraced waiting as seen in the practice of *waiting on the Lord* and waiting for the Lord's Second Coming. I then turn towards 1 Corinthian's attention on waiting as seen in the eschatological thread that flows throughout the letter and contend that we as believers are called to embody an eschatological waiting alongside survivors of sexual violence. The next chapter underscores the praxis of embodied learning. By employing Jack Mezirow's transformative learning theory, I assert that learning may be transformative, which causes it to be an inherent characteristic of pentecostalism. If pentecostals are potentially to be transformed through learning, it requires for us to embody both listening and waiting, which implies an open and a teachable stance.

This stance means I embrace my finitude before upholding Western culture's can-do attitude of superhumanity that tends to defy our limitations. I then turn to 1 Corinthians 3 and 4 to underscore the importance of humility in order to remain teachable, which calls for a God-centered approach to ministry over and above a human-centered one. Chapter 9 is a conclusion that also proposes ideas as to where we as pentecostals are to go from here.

SEEING, HEARING, AND BELIEVING THE TERMS

Prior to moving forward, I see it as essential to define three terms that are central to this study: *pentecostalism*, *sexual violence*, and *healing*.

Pentecostalism

For the definition of pentecostalism, I am drawing from the participants' descriptions. I invited the participants to tell me during the interviews what being a pentecostal meant for them and/or how they defined pentecostalism and/or a pentecostal, and I found three general elements that surfaced in their descriptions. First, *regularly experiencing God* was a priority for several of the participants. Survivor-participant Frances spoke of being "open to the movement of God in ways that are surprising." Counselor-participant Joel echoed this when he commented about his asking God during a counseling session: "OK, God, what are you doing here?" Counselor-participant Megan said that being a pentecostal for her was "having access to the Holy Spirit in a dynamic and living way." It meant "having access to something that is greater than our stories that will help bring healing, but also bring life and light into places that, at least in the work that I do, are very, very dark." Counselor-participant Kiley also explicitly emphasized experience when she said, "Our faith is such an experiential faith," which included "bodily experiences." Several participants associated the gifts of the Spirit with pentecostalism, such as survivor-participant Elizabeth. For her, pentecostalism was "more robust" than non-pentecostal traditions in that pentecostals believe that God is the giver of the gifts. She values this because she "really needs spiritual divine intervention for getting through some of the things that life hands" her. A couple of survivor-participants viewed pentecostalism as including the experience of the baptism of the Holy Spirit, such as Frances and Sutton, but Frances qualified her remark by saying that Spirit baptism did not have to be accompanied by tongues. Survivor-participant Jade centered on Jesus when she spoke of Spirit baptism. She saw pentecostal faith as believing "that Jesus is our Healer and our Savior, and that he baptizes in the Holy Spirit, and that he is going to come back again and return again as a king." Survivor-participant Destiny saw being pentecostal as her life being involved with the triune Godhead when she said, "[It] is about understanding the Trinity, and the different ways that the Trinity functions in our lives."

Second, some survivor-participants stressed the importance of *Scripture*. For Jackson, being pentecostal meant "believing everything in the Bible, and believing that it applies to us today and just the same as it did two thousand years ago." Mackenzie included the statement, "what happened in Acts still occurs today" in her description of pentecostalism.

Third, multiple participants accentuated the *daily living out* of one's faith *in the power and healing presence of the Spirit*. Counselor-participant Dayton said, "It means operating in the fullness and the gifting of the power of the Holy Spirit, and (I think more specifically for me) ... the healing ministry of Jesus." He particularly referenced pentecostals "engag[ing] the Holy Spirit in power and liv[ing] that out." Survivor-participant Dominique underscored the aspect of power when she said that being pentecostal meant having God's power of healing inside of her. This power for her meant that limits were not placed on her since nothing was impossible for God. For her, there are no limitations on what God could accomplish in her life since God is all powerful. Counselor-participant Shauna's view of pentecostalism included all three of the above aspects: "Being Charismatic means honoring the whole counsel of the Word of God by reverencing the holiness of God, the tenants of the faith, and the power of the Holy Spirit and the role of the spiritual gifts in the church today to empower believers to love people well through His [God's] grace expressed in love through us."

Based on their responses, I formulated a theme (code) that describes pentecostalism or a pentecostal as having: *an active, experiential faith, grounded in Scripture, that is daily lived out both personally and communally in the power and healing presence of the Spirit*. On a related note, I use a small *p* when speaking of all sects of pentecostals and Charismatics and a capital *P* when referring only to Classical Pentecostals who are represented by those denominations (Assemblies of God, Four Square, Canadian Assemblies, etc.) formed out of nineteenth- and twentieth- century revivals; these denominations have frequently adhered to the belief that the initial physical evidence of the Holy Spirit's baptism is speaking in tongues. I also use a capital *C* for Charismatics when delineating those pentecostals who have remained in mainline denominations.

Sexual Violence

While interviewing survivor-participant Jade, she inquired as to why I used the term "sexual violence" rather than the term "sexual abuse." When I considered employing the term "sexual abuse," I personally linked it to children because of the phrase "childhood sexual abuse." In like manner, the term "sexual assault" in my mind failed to include *childhood sexual abuse*. Therefore, I selected *sexual violence* because it enveloped both *sexual abuse* and *sexual assault*. As the organization RAINN states, "The term 'sexual violence' is an all-encompassing, non-legal term that refers to crimes like sexual assault, rape, and sexual abuse."[44] Furthermore, I teach and personally embrace *Compassionate Communication*, which is also called *Non-violent Communication*. Drawing from this theory, *violence* has a broader sense as it includes the way persons communicate verbally to others or themselves by blaming, judging, or using all-or-nothing words and phrases such as *always* or *never*.[45] With that being said, I employ the National Sexual Violence Resource Center's (NSVRC) definition, which defines sexual violence as, "someone forc[ing] or manipulat[ing] someone else into unwanted sexual activity without their consent."[46]

Healing

The purpose of this book is to teach survivors, church leaders, non-church leaders, scholars, and non-scholars how particular persons heal from sexual violence. It is an invitation to see, hear, and believe the stories of sexual violence and of healing, whether they be stories told on these pages or those that are heard but remain unpublished. The upcoming pages will teach that healing from sexual violence is not instantaneous,

---

44. RAINN, "Types of Sexual Violence."

45. I explain this more fully in Engelbert, *Who Is Present in Absence?*, chapter 6.

46. NSVRC, "What Is Sexual Violence?: Fact Sheet," under heading "What is sexual violence?"

which is in contrast to the idea of a cure. There is no cure for the damage thrust upon a survivor. The word "cure" is often used in the medical community, and it refers to eliminating or treating a "disease, condition, or injury" "with medical treatment" or solving a problem.[47] It suggests a remedy. It means the sickness is gone. Another word often associated with healing from sexual violence is *recovery*. As grief counselor Alan Wolfelt asserts when discussing a grief journey (which in many ways is what healing from sexual violence is), *recovery* indicates that a person will return to a prior state of normalcy. However, life will never be the same as it once was.[48] The participants demonstrate that healing from sexual violence is a journey and is not completed until we see Jesus's face. It involves a process of moving towards wholeness in every dimension—cognitive, spiritual, relational, emotional, as well as physical.[49]

THE INVITATION TO SEE, HEAR, AND BELIEVE

I listed previously in this chapter some facts and figures about sexual violence. It is sometimes easy to scan numbers like those aforementioned statistics and only see them as nameless, faceless, numerical digits that have very little impact on my community and my personal life. Yet, as one who has pastored and who is also a survivor of sexual violence, these statistics have a definitive shape. They move from cold numerals that are nameless and faceless to personal lives with real names, real faces, real wounds. In one particular church that my husband and I pastored, which averaged approximately fifty attendees on any given Sunday, I can recall the names and faces of seven congregants plus me, who had previously experienced sexual or domestic violence—and these were the ones that I knew. And so, the above numbers are not icy-cold integers but real people with real stories and real wounds. In this light, I have reflected on

---

47. *Dictionary*, "cure."

48. Wolfelt, *Companioning the Bereaved*, 158.

49. Previously, I defined *healing* as "God restoring or reconciling all of creation to become what God has designed. Because this study focuses on human beings, I particularly highlight the healing of the whole person, which includes not only the physical body but also the emotional, spiritual, and relational aspects as well. Thus, while healing may not occur in the physical body (a cure) for a person, I believe in the continuing work of the Spirit to generate ongoing healing in other ways, transforming the person to be more complete in order to be the human being that God planned from before the beginning of time." Engelbert, *Who Is Present in Absence?*, 13.

SEE, HEAR, BELIEVE THE STORY: THE INTRODUCTION   23

a possible response if I were to travel back in time and pastor the same churches again. I have concluded that I would do some things differently.

If I had known then what I know now . . .

- I would have been among the pastors who had heard of #Church-Too (and among the smaller percentage of those who had heard of #pentecostalsisterstoo).
- I would have been among the pentecostal pastors who would have been more inclined to preach on sexual and domestic violence after being made aware of #MeToo.
- I would have taught the congregation about domestic and sexual violence. The congregants would have heard that rather than healing being a one-time event, or even being completely finalized, healing for the survivor of sexual violence is an ongoing process.
- I would have related how many survivors, be it domestic or sexual violence, have been silenced and have a need for someone to hear their stories.
- I would have invited congregants to help break the silence by becoming people who listen. I would have offered ways to cultivate the characteristic of listening, a path that demonstrates a *power with* the survivor instead of a *power over* the survivor. Such an invitation would have been framed theologically as participating in the ministry of Christ, being present to others as Christ is already ministering his presence to them in and through his very being.
- I would have taught that while cultures throughout the ages have asserted *power over* women, God demonstrates that the divine is *with* survivors in the person of Jesus, providing dignity, equality, and mutuality.

If I had only known then what I know now . . .[50]

The next several chapters are an invitation *to see* the survivors. They are a call to avoid being like Freud who heard stories from Victorian women but eventually did not see them as survivors. He refused to believe that so many women were being sexually violated in Victorian

---

50. These paragraphs were adapted from a blog, Engelbert, "If I Had Known Then What I Know Now."

homes. This book is a qualitative study in that it makes the survivors personal. While their identities are disguised, their stories generate a sense of personalness. This personalness means that each survivor may be a person in your church. Listening to your sermon. Sitting next to you in the pew. Leading from your church's pulpit. The invitation is to see them, hear them, and believe them.

2

The Body's Telling of the Story

I think the surprising part [for me] with this particular population [is] there's something about sexual abuse. When that boundary has been crossed, that behavior becomes [an] identity. There is an internalization of an event that no longer can be viewed as an event, but now [it] is viewed as part of self. I don't know if there's any other environmental exposure that we're exposed to that has that kind of impact. [It] flips from an event that happened on a timeline [to] now becom[ing] part of our identity. And that's where that toxic shame really settles in.

—Joel, a counselor-participant

Once the numbness starts to wear off, many may start to struggle with confusion, frustration, shame thinking there is something wrong with them as they may not make the connection of the surfacing emotions, nightmares, symptoms, intrusive memories etc. as part of the trauma response. Helping survivors understand the natural symptoms and course of trauma is important. Helping survivors engage in the healing process of starting to re-connect to their bodies and to the events in order to start the grieving journey.

—Shauna, a counselor-participant

I would say [to survivors] that sexual violence is an incredible violation of a person in terms of a person's sense of self, identity, and ability to accept

God's dignity in oneself. It really shatters a person at their core, and it's a journey of restoring the imago Dei *in a person.*

—Dayton, a counselor-participant

Survivor-participant Mackenzie said that the most surprising aspect in her healing journey was her capacity to bury the story of sexual violence for fifty years. In 2015, Mackenzie became curious about a particular book that her daughter was reading for a Bible study. As she glanced through the book's index, she saw a reference to a story of a woman, an RN who had written Bible studies on overcoming sexual abuse. This woman recounts her own story of childhood sexual abuse and addresses readers who may be struggling with things that are overpowering them. Mackenzie said, "It was like the Lord opened up my eyes that I had been sexually abused." This blocking out of sexual trauma is not unusual as psychiatrist Judith Herman makes clear: "The ordinary response to atrocities is to banish them from consciousness."[1] When Mackenzie broached the subject of childhood sexual abuse with two of her older sisters, she learned that the three of them had been sexually abused by the same relatives. While her sisters had been discussing it for several years, they had not mentioned it to Mackenzie because they believed that she had been too young to recall the abuse.

I recounted in the previous chapter my own story of how I had banished my experience of sexual violence from my consciousness. It was my personal experience of healing that engendered curiosity as to how other survivors experienced healing from sexual violence. In this chapter, readers are invited to learn from the experiences of counselors and survivors on how sexual violence impacts a person's whole being. Two threads are flowing through this chapter and much of the remaining chapters: story and body. These are two common themes both in pentecostalism and in healing from sexual violence. This chapter engages story and body by exploring the intersection of psychology, experience, Scripture, and Christology. Drawing from trauma theory, participants' experiences, and 1 Corinthians, the purpose of this chapter is to highlight the impact of sexual trauma and connect it with Scripture. This will be accomplished in three movements: (1) by providing a brief overview of trauma theory, particularly underscoring body memory; (2) by highlighting the

1. Herman, *Trauma and Recovery*, 8.

experiences of the participants to show the impact of sexual violence; and (3) by exploring how the Lord's Supper is a retelling of Christ's trauma story and a way for survivors to place themselves in God's story.[2]

THE THEORY OF TRAUMA

One aspect frequently mentioned by the participants was the importance for the church to gain an understanding of trauma theory (see chapter 8). If pentecostals are to provide healing support to survivors of sexual trauma, it begins here—with an introduction to the theory of trauma. To accomplish this task, this section includes the following two elements: (1) define and characterize trauma, and (2) provide an overview of the impact of trauma on the brain and the body. The word "trauma" is frequently heard in both professional and nonprofessional conversations. At one end of the spectrum, professional researchers and/or psychiatrists may present new theories about healing from trauma to other professionals in their field, but at the opposite end of the spectrum, good friends may describe their experiences at Black Friday sales as being *traumatic*. With such diverse usage, a definition of trauma is necessary for the sake of clarity. Theologian Shelly Rambo's description points to trauma as being overwhelming: "Trauma is often expressed in terms of what exceeds categories of comprehension, of what exceeds the human capacity to take in and process the external world... Trauma is described as an encounter with death."[3] Rather than being a physical death, Rambo explains that trauma is an event(s) that destroys one's understanding of the world and how one functions within it. Since what is known in the world is no longer "true and safe," life is no longer fundamentally defined in the same manner. Instead, life is "always mixed with death."[4] Similarly, neurologist Robert Scaer notes, "A traumatic event is basically a life threat that is linked to a state of helplessness."[5] Thus, in an event of trauma, persons are unable to cope using their internal resources, temporarily rendering persons powerless.

---

2. Portions of this chapter were presented at a SPS meeting. Engelbert, "Tell Me the Story of Trauma."
3. Rambo, *Spirit and Trauma*, 4.
4. Rambo, *Spirit and Trauma*, 4.
5. Scaer, *8 Keys to Brain-Body Balance*, 143.

While a traumatic event is not always associated with a physical death, it is generally understood to fall within particular parameters, which may produce various symptoms within one's being. Body-psychotherapist Babette Rothschild outlines three established parameters of trauma: (1) experiencing an event that is threatening to one's body and/or life; (2) witnessing an individual experiencing a violent act, be it malicious or not; and (3) hearing that a "close associate" has experienced a violent event and/or unexpected death.[6] A word of caution is in order as these parameters are not to be mistaken as definitive principles for identifying those who will develop traumatic symptoms. Not all who have had one or more of the above experiences will exhibit traumatic symptoms, and neither will an experience that traumatizes a child necessarily traumatize an adult (e.g., tonsillectomy). This is in part because trauma is not only an event, but it also involves responses, such as psychological and biological responses (the latter is addressed below). This means that trauma includes both external (an event) and internal (response) aspects. In addressing this point, Beste mentions how the question remains whether it is the severity of the event or the person's disposition, coping abilities, and emotional/physiological make up that determines if one is traumatized.[7] It is now recognized that multiple factors govern "the degree to which an event will overwhelm and traumatize a person," including the "nature of the event" as well as the person's own being and previous experiences (e.g., family system, previous traumatic experiences, personal biological aspects, etc.).[8] That is, the level of traumatization involves both the exterior and the interior worlds of a person.[9]

Yet, it is not only the victim's internal nature and the nature of the horrifying event that matters but also the nature of society or community. Alexander McFarlane and Bessel van der Kolk state that when an affirming community validates a person's experience of a horrifying trauma, it helps in "preventing and treating posttraumatic stress"; however, the authors also note that "validation and support" may become more difficult when the communal or societal "needs" clash with the survivor's ongoing "needs."[10] Many societies believe that persons are able to "control

---

6. Rothschild, *Body Remembers*, 6–7.

7. Beste, *God and the Victim*, 6.

8. Beste, *God and the Victim*, 6–7.

9. Rambo speaks of trauma being both "the actual occurrence of a violent event(s) and a belated awakening to the event." Rambo, *Spirit and Trauma*, 7.

10. McFarlane and van der Kolk, "Trauma and Its Challenge to Society," 25.

their own destinies."[11] For such societies, the world is seen as basically "just" in "that 'good' people are in charge of their lives, and ... bad things only happen to 'bad' people"; thus, the ongoing "presence of victims as victims" contradicts and "insults" society's dearly held conviction that "human beings are essentially the masters of their fate."[12] Therefore, survivors may not find a validating and supportive society or community when their "helplessness persists or when the meaning of the trauma" must remain hidden. As such, survivors are more than likely to continue to manifest reoccurring memories of the trauma, which are exhibited by ongoing hostility, withdrawal, and aggression.[13] This is an important factor for pentecostal communities to consider when evaluating if their responses are healing or harming survivors of sexual violence. To assist in providing more supportive responses and a better understanding of trauma, it may be helpful to outline how ordinary events differ from Rothschild's parameters of traumatic events, which cause traumatic symptoms to appear. To accomplish this, I turn towards a brief overview of the parts of the brain and the impact of trauma on the brain and the body.

Trauma's Impact on the Brain and the Body

At risk of this segment's sounding highly technical, I turn to neurology's perception of how the brain functions. I believe taking this risk is necessary as it will help to develop a more comprehensive picture as to how sexual violence impacts the whole person. Drawing from psychiatrist van der Kolk, the brain may be broadly divided into three sections: reptilian, mammalian, and prefrontal cortex. The reptilian brain is in the brain stem, which controls the respiratory system, digestive system, cardiovascular system, etc. Since the reptilian brain develops while humans are in the womb, van der Kolk comments it "is responsible for all the things that newborn babies can do."[14] This includes the taking of breaths, the consumption of food, and the beating of the heart. The mammalian brain refers to the limbic system, which van der Kolk describes as "the seat of the emotions, the monitor of danger, the judge of what is pleasurable or

---

11. McFarlane and van der Kolk, "Trauma and Its Challenge to Society," 26.
12. McFarlane and van der Kolk, "Trauma and Its Challenge to Society," 28.
13. McFarlane and van der Kolk, "Trauma and Its Challenge to Society," 25.
14. van der Kolk, *Body Keeps the Score*, 56.

scary, the arbiter of what is or is not important for survival purposes."[15] The limbic system includes (but is not limited to) the thalamus, amygdala, and hippocampus. The thalamus, the relay center,[16] receives signals from the senses (eyes, nose, ears, etc.) and sends these sensations to the amygdala, the body's alert system.[17] That is, the amygdala is like the body's flashing lights and siren, warning, "Danger! Danger!" Van der Kolk calls it "the smoke detector," which ascertains "whether incoming input is relevant for our survival."[18] The amygdala sends a message to the hippocampus, which, according to Rothschild, categorizes the message based on previous experiences and places the event on one's personal timeline.[19] Unlike the reptilian brain, van der Kolk notes that the limbic system develops within "the first six years of life" and continues to be shaped by one's experiences. It is seen operating when children cry when placed with a stranger as their amygdala becomes like a siren alerting the children to danger, the unfamiliar. The prefrontal cortex is the last to develop and involves the region of the brain that includes reasoning, speech, empathy, planning, self-awareness, etc. Very few pathways connect the prefrontal cortex (which is also called the *rational brain*) to the reptilian/mammalian parts of the brain (which is also called the *emotional brain*), so it has limited activity during a threatening event.[20] As counselor-participant Megan indicated, the language center "goes offline" (the brain's Broca area), so people may appear blank with nothing to say and may not "think straight," becoming forgetful. This additionally means that using reason is ineffective in the face of trauma.

The above basic description of the brain is foundational to portray how traumatizing events impact the brain/body differently than ordinary events. Consider my walking through a neighborhood when a German

15. van der Kolk, *Body Keeps the Score*, 56.

16. Rothschild, *Body Remembers*, 22.

17. van der Kolk says the thalamus mixes the input of one's "perceptions into a fully blended autobiographical soul, an integrated, coherent experience of 'this is what is happening to me.'" van der Kolk, *Body Keeps the Score*, 60.

18. van der Kolk, *Body Keeps the Score*, 60.

19. Rothschild explains, "Hippocampal processing gives events a beginning, a middle, and an end . . . one of [PTSD's] features is a sense that the trauma has not yet ended. It has been shown that the activity of the hippocampus often becomes suppressed during traumatic threat; its usual assistance in processing and storing an event is not available. When this occurs, the traumatic event is prevented from occupying its proper position in the individual's history and continues to invade the present." Rothschild, *Body Remembers*, 12.

20. van der Kolk, *Body Keeps the Score*, 56–60.

Shepherd menacingly approaches me. Upon seeing and hearing the dog, my limbic system is alerted. The senses of sight and sound send a message to the thalamus (the relay center), which messages the amygdala (the brain's warning system), and signals are sent to the brain to increase blood pressure, heart rate, breathing, etc. to prepare the body to flee or fight.[21] If I turn and yell at the dog, "Go home!" and the dog flees, I have successfully thwarted the dog's attack, causing my body to return to normal due to the termination of the threat. This success contributes to the formation of a cycle of competence within me, as I have effectively protected myself from danger.[22]

But what occurs when I cannot thwart the attack of the German Shepherd? As in the previous example, the brain and the body respond by preparing the body to flee or fight; however, a change in the brain/body transpires when my yelling at the dog is futile. When the German Shepherd, instead of fleeing, lunges at me and pushes me to the ground, I am placed in a helpless position as the dog forces its attack. This sense of helplessness is a contributing component to the development of traumatic symptoms. When fight/flight is unsuccessful and the person is restrained in some manner, the body maintains an alert status so that the trauma continues to exist in the person's body.[23] Helplessness keeps the energy within the body so that it is not released, which establishes a cycle of panic and fear as the body continues in fight/flight mode.[24] This means the body remembers the trauma by storing the event, thereby exhibiting symptoms of the trauma. Such symptoms are categorized as follows: (1) physical symptoms, e.g., survivor-participant Dominique previously had cold sweats; (2) avoidance behaviors, e.g., refraining from sleeping at

---

21. van der Kolk states, "The amygdala's danger signals trigger the release of powerful stress hormones, including cortisol and adrenaline, which increase heart rate, blood pressure, and rate of breathing, preparing us to fight back or run away." van der Kolk, *Body Keeps the Score*, 61.

22. van der Kolk, "Body Keeps the Score," YouTube video.

23. van der Kolk writes, "If the fight/flight/freeze response is successful and we escape the danger, we recover our internal equilibrium and gradually 'regain our senses.' If for some reason the normal response is blocked—for example, when people are held down, trapped, or otherwise prevented from taking effective action, be it in a war zone, a car accident, domestic violence, or a rape—the brain keeps secreting stress chemicals, and the brain's electrical circuits continue to fire in vain. Long after the actual event has passed, the brain may keep sending signals to the body to escape a threat that no longer exists." van der Kolk, *Body Keeps the Score*, 54.

24. van der Kolk, "The Body Keeps the Score," YouTube video.

night; (3) visual images, e.g., flashbacks, nightmares; and (4) emotional sensations, e.g., anger, shame, anxiety.[25]

While the body recalls the traumatic event, it does so in bits and pieces. As such, traumatic memories of the attack are preserved, not as a full story with a beginning, middle, and ending, but in fragments of sights, sounds, smells, touch, emotions, and images. This becomes evident when I see a large dog and my blood pressure, heart rate, and breathing increase as the amygdala places the body in fight/flight mode. Remnants of the incident may emerge when I trip and fall, which places me in a similar position on the ground as experienced in the attack, causing me instinctively to move my arm to protect my face. I may recall the attack in full detail but relate it without any emotion or may remember fragments of the trauma but be easily startled or overreact emotionally (shame, anger, fear, etc.) to various situations. My struggle with shame may emerge as I chastise myself for failing to stop the dog's attack or for my subsequent fears. As van der Kolk notes, "One of the hardest things for traumatized people is to confront their shame about the way they behaved during a traumatic episode, whether it is objectively warranted . . . or not."[26] I may not only avoid walking in the neighborhood, but I may limit my time outdoors in my yard to assure myself of protection, and when I am in the yard, my blood pressure and heart rate may be elevated. I may develop compulsive organizing proclivities that point toward a desire for some semblance of control since power had been stripped from me during the original event. If the attack occurred at night, I may struggle to sleep when it is dark due to the higher risk of harm. Hence, unlike the successful thwarting of the attack in which the experience becomes an event of the past that is forgotten with little or no impact on the person's life, the event is traumatic when the past continues to intrude into the present as if the trauma is occurring again and again.[27] This means that instead of being assimilated in time like ordinary events,

---

25. Rothschild writes, "Symptoms associated with PTSD include (1) reexperiencing the event in varying sensory forms (flashbacks), (2) avoiding reminders of the trauma, and (3) chronic hyperarousal in the autonomic nervous system (ANS). *DSM-IV* recognizes that such symptoms are normal in the immediate aftermath of a traumatic event." Rothschild, *Body Remembers*, 7.

26. van der Kolk, *Body Keeps the Score*, 13.

27. van der Kolk writes, "For most people the memory of an unpleasant event eventually fades or is transformed into something more benign. But most of our patients were unable to make their past into a story that happened long ago." Van der Kolk, *Body Keeps the Score*, 19.

Rambo says the trauma remains "an open wound."[28] Figuratively speaking, it is as if the body longs to heal the wound by attempting to tell the story of the traumatic event, but it can only do so in incomplete blurbs. Such is the case, as will be shown below, for many survivors of sexual violence. It is understandable, then, why many practitioners see the body as an additional resource for healing from trauma since trauma impacts the reptilian/mammalian parts of the brain.[29]

THE PARTICIPANTS' BODIES TELL A STORY

Having briefly defined some elements of trauma theory, I turn towards the stories of the participants to help connect theory to experience. Readers will be introduced in this section to various ways the body attempts to tell the story of trauma. Some indications recounted below on how the participants exhibited the impact of sexual violence had (at the time of the interview) either diminished in intensity or were no longer a part of their lives. One way some of the participants' bodies told their stories of trauma was through dissociation, as seen in this chapter's opening story of Mackenzie. The National Alliance on Mental Illness (NAMI) defines dissociation as "an involuntary escape from reality characterized by a disconnection between thoughts, identity, consciousness and memory," which often occurs with trauma.[30] NAMI provides the following five types of symptoms of dissociation: "significant memory loss of specific times, people and events; out-of-body experiences, such as feeling as though you are watching a movie of yourself; mental health problems such as depression, anxiety and thoughts of suicide; a sense of detachment from your emotions, or emotional numbness; [and] a lack of a sense of self-identity."[31] NAMI points out that it is quite common not to recall a traumatic event, such as abuse.[32] This lack of recall is the body's attempt to protect itself, which, unfortunately, is an illusion.

---

28. Rambo, *Spirit and Trauma*, 7.

29. For example, Peter Levine, Rothschild, and van der Kolk are three noted practitioners who engage in a variety of treatments to foster body awareness of trauma survivors.

30. National Alliance of Mental Illness, "Dissociative Disorders," heading "Overview."

31. National Alliance of Mental Illness, "Dissociative Disorders," heading "Symptoms."

32. National Alliance of Mental Illness, "Dissociative Disorders," heading "Overview."

Other participants, besides Mackenzie, implied experiencing dissociation when they spoke of not remembering the abuse until later in life. Herman notes that, initially, dissociation may be an essential adaptation for survivors; however, later after the danger is gone, it impedes "the integration necessary for healing" since dissociation keeps "the traumatic experience walled off from ordinary consciousness."[33] Such a walling off may also occur through self-medicating, such as when Mackenzie periodically used alcohol and opioids to numb the pain. Destiny remembered the childhood sexual abuse when she was in her mid-thirties, which led her to try to attend to the issues. She admitted to continuing to have what she called *memory gaps*, which she now considers a gift from God. For her, God has taken the very hurtful memories and is keeping them for her. More than one counselor-participant referenced dissociation as a frequent response to sexual violence, which survivors must process. Joel said that one of the challenging aspects of counseling survivors is helping them to learn to be present to their emotions. Learning to be present is different for each client and is complicated by their own fears. The inability to be present to their emotions is exemplified when some survivors, e.g., Dominique, cut and/or claw at themselves or experience suicidal ideation, such as Destiny, Jade, and Dominique. Suicidal ideation intimates a desire to end or permanently close off the painful feelings rather than be present to them. In contrast to shutting off the feelings, the survivor is invited to become present to, or to embrace, them. One way to learn to be present is to discover the art of self-empathy. Counselor-participant Dayton alluded to this by encouraging pentecostal survivors to offer grace and compassion to themselves as they hold space for the damage that has been done to them and attempt to integrate all parts of the self that they have compartmentalized and/or from which they have dissociated. Counselor-participant Megan referred to this as being a "good host" to one's trauma.

Several survivor-participants provided examples of their bodies recalling the sexual violence through images, such as nightmares, memories, or explicit and/or implicit flashbacks. While Dominique's nightmares have now ceased, Destiny spoke of nightmares as being an ongoing issue. Destiny said, "If I do something in my life that challenges me or maybe . . . things are [not] going well, I will have nightmares . . . Two nights ago, I was shot in my dreams." She spoke of being terrified by her nightmares,

33. Herman, *Trauma and Recovery*, 68.

which often involved either snakes or someone's trying to kill her. Both Dominique and Sutton brought up about smells generating memories or flashbacks. This supports the words of body-psychotherapist Peter Levine: "'[T]raumatic memories' tend to arise as fragmented splinters of inchoate and indigestible sensations, emotions, images, smells, tastes, thoughts, and so on."[34] Jackson recalled being triggered by a life event: "When my oldest son turned five, [it] brought up a flood of emotions and feelings because that was the age I was when it first started happening to me." As he gazed at his little boy, he wondered, "How could someone do that to a five-year-old boy?" Jade believed she had flashbacks prior to remembering the abuse so that she could not fully understand what was happening. When she and her husband had their first child, a little girl, they hired a babysitter for when they attended the church's midweek service. On the way home from church, Jade would begin crying, saying, "I think [our baby] is in her crib crying. I can hear her crying." However, when the young parents arrived home, they discovered that their baby was sleeping peacefully. Since Jade's sexual abuse began prior to her walking, Jade later understood that she was having memories of her own crying in a crib, but she failed to realize she was the one crying. Instead, Jade thought it was their baby. Her story indicates that it is unnecessary for survivors to recall the details of the sexual violence for it to have an impact on them. Rambo describes flashbacks like Jade's as "an event that was never cognitively registered and organized. The body directly experiences in the *present* what the mind could not grasp in the *past*" (italics in original).[35]

Several survivors disclosed having issues around sex and sexuality. This coincides with Levine's discussion that healing from the wounds of childhood sexual abuse "ultimately includes the reclamation of the capacity for pleasure and intimate, joyful sexuality."[36] Jackson referenced his struggle with pornography, which he does not completely blame on the sexual abuse but sees the two as being linked. Dominique wrestled with whether she could be a lesbian or a bisexual prior to her marriage, and both Frances and Dominique spoke of having issues in connecting romantically and/or sexually with their husbands. Mackenzie struggled with sadomasochistic fantasies both before and during marriage due to the sexual abuse that she experienced. These experiences illustrate what

34. Levine, *Trauma and Memory*, 7.
35. Rambo, "Trauma and Faith," 237.
36. Levine, *Trauma and Memory*, 127.

counselor-participant Kiley sees when some survivors are surprised as to the degree that sexual violence has impacted their beliefs or views about sex, including their having misinformation or a lack of knowledge about their own sexuality.

Multiple survivors underscored how their bodies told the story of their experiences of sexual violence through various emotions, particularly depression, fear, and/or shame. Jade and Destiny spoke of experiencing depression. Jade's depression became so severe that she made a plan to take her own life. Destiny endures an ongoing fear of abandonment, although it has lessened. When someone says to her, "I'll be back in fifteen minutes," she becomes anxious about being abandoned after the person is gone for twenty minutes. Destiny explained, "I have to really talk myself down from those things." She has to tell herself, "I am not abandoned. I can trust this person, and this person has my best at heart." Destiny also was fearful of being sexually assaulted, so she built a "protective mechanism" to avoid being "thin and pretty." She described her plan: "If you're a little bit more heavyweight, men don't look at you the same way, [and] that makes you safer." Therefore, she tries to stay in what she called the "safe zone," a little overweight, so she is less "likely to be raped or attacked." This is a way to protect herself from any unforeseen threat looming in an unsafe world, as discussed above.

Several survivors highlighted their experiences with shame. Sutton found that the most challenging part of his journey was "the seemingly random emergence of memories that [brought] shame, guilt, and fear." Mackenzie spoke of being unaware of the degree of self-hatred and self-loathing she carried until she began her healing journey from sexual violence. Dominique and Frances portrayed how the feelings of shame interfered in their relationship with God. For Dominique, she rightly viewed God as pure, holy, just, and righteous but incorrectly interpreted her experiences of sexual abuse as her having committed adultery, which kept her from relating to God. Shame was visible when she said, "I felt like I was a bad girl who wanted to be a good girl but felt like I could never be a good girl." Herman explains this response: "When it is impossible to avoid the reality of the abuse, the child must construct some system of meaning that justifies it. Inevitably the child concludes that her innate badness is the cause. The child seizes upon this explanation early and clings to it tenaciously, for it enables her to preserve a sense of meaning, hope, and power... If she is bad, then she can try to be good."[37] Herman continues by pointing out that this kind of self-blame "is congruent with the thought processes of traumatized people of all ages, who search for faults in their own behavior in an effort to make sense out of what has happened to them."[38] Survivor-participant Jackson confessed to never feeling like he was good enough, which connotes shame. He saw this as contributing to his overworking at his previous job because he was driven to prove his worth. He also perceived that this appeared in his relationship with God. When he sinned and asked God to forgive him, his feelings of guilt would sometimes continue for weeks. Practical theologian Stephen Pattison speaks to this matter when he writes about what transpires if shame and guilt are not differentiated: "[S]hamed people may label their condition as one of guilt: they may then wonder why their attempts at repentance and reparation do little to restore their sense of self-acceptance and belonging within their reference communities and relationships."[39]

Shame also surfaced in more than one conversation with the counselor-participants. Megan spoke about seeing shame in relation to any kind of arousal, delight, or kindness that occurred, such as when the perpetrator may say, "I love your smile." Megan alluded to the power of shame as it caused some clients to be in counseling for years before they felt safe enough to speak of those tender places where shame had set up house. Such feelings of shame may not encompass the whole event but center on one moment in the story, causing survivors to keep it well shielded from others. Megan clarified, "Those are the hardest places to get to because they're the ones we fiercely guard against because they're the ones [where] we're at war with ourselves." According to Rothschild, many who have experienced trauma have a sense of shame because they failed to protect themselves successfully by fleeing or fighting but froze in place. She writes that when it is understood "that freezing is automatic," it "often facilitates the difficult process of self-forgiveness."[40] This possibly describes Dominique who recounted her difficulties in forgiving herself because she failed to stop the abuse when she was thirteen years old (she waited until she was fifteen) or because she did not remove herself from harm's way by moving out of her family home at age eighteen (staff at a

---

37. Herman, *Trauma and Recovery*, 151.
38. Herman, *Trauma and Recovery*, 151.
39. Pattison, "Shame and the Unwanted Self," 12–13.
40. Rothschild, *Body Remembers*, 12.

psychiatric hospital strongly encouraged Dominique not to return to her family home since it was unsupportive, unhelpful, and unsafe). Rothschild's description of freezing in place is illustrated through Dominique's words: "I probably get more upset with me [for] being so fearful and scared and [for] not moving forward." Rothschild also comments that sometimes for people, who have been diagnosed with PTSD, shame is a result of believing that "on some deep level that they have let themselves (and perhaps others) down and/or that something integral is wrong with them that they fell victim to the trauma."[41] In essence, shame is the invisible steel cage that holds people captive.

If pentecostals, however, are to grasp a deeper level of the impact of sexual violence on a person, they must, as counselor-participant Joel insists, distinguish between guilt and shame. Joel explains, "When we're guilty of something, if we stop the behavior . . ., the guilt tends to go away. If I'm guilty for being late at work, if I quit being late for work, then the guilt probably goes away." However, Joel goes on to say that if he views himself as a liar and feels shame because he is a liar, his shame will not be fixed by his putting an end to his lying. According to Joel, the difference between the two scenarios is that his lying, in the latter example, has become a part of his identity: "Healing has to start with identity. It's not so much what happened to us. It's . . . what do we believe about ourselves" after the event. Joel's comments mirror Pattison, who notes, "A guilty person is a responsible self who has committed an offense." That person is able to take responsibility for said offense, apologize, and put "things right with the offended person." In this case, a guilty person's "identity is not impaired." However, with shamed persons, "their whole identity . . . is inadequate and impaired." In short, "[s]hame is a judgment on the whole self, not just on an aspect of action of behavior."[42] It is unlike guilt, in which people stop committing the offensive act to free themselves of it. It is unlike the feeling of sadness, in which individuals release the emotion through crying to rid themselves of it. Instead, as Rothschild explains, "[a]cceptance and contact appear to be keys to relieving shame." The "nonjudgmental, accepting contact of another human being"[43] is what is necessary to dispel shame. In other words, empathic relationships are essential to nurture healing for survivors. This is the type of empathy that is embodied in Christ's story of trauma, to which I now turn.

41. Rothschild, *Body Remembers*, 62.
42. Pattison, "Shame and the Unwanted Self," 12.
43. Rothschild, *Body Remembers*, 62.

TELLING CHRIST'S TRAUMA STORY

The above theory and experiences of the participants reveal how the body tells the story of trauma. A survivor's body may attempt to protect the survivor through dissociation, hiding the sexual violence from the consciousness. However, trauma is an open wound that defies time by bringing the past into the present by a variety of means, like flashbacks, triggers, nightmares, suicidal ideation, smells, self-medicating, and emotions, e.g., depression, fear, and shame. In the preceding chapter I mentioned how pentecostals have traditionally placed themselves into God's story by mirroring the stories of miracles in the book of Acts. Several participants corroborate this in their descriptions of their experiences of being baptized in the Holy Spirit as evidenced by speaking in tongues. Survivor-participant Mackenzie gave an example of divine healing when she spoke of meeting "a young man who was dead, and the Lord brought him back to life."[44] Survivor-participant Destiny experienced a divine intervention of healing when both her knee and her husband's shoulder were "miraculously healed." Survivor-participant Elizabeth spoke of a miraculous healing from acute inflammatory demyelinating polyneuropathy (AIDP), or commonly known as Guillain-Barre, in which the immune system begins to attack the nerves, leading to weakness, numbness, and/or paralysis. Unfortunately, survivors rarely have healing stories from sexual violence that imitate the miraculous, instant, divine interventions of the healing stories of the book of Acts. As Dominique acknowledged, instant healing may occur with some healings, such as physical healings, but she did not experience this in her healing from sexual violence. While survivors may be unable to place themselves in God's story through a miracle of complete healing from sexual violence, I believe they can place themselves in God's story through their experiences of trauma. Survivors may insert themselves into a biblical trauma story—the story of death by way of the cross, the central feature of the gospel. They may identify with Christ's story of trauma and shame, thereby seeing themselves in God's own story.

First Corinthians speaks of the retelling of the story of the cross through the partaking of the Lord's Supper, which is the retelling of a death experience—trauma. I am drawing from 1 Corinthians because of

---

44. This true to life story of this young man is told by Smith in *Breakthrough: The Miraculous True Story of a Mother's Faith and Her Son's Resurrection* and in the 2019 movie *Breakthrough*.

the pentecostal emphasis that has historically been placed on chapters 12 and 14. Similar to a story of trauma, the story that is retold through the partaking of the Lord's Supper is not one that contains a conclusive ending in the past. Instead, it is a story of trauma that seems to defy time, mixing the past and present as it moves towards a future. These elements of past, present, and future are displayed in 1 Corinthians when Paul outlines the words of institution of the Lord's Supper. For a sexual trauma survivor, these words may serve as a message of the healing presence of Christ, which is able both to eclipse time and to emerge in time by entering a survivor's death experience.

Prior to portraying how survivors place themselves in God's story, I first set forth a frame of reference by highlighting Paul's first visit to Corinth as described in Acts. This is followed by providing some background to the first letter to the Corinthians and then describing the circumstances that arose in the Corinthian church, which engendered Paul to include the words of institution of the Lord's Supper. Lastly, I explore the past, future, and present that are held within the story of the Lord's Supper and relate it to a story of trauma.

The Backstory of the Corinthian Church

Before considering 1 Corinthians, I draw the reader's attention to Luke's record of Paul's visit to Corinth (Acts 18) as it lays a foundational theme for my discussion. According to Paul's general pattern in other cities, Paul initially visits the local synagogue, preaching "Jesus is the Messiah" (Acts 18:5); however, the Jews oppose Paul and speak harshly against him. Paul responds by saying to them, "Your blood be on your own heads! I am guiltless! From now on I will go to the Gentiles" (Acts 18:6). While not all Jewish hearts are opposed to the gospel, as seen in the conversion of the synagogue president (Acts 18:8), Luke implicitly indicates Paul's discouragement by recording God's ministry to Paul. God comes to Paul in a vision during the night (perhaps both literally and figuratively), instructing Paul not to be afraid as God is present with him (Acts 18: 9–10). That is, God enters into Paul's impossible, hostile situation and ministers to him. Paul experiences God as a minister in his darkness, when God comes to the apostle in God's very being, an event of ministry.[45] This

---

45. I am drawing from practical theologian Andrew Root who writes, "To say that God is uniquely the arriving God—a living God who makes himself known as an event in history—is to claim that *God's being is in God's becoming* . . . To say it like this is

ministry event changes Paul, encouraging and empowering him to stay in Corinth for an extended time. Paul, having received ministry in his death experience, turns to minister to others in their death experiences.[46]

When speaking of death experiences, I am not only highlighting a physical death, but I also am including impossibilities, voids, or hopeless situations. Death experiences encompass certain situations in Scripture such as Abraham and Sarah, whose void was their inability to have children. It may also be said of the Israelites in the book of Exodus, who were slaves of the Egyptians, in which freedom was an impossibility. Yet, in each of these experiences, God enters humanity's history through acts of ministry. God reveals God's self as a minister by encouraging Paul, by providing Abraham and Sarah with a child, and by delivering the Israelites out of Egypt. In each case, God reveals who God is through an act of ministry by entering the time and space of humanity. By entering into human history, God becomes the main actor in the story by an act of ministry in God's being.[47] Humans would not know God except through God's acts of ministry within time and space. This theme is reiterated through the crucified Christ, which Paul accentuates throughout the first epistle to the church in Corinth, particularly in chapter 11. That is, Christ enters into humanity's death experience through his crucifixion, and we enter into his death experience as we partake of the Eucharist.

Living the Story of Christ Crucified

Throughout this first letter to the Corinthians, Paul points toward the story of the crucified Christ, not only in chapter 11 (as will be discussed below) but also when Paul literally writes in 1:23, "But we preach Christ crucified" and again in 2:2, "For I decided to be concerned about nothing among you except Jesus Christ, and him crucified" (see also 1:13). Such an emphasis is in stark contrast to Roman culture, which had influenced the Corinthian church's understanding of power. New Testament scholar Michael Gorman defines *power* as "the ability to exercise significant control

---

simply to claim that the only way for us to know God (and therefore experience God's being) is to encounter God's historical arrival" (italics in original). Root, *The Pastor in a Secular Age*, 183–84.

46. I develop this theme more clearly in Engelbert, *Who Is Present in Absence?*.

47. Root says, "God's arriving happens in time, producing a history." Root, *Pastor in a Secular Age*, 185.

or influence, either for good or for ill, over people and/or history."[48] In Paul's day, the gods were perceived to have the most power, which was followed by "humans who somehow had a share in these suprahuman powers."[49] The humans with supreme power and honor were those who ruled the empire, with the emperor being viewed as close to divine (if not fully divine) as a human could be. Below him was a hierarchy of governmental officials, who each had been allocated a measure of power and honor according to his rank. Gorman explains, "The higher up the ladder people were, the greater the honor they were due and the closer to the divine realm they were believed to be."[50] Gorman notes that the greater affluence, prestige, accomplishments, education, proper lineage, outward beauty, and persuasive speech one had, the more power and honor one received; thus, the culture centered on competition within a system of "meritocracy." If one failed to have such qualities, or even lost them, the result was "shame" and being perceived as "weak."[51]

The above discussion on power is significant for survivors in light of psychoanalyst/psychotherapist Lyn Yonack's assertion that sexual violence is more about power than sex. Yonack writes, "Although the touch may be sexual, the words seductive or intimidating, and the violation physical, when someone rapes, assaults, or harasses, the motivation stems from the perpetrator's need for dominance and control. In heterosexual and same-sex encounters, sex is the tool used to gain power over another person."[52] As Yonack notes, the perpetrator is in "a more powerful or dominant position in relation to the victim," and in some cases the perpetrator is in the position to grant the victim something she seeks like a job, a good grade, a promotion, etc.[53] In other words, the strong and influential overpower the so-called weak, often leading to shame, a topic which surfaces on these pages again and again.

However, Paul resists the pull of his culture and welcomes a life of "cruciformity," a term used repeatedly by Gorman. Gorman defines "cruciformity" as a daily "conformity to the crucified Christ."[54] Gorman

---

48. Gorman, *Cruciformity*, loc. 3151–52.
49. Gorman, *Cruciformity*, loc. 3153.
50. Gorman, *Cruciformity*, loc. 3165.
51. Gorman, *Cruciformity*, loc. 3164–68.
52. Yonack, "Sexual Assault Is about Power," heading "All about power."
53. Yonack, "Sexual Assault Is about Power," heading "All about power."
54. Gorman, *Cruciformity*, loc. 76. Gorman continues, "[T]his conformity is a dynamic correspondence in daily life to the strange story of Christ crucified as the

argues that "cruciformity" is not the "'center' of Paul's theology" but is an "'integrative narrative experience'" of Paul's whole life.[55] It is not a surprise, then, that in this epistle, Paul first establishes himself as an example of cruciformity before calling the Corinthians to live out a life of cruciformity, which will be developed more fully in upcoming chapters. In the same way God ministered to Paul in his death experience in Corinth, Paul now ministers to the Corinthians by entering into others' death experiences, becoming like the crucified Christ, in order that others may be persuaded to believe in Jesus as Savior. As Paul embodies the story of the Crucified One,[56] he also, as Gorman writes, instructs the Corinthians "to live out the story of Christ crucified in their community."[57] The apostle is advocating for a life characterized by cruciformity rather than a life characterized by competition. For Paul, the cross is the story of God's power (1:18). In this chapter I underline Paul's exhortation to the Corinthians to live out the story of the crucified Christ in and through their partaking of the Lord's Supper (1 Cor 11) in the same way Christ has entered into their death.

The Retelling of Christ's Trauma Story

The Corinthians were coming together (1 Cor 11:17, 18, 20, 33, 34) to retell the story of the crucified Lord by regularly partaking of the Lord's Supper. However, Paul is clear that they are not partaking of the *Lord's* Supper (v. 20) but are eating of each one's *own* supper (v. 21). While the Corinthians are attempting to retell the story of the crucified Lord, they are embodying the telling of their *own* story. Their own story includes social stratification where the rich exhibit power over the poor and behave in a manner of superior importance. The telling of *their* story involves the exemplification of "extremes," to use pentecostal Gordon Fee's word.[58] Paul juxtaposes those who remain hungry, signifying nothing to eat, with those who are drunk, signaling the overindulgence of food and wine (v.

---

primary way of experiencing the love and grace of God." Gorman, *Cruciformity*, loc. 77. Gorman perceives this theme throughout Paul's epistles. See Gorman, *Apostle of the Crucified Lord* and *Cruciformity*.

55. Gorman, *Cruciformity*, loc. 4366–78.

56. Gorman writes, "Paul wanted his life and ministry to tell a story, a story that corresponded to the 'story of the cross,' to his gospel." Gorman, *Cruciformity*, loc. 344–45.

57. Gorman, *Apostle of the Crucified Lord*, 282.

58. Fee, *First Epistle to the Corinthians*, 543.

21). Paul then juxtaposes those who have "houses" in which to eat and drink, suggesting ownership, to "those who have nothing."[59] The apostle indicates that through their actions, the wealthy Corinthians are "shaming" those who have nothing (v. 22). Thus, rather than being a place of healing of sociological relational differences that are present in society, the Christians from the upper-class fashion the Lord's Supper into an occasion for division, for shaming. This is not to be! No class distinctions are to exist at the *Lord's* Table, for as Paul writes, "For in one Spirit we were all baptized into one body. Whether Jews or Greeks or slaves or free, we were all made to drink of the one Spirit" (12:13).[60] There is no shaming in Christ based on ethnicity or status, and to do so, as Paul conveys, may be a sign of "contempt for the church of God" (v. 22). And I might add that for survivors, neither is there to be shaming, whether one is a survivor of sexual violence or not. As a matter of correction, Paul reminds the Corinthians of Jesus's words that were said at the institution of the Lord's Supper. Such words not only describe God's ministry to humanity but also capture the past, future, and present aspects that are part of eating at the Lord's Table.

The partaking of the bread and wine retells the story of the *past* life and death of Jesus Christ. As believers chew and eat the bread and sip and swallow from the cup, they experience with their senses the life and death of Jesus, the body and blood of the Lord. Pentecostal scholar Chris Green writes, "In the present-day liturgical breaking of the bread and the offering of the cup, we 'see' Christ crucified before our very eyes (Gal 3.1) and 'hear' his death proclaimed (1 Cor 11.26)."[61] The Lord's Supper calls to mind the event of God's coming to humanity, entering our time through an act of ministry in God's very being. Namely, it underscores God is a minister. It recognizes the incarnation, in which the divine joins us in our death experience through his living and dying as Emmanuel. Jesus entered into humanity's death experience when Jesus ate with sinners, thereby he embodied the divine's friendship with and acceptance of humanity, and when he died for sinners, thereby he reconciled sinners to God.[62] As such, he joined our death experiences of fear and shame.

---

59. Fee, *First Epistle to the Corinthians*, 543.

60. Paul also states in Gal 3:28: "There is neither Jew nor Greek, there is neither slave nor free, there is neither male nor female —for all of you are one in Christ Jesus."

61. Green is describing what it means to remember. Green, *Toward a Pentecostal Theology of the Lord's Supper*, 254.

62. Green writes, "At one level of significance, the Eucharist simply directs our

Besides the retelling of the past, the partaking of the Lord's Supper includes the telling of the *future*. The Lord's Supper contains an eschatological element, an aspect that is highlighted by Paul's words, "you proclaim the Lord's death until he comes" (11:26). Theologian Thomas F. Torrance holds that the eschatological element must be underscored in the Lord's Supper. To fail to do so is a denial of divine action, "the new creation," so that the church's story becomes focused on human action, the sustaining of a faith in a Christ "who has not really made all things new in the power of the resurrection." Such a denial of divine action engenders the church to continue to be held captive "in the wrapping of human systems and decisions."[63] This is pointedly illustrated by the elite Corinthians who uphold the non-eschatological values of the culture's social stratification at the Table. And it is seen when those in power in our contemporary church culture fail to maintain eschatological values by sexually violating those under them. When believers appropriately embrace the eschatological emphasis of the Lord's Supper, they acknowledge that they are participating in God's ministry and are a church resulting from divine action. It is God, through the divine-human one, who has entered humanity's time and space through the event of the virgin birth, and it will be God who will be "all in all" (15:28) in the forthcoming eschaton.[64]

When the church partakes of the Lord's Supper, it is being pulled toward the future—the eschaton. First, the church is being pulled toward a new heaven and new earth as the Lord's Supper is a foretaste of the Marriage Supper of the Lamb. Second, since the "whole Christ" is present at the Table,[65] the future is present in Jesus Christ as he is what we

---

attention to the historical realities of the life of one Jesus of Nazareth, to his subversive table-fellowship and his Last Supper, and to the event of what the church understands as his once-for-all agonizing death for us and for the world." Green, *Toward a Pentecostal Theology of the Lord's Supper*, 254.

63. Torrance, *Atonement*, 422.

64. Torrance remarks, "The perfect union of God and man that has broken into time in the virgin birth, inserted itself into history at the cross, and yet is not the prisoner of fallen time because of the resurrection, entails a new creation that travels through old time inasmuch as Christ Jesus lives on." Torrance, *Atonement*, 421.

65. Green, in writing about "a revisioning of the 5-fold gospel," states, "[T]he Christ who is present at the Table is the whole Christ, identical with the man Christ Jesus whom the Scriptures and creeds together identify as God's eternal Son, head of the church, and judging savior of the creation." Green, *Toward a Pentecostal Theology of the Lord's Supper*, 272. Green continues, "Jesus is 'coming king' in the church's sacramental experience, just as he was in the incarnation and shall be in the *parousia*—with this

shall be. According to Torrance, through his resurrection, Jesus is the Healer of "space and time" and "every threat of death or nothingness."[66] The Healer is the one who embodies the coming together of time and eternity because Jesus Christ is fully God and fully human, which means the past and the future are simultaneously present in Jesus Christ. If space and time are healed in Christ, survivors of sexual trauma have hope that their trauma will be fully healed in Christ: as he is, they will be.

While the Lord's Supper is a retelling of an event of the past ("on the night in which he was betrayed," 11:23) and while it points toward the future ("until he comes," 11:26),[67] it is also an event in the *present*. It simultaneously brings the past and the future into the present.[68] Green affirms, "[T]he Eucharist is uniquely the event in which Christ's past, the church's present, and creation's future come together—if only mysteriously and hiddenly."[69] As we partake of the Lord's Supper, we are reminded that we currently live in "the middle," to use Rambo's concept. On the one hand, the present involves who Jesus Christ is now: He is now the glorified One who is seated at the right hand of God. This reality is currently operating in today's church, which the partaking of the Lord's Supper reminds us. As believers eat the bread and drink the cup, it calls to mind that they are now raised with Christ in the divine life (Eph 2:4–7; Col 3:1–3) through the Spirit because of Jesus Christ's incarnation, death, resurrection, and ascension. Since Christ has died and been raised, believers presently experience the benefits in Christ, such as righteousness, adoption, forgiveness of sins, etc. (Eph 1:3–8). As Green asserts, "To 'remember' rightly, then, is to receive the meal in such a way that Christ is present to us and the benefits of his victorious death are made effective in our lives. It does this by drawing the believing community into authentic and

---

difference only: in the End, his kingdom shall be finally and fully established beyond dispute" (italics in original). Green, *Toward a Pentecostal Theology of the Lord's Supper*, 272.

66. Torrance, *Atonement*, 286.

67. Torrance sees "the two fundamental moments within which the eucharist has its place: 'the night on which he was betrayed' and the 'till he come,' as St Paul puts them." Torrance, *Atonement*, 419.

68. Torrance writes, "The eucharist is . . . bound to history and related to the advent of Christ at the end of history. It reaches into the past, to the death of Christ, and sets it in the present as reality operative here and now in the church. On the other hand, the eucharist reaches out beyond the present into the future and becomes the means whereby the church in the present is brought under the power of the advent of Christ." Torrance, *Atonement*, 419.

69. Green, *Toward a Pentecostal Theology of the Lord's Supper*, 257.

transformative encounter with the Spirit-mediated presence of the living Christ . . . In the Eucharistic encounter, believers are bound together not only with Christ, but also with one another and with the whole created reality."[70] Thus, Jesus, who is Savior, Sanctifier, Baptizer, Healer, and Coming King, is present, and his body (the church) encounters and is united with him and each other through the Spirit.

On the other hand, believers' existence (even after Christ's death) is similar to that of trauma survivors who live in the wake of a traumatic event. While believers are raised with Christ in the divine life, they are also living in a fallen world. That is, believers embrace a proleptic life—the now-but-not-yet.[71] Pentecostals have a reputation of upholding the resurrection and speaking of hope, but in Rambo's words: "Many familiar versions of the redemptive narrative skim the surface of the abyss. The gloss of redemption is, perhaps, the greatest enemy to those who survive trauma; it provides a promise often unaccompanied by forms of life that can deliver on that promise. Life, for many, does not triumph over death. Instead, life persists in the midst of death and death in the midst of life."[72]

The Lord's Supper and trauma are essentially ongoing reminders that pentecostals exist proleptically. The retelling of the story of Christ's crucifixion and the foretelling of our future continually remind pentecostals that they live in the now-but-not-yet, wedged between the past and the future. As the church comes together at the Table, the community is participating in their ongoing longing and striving for healing. Paul instructs the Corinthians that each time they eat the bread and drink the cup, they are proclaiming Christ's death "until he comes" (v. 26). That is, Christ has not yet returned, which means God's promise to be "all in all" (15:28) is yet to be. The partaking of the Lord's Supper, then, signifies that believers are in mourning as they await the return of Jesus Christ. This implies that pentecostals live in the middle, the now-but-not-yet. Thus, while the Lord's Supper is a foretaste of the eschaton and the victorious Christ is now present, pentecostals must exercise caution. They must resist an overemphasis on a theology of glory by responding appropriately

---

70. Green, *Toward a Pentecostal Theology of the Lord's Supper*, 255.

71. Fee writes, "By these final words ['proclaim the Lord's death until he comes'] Paul is reminding the Corinthians of their essentially eschatological existence . . . They have not yet arrived (4:8); at this meal they are to be reminded that there is yet a future for themselves, as well as for all the people of God." Fee, *First Epistle to the Corinthians*, 557.

72. Rambo, *Spirit and Trauma*, 165.

to ongoing suffering, like the triggers of survivors.[73] This means for survivors of sexual trauma, who partake of the Lord's Supper, that their experiences of ongoing triggers, such as nightmares, flashbacks, smells, and emotions, are normalized. They may realize that Jesus is intimately present in their past, future, and present while they are present to him in his past, future, and present. Thus, they are reminded at the Table that they live proleptically: they are in Christ who heals both time/space and their death experiences so that they are healed positionally while they simultaneously are experiencing ongoing healing in time/space. It is this Christ, who presently embodies their wholeness in the future and who continues to minister in their present death experiences through the power and the presence of the Spirit. It is this Christ who places their stories in God's story. It is this Christ who has entered into the survivor's trauma, an encounter with death through his trauma.

CONCLUSION

This chapter has underscored that learning about trauma theory is an important starting point both for understanding healing from sexual violence and for becoming a healing church community for survivors. I have stressed the impact of trauma on the brain and body as seen in the theory of trauma and in the experiences of the participants. According to trauma theory, survivors have open wounds of encounters with death in which the past is in the present. This means that survivors' lives continue to be mixed with death as their stories of sexual violence are retold through images, such as flashbacks; emotions, such as shame; avoidance behaviors, such as avoiding sexual intimacy; or physical symptoms, such as cold sweats. In short, their sexual trauma is being retold through their bodies. It is through their trauma that survivors may place themselves in God's story via Christ's story of trauma—his death. Thus, rather than only focusing on complete healing in this life from trauma's impact, pentecostals are invited to become informed of how trauma is an open wound, thereby entering into a survivor's death—their experience of trauma.

---

73. In writing about the Eucharist as "a new creation event," Green cautions us not to overly emphasize a theology of glory, forgetting "that the triumphant Christ who comes from the new creation in the Spirit to us at the table is even yet the *crucified* one"; thus, we, too, are to "take up" our "cross and allow the Spirit to lead" us to where we "do not want to go" (italics in original). Green, *Toward a Pentecostal Theology of the Lord's Supper*, 271–72.

The story told through the Eucharist is a trauma story that reveals God is a minister. Through the partaking of the Lord's Supper, we are embodying the story of how God joins in humanity's death experience through Jesus Christ, and more specifically how God joins the survivor-participants in their death experiences of trauma. This places their stories in God's story. One way the retelling of the crucified story occurs is when pentecostals participate in the physical swallowing of the bread and cup, thereby entering into the death experience of Christ as he enters into the death experiences of others, especially survivors. As such, pentecostals are invited to become present to trauma stories as Christ has become present to survivors' trauma stories. They are being invited to join in the struggle of brokenness as they also yearn for complete reconciliation, or healing. In the partaking of the bread and the cup, the church shares in Christ's brokenness, joining in each other's brokenness, thereby embracing all stories. Through this embodiment of participating in the Eucharist, they are proclaiming Christ and Christ crucified, which is a divine intervention. I continue in the next chapter with how the repeated telling of the story of trauma, both that of Christ and of the survivors, is healing.

3

Telling the Story as Healing

[Pastors] need to hear our stories. Because if they don't know that we have stories, they can't support us.

—Destiny, a survivor-participant

People have this façade. They have this curtain that they live behind . . . For us to be open with each other, to be able to tell our stories to each other, it's powerful. It's why grief groups are so powerful. There's no curtain. No judgment.

—Joel, a counselor-participant

For every time you eat this bread and drink the cup, you proclaim the Lord's death until he comes.

—Paul, an apostle of Jesus Christ

JACKSON WAS SIXTEEN YEARS old when he began his "forgiveness journey," which he equated to his healing journey from sexual violence. No one else knew about the abuse up to this point for he had "stuffed it down inside." His attempts to bury it, however, were ineffective: "If you don't resolve them [things like abuse], they start to well up in your behavior or in your thoughts [or] in your attitudes towards different things." The evidence of the concealed abuse was most visible in his attitude toward his abuser: "I got to the point where I hated the guy who had molested me."

Alone in his pain, Jackson identified with stories of individuals who were experiencing domestic abuse until they went "off the deep end," killed the spouse, and landed in jail, losing everything. These individuals had become convinced that killing the spouse was their "only option," which mirrored Jackson's feelings. Yet, he recognized that his thoughts were in opposition to his Christian beliefs, prompting him to read scriptural passages about forgiveness. Characteristically, he was a forgiving person. He had forgiven others, from the bullies at school to his mom and sister when he fought with them. But Jackson could not forgive the man who had sexually abused him. He admitted that he "did not want to let go of this."

After an internal wrestling match, reading others' stories, and studying the Scriptures, he eventually arrived at a place where he forgave the man. This became his first major step toward healing from sexual violence. His decision to forgive was quickly followed by communicating his story about the sexual abuse to others for the very first time. He began by informing his mom and his sister, and he later told his girlfriend (who eventually became his wife) after they had become more serious in their relationship. Today, Jackson continues to adhere to the importance of forgiveness. He has claimed Matthew 6:14 as his life verse: "For if you forgive others their sins, your heavenly Father will also forgive you." Jackson also is not one to abide by the lone-cowboy or just-Jesus-and-me mentality that was advocated by his mom. He deeply believes that God has "put us in community to need other people."

The telling of and the listening to each other's stories matter. Our stories are of considerable importance for us as humans, whether we are relating or hearing them. It is the basic foundation of this research project. As I engaged in this qualitative research project, I immersed myself into the narratives of the participants. Listening to the participants during extended interviews formed the heart of this research. After transcribing each recorded interview, or story, word for word, I read each one again and again, searching for themes that were contained in the stories. I then endeavored to pinpoint which themes were shared among the survivors and which were included among the counselors. This was followed by determining the main themes overall (the entire process of finding themes is referred to as *coding*). The broad themes form the basis of the chapters of this book. Drawing from each theme, I retell the stories of the participants. At the same time, the story of my life intersects with this process. This project is not cordoned off in a separate space apart from my own story. I cannot separate the essence of who I am from the research. My life story intermingles as I listen to the stories, identify themes in the stories, and write each chapter, while I am correspondingly being changed.

Stories are powerful. Both storytelling and storylistening have the potential to heal us.[1] Healing through stories involves cooperation as it necessitates the working together of the teller and the listener. It beckons for both to recognize the healing nature of stories so that the teller will courageously voice the story, and the listener will perceptively nurture a supportive environment. This chapter centers on the healing characteristics of stories to generate healing transformation in the teller and the listener. My main purpose is to highlight the significance of the survivors' telling of their stories for healing and how this is congruous with a retelling of Christ's trauma story. This will be accomplished in four movements: (1) by recounting the participants' experiences of telling their stories; (2) by demonstrating the importance of stories for human beings; (3) by underscoring the healing nature of stories, both in the telling and the listening; and (4) by portraying how the retelling of Christ's trauma story is healing.

THE TELLING OF THE PARTICIPANTS' STORIES

The importance of telling the story of sexual violence became evident to me during the coding process. While I was searching for themes in the transcriptions, it occurred to me that all the survivor-participants had told their story of sexual violence to another person during their healing journey. Many of them, like Jackson's story above, had embarked on

---

1. Such healing may even occur in a research project such as this. Rosenthal argues that when one is conducting qualitative research, the participants may experience a healing process through the telling of their stories. If the trauma is not shared, according to Rosenthal, it may have an isolating impact. Rosenthal states, "If people cannot tell their traumatic experiences, then they cannot share what they have experienced with others, and they experience themselves at a distance as well as a relationship of being excluded in relation to those who themselves did not experience something similar." Rosenthal, "Healing Effects of Storytelling," 924. However, if healing is to occur, Rosenthal stresses the importance of the researcher to foster a healing environment by being supportive while also protecting the participants from digging too deeply into their pain, which can lead to their becoming overwhelmed. Rosenthal, "Healing Effects of Storytelling," 915–33.

a healing journey when they related their story to someone else. All of them spoke of telling more than one person about their experience of sexual violence. Whether it was explicitly or implicitly, they all referenced their need for others to walk with them throughout their healing journey. Research supports this as 65 to 81 percent of survivors tell their story to someone else.[2] To honor the priority placed on the telling of stories, I begin this section by highlighting the counselors' comments about storytelling prior to recounting the survivors' experiences in telling their stories.

Storytelling and Counselors

The significance of storytelling lies at the very core of a counselor's occupation. Much of what is involved in being a counselor encompasses the priority of healing through the telling of stories. If healing is portrayed as a journey, the counselor is the one who accompanies the other as the story doubles back, winds around, and faces difficult odds. The counselor joins survivors when the story's scenes contain unexpected plot twists with steep ravines or rocky rapids. The counselor is present as survivors unearth the hidden layers beneath the surface, the unseen messages they have unknowingly breathed day in and day out, what is referred to as the *subtext* of their stories. The counselor bears with survivors when their story engages a conflict along stony paths or up and down sheer mountains. But the counselor also remains beside them when their story includes a relaxed stroll along a more predictable trajectory. Thus, by traveling with survivors through their highs and lows, the counselor is inhabiting the priority of storytelling.

According to counselor-participant Joel, one of the most challenging aspects for survivors on their healing journey is telling the story of their trauma. Counselor-participant Megan seems to agree when she notes that an important part of the healing journey is "the process of actually being able to tell the story." Joel perceives it is difficult for those in the church to speak about sexual violence because church culture resists discussing these kinds of matters, even though many congregants experience the pain of sexual violence. For instance, Joel mentions that churched youth are the most difficult "to work with in treatment because"

---

2. Yuvarajan and Stanford, "Clergy Perceptions of Sexual Assault Victimization," 589.

of "the shame of talking about it." To navigate this, Joel uses "well-placed compassion and humor" to help people tell the story of their trauma. This helps survivors realize that there's nothing they can do that will surprise or scare the counselor. Survivors eventually recognize that the counselor accepts them because the event is "just something that happened. It's just a story. It's not today." Until they reach this place, the survivors are "living as if it is today. That's the whole point: their past, present, and future is all happening at the same time, and that's why it's so intense."

Kiley implied the importance of being able to relate one's story when she spoke about survivors' attempts to tell their stories, but potential companions shut them down. Some individuals silenced survivors by blaming them or by responding with clichés like, "Well, God doesn't give us more than you can handle." Kiley viewed such responses as "super counterproductive" and "sometimes damaging." This may be a reason for Megan's advice to pentecostal survivors, in which she underscored healing through storytelling: "Don't give up. Keep looking until you find someone that can hear your story and help you heal."

Storytelling and Survivors

As an attestation to Megan's above point, each of the eight survivor-participants had people in their lives who were willing to hear their stories, helping the survivors move toward wholeness. Jade was one of those who began her healing journey by talking to another. Jade was married and a mother when her memories surfaced about being sexually abused as a child, whereupon she informed her pastor. After she talked to him about the two small flashbacks she had experienced, which she described as tiny pieces of images that she had recognized as sexual abuse, he prayed with her. Unfortunately, these two memories were just the dawning of the barrage of memories that was about to engulf her. While getting out of bed later that night to fetch a bottle for her baby, Jade was flooded with memories. She described it like a knife being thrust into her stomach and opening her up. She was at a loss. What was she to do with these memories? What was she to do with the knowledge that people, who she loved, had abused her for an extended period? She returned to her pastor to tell him about the additional memories that had surfaced. He, in turn, wisely referred her to someone else for he knew he was not qualified as a counselor to help her walk through her story.

Similar to Jackson's story, sometimes the survivor first tells a family member about the sexual violence. It had been six months since Sutton's family had moved away from the town where Sutton had been sexually abused by a Sunday School teacher when his sister received a letter from a friend who attended that church. The friend reported about the church's discovery of the Sunday School teacher's abuse of multiple middle-school-aged boys and was wondering if Sutton had been among them. Sutton stated, "I broke when my sister read it to me." He then revealed to both his sister and his parents about being sexually abused. Sutton described this major turning point in his healing journey: "This allowed the suppression of the abuse to be abandoned, and others and myself to come to the weight of what was done to me." His parents responded by scheduling several counseling sessions with a pastor, who was not specifically trained in counseling. Besides these initial conversations, Sutton also talked with his wife about the sexual abuse when they were newly married, which he described as "a liberating and painful but healing experience." In addition to the one-on-one conversations, Sutton has shared his story in small groups about his being sexually abused by a church leader, albeit in general terms, which has also been helpful during his healing journey.

The first person that survivor-participant Mackenzie told was her husband after she became aware at age fifty-three that she had been sexually abused as a child. She had read about the need for survivors to have someone walk with them because this was not a journey to be taken alone. Thus, "from the very get-go" when she told her story to her husband, he agreed to support her on her healing journey. Shortly thereafter, she confided in the women's ministry director at her church, who suggested that they meet regularly. Later, the women's ministry director told Mackenzie: "The reason I stuck with you is because I couldn't bear to leave you in that state you were in. You needed help." Mackenzie said, "She's been with me this whole time. She's been through some rough things with me, but she has stuck with me." Besides one-on-one support, Mackenzie spoke of having a group of women who have been very helpful to her during her healing journey. She lovingly referred to them as the *Laugh Out Loud Ladies*. The women pray and study the Bible together as well as have fun together, such as celebrating their birthdays, eating ice cream, and going to movies.

Concerning her not going at it alone, Frances said, "Jesus had a team." She spoke of conversing with a variety of people, such as her pastor and other pentecostals. An important healing aspect for Frances has been the opportunity to ask questions in a place that was safe both for her to question and for other Christians to answer. At the time of the interview, Frances was connected (a word she frequently used throughout the interview) with a small pentecostal group in which they provided a space to explore together, which was very healing for her. For Frances, God is involved in her story for she perceives it was God who brought people on her path to help her on her journey.

Jade also said that one of the most helpful resources for her was finding someone who believed her and prayed with her, which was her pentecostal friend. Over the course of Jade's journey, she and this friend shared everything. Jade said, "I could talk to her. We would sit sometimes on Sunday nights in our car and pray for one another after the service. We would sit there for hours, talking and praying with each other." Jade described this friendship as "one of the most beneficial things for me. There was someone else who believed me and was willing to walk with me and go on that journey of healing with me." Unfortunately, not everyone in Jade's life was willing to journey with her as she processed the memories. She experienced numerous pentecostals across the board as being very judgmental. Many of them said to her, "That happened a long time ago, Jade. That's done now. It's over." Dominique, too, had moments when she needed to tell her story, but people shut her down by saying, "If you just prayed about it, it would just go away."

As mentioned above, Sutton shared publicly about being sexually abused, but he was not the only one. As a self-employed musician, Jackson had been performing concerts at various churches when a friend suggested that Jackson was "missing something by not sharing" his story at his concerts. Jackson admitted that he "was terrified" when, at age thirty or thirty-one, he began telling his story publicly at a concert venue. He soon discovered that the beneficial impact of telling his story publicly was two-pronged: It helped other people, and it was a valuable part of his healing process. Another major turning point in Jackson's healing journey was sharing his story publicly through writing. Originally, his goal for writing about being sexually abused and God's redemption of it was not for his benefit; however, as he wrote, he realized the writing process was very healing. He described moments while writing when tears poured out of his eyes. He said, "You think you're done crying over something, but different things in life sometimes bring that back." For Jackson, writing and publishing his story "was a big step" on his healing journey.

Besides Jackson, Elizabeth also wrote and published about her healing journey. For her, writing and publishing was an act of obedience that corresponded with Hannah's agreement to take Samuel to the temple: "Writing the book is like before you give birth. After it's published, it belongs to God." For Elizabeth, having a published book means her story is no longer private. She views the writing and publication of her story as a way to hold her accountable so that she is unable to go back to privacy, which she prefers. It is now out there that "this is something that happened," which is her "new story."

To close out this section, I return to Joel's comments on the challenge for church survivors to overcome the shame of telling the story of sexual trauma. Elizabeth desires other pentecostal survivors to know that storytelling quells the shame that shrouds sexual violence. Elizabeth explains, "Shame is buried, and it keeps us in the dark," but it dies when light is shed on it. Instead of keeping things hidden, like we tend to do, Elizabeth encourages survivors to give voice to their experiences of sexual violence. Yet, she assures them that it is not necessary for the story to contain all the gory details. Survivors have the power to share only the elements of the story with which they are comfortable. According to Elizabeth, if survivors relate only one thing from their story, they are shining light on their shame so that it can no longer live in that dark place. Perhaps the proof of healing from shame is seen when I asked Elizabeth how she is different today, and she replied that she is now able to speak about being sexually violated. The healing power of telling the story appears as shame dies when the story is told, and that continues to strengthen survivors to tell their stories.

The above accounts of the participants have implicitly demonstrated how we are storied humans. We are people of stories, no matter if the stories are told privately or publicly or if they are spoken or written. In the next section, I focus on how we naturally are drawn to stories, both in the telling and/or the hearing of them.

HUMANS AS STORIED PEOPLE

As humans, we are storytelling and storylistening beings. We are storylovers. Author Jonathan Gottschall in *The Storytelling Animal: How Stories Make Us Human* maintains that humans are compelled by the power of stories. For Gottschall, humans thrive on living a life permeated with imagination. From the time we are children to when we are seniors, we never seem to outgrow our infatuation with stories. It remains a challenge to pry our attention away from listening to *the rest of the story* (to borrow from Paul Harvey) when we hear those familiar words "once upon a time." According to Gottschall, we repeatedly find ourselves lured by stories. We continue to be charmed by them whether it is the American coverage of the Olympics with stories of athletes overcoming insurmountable odds or the 400th television episode of *NCIS*. Why else would over a 100 million people view the finale of *M*A*S*H* in February 1983? Any attempt to withstand the allure of stories is probably useless (or to borrow from the Borg of Star Trek infamy, *resistance is futile*). For instance, recall the last time you mentally constructed a possible outcome if you were to have a difficult conversation with a friend. We cannot stop ourselves from imagining various scenarios that may arise if we said this or if we said that. We conjure up a possible chain of events that includes what we will say and our friend's response. We become playwrights as we create a script complete with each person's lines, stage directions, and the final scene, outlining what may transpire when we relay how our friend's words had hurt us.[3]

Not only do we become engrossed in stories while we are awake, but Gottschall also points to our dreams as evidence that we are storytellers.[4] By definition, according to researchers, a dream's very essence is a story: dreams are "intense 'sensorimotor hallucinations with a narrative structure.'"[5] When researchers discuss dreams, they incorporate an emphasis on the elements of story by employing the narrative terminology of "plot, theme, character, scene, setting, point of view, [and] perspective."[6] Gottschall's own description of dreams entails referring to them as "night stories" that involve a "protagonist" (often the one who is dreaming), "who struggles to achieve desires."[7] Wolfelt illustrates this when he suggests that dreams about the person who has died are how we continue to engage in a normal part of the grief process, our yearning for that person. Mourners may dream about the person who has died as an indication of their struggle to be with that person again.[8]

3. I am drawing from Gottschall, *Storytelling Animal*, chapter 1.
4. Gottschall, *Storytelling Animal*, chapter 4.
5. Gottschall, *Storytelling Animal*, 70.
6. Gottschall, *Storytelling Animal*, 70.
7. Gottschall, *Storytelling Animal*, 70.
8. Wolfelt, *Understanding Your Grief*, 73.

Our enjoyment of stories is not simply an activity in which we take delight. We also have an innate proclivity toward stories. Our bent toward stories is a part of us—it is deeply engrained in our very way of being—as it is how we integrate life.[9] As a clinical professor of psychiatry, Daniel Siegel explains that our ability to form stories (the narrative function) is "about making sense of events and the mental experiences of the characters."[10] This appears as a natural response to life's little and large adventures. If we were in a near accident, what is the one thing we do in the hours or days after the event? If we won a sweepstakes or if we finally caught the fish that previously had gotten away, what is one of our first responses? If we attend a funeral of someone for whom we cared deeply, what is an activity in which we spontaneously participate? If our response to each of these questions is that we "tell someone" or "share the story," we are not alone. Bernard Rimé cites studies in which 90 to 96 percent of the participants shared emotional episodes with others, whether the episodes elicited negative or positive emotions in the teller.[11] If making sense out of life's experiences is part of who we are, then chances are one of our first responses to life's near-misses, our small triumphs, or major tragedies is: tell the story. According to Siegel, this ability to create stories about our experiences begins early in life—at about age three.[12] And in all likelihood, the stories that we tell throughout our lives will be told more than once because making sense of life's events necessitates that many stories be told again and again and again.

9. McKnight and Barringer speak of this in their book in which they underscore sexual violence in the church, particularly the story of Bill Hybels and Willow Creek Community Church. It relates experiences of survivors who were sexually assaulted by various church leaders. The book is divided into two parts: part one describes the shaping of a church and how it becomes deformed by outlining signs and symptoms of toxic churches, and part two offers a description of qualities of churches that may be depicted as good (*tov*). McKnight and Barringer talk about how church cultures become either empathic or toxic when they write about humans being storytellers: "Scientists who study the brain and the mind (which are distinct entities for the specialist) tell us that when our brains are not focused on a task, when they are in downtime, our minds naturally go into storytelling mode—weaving an ongoing narrative about the past, present, and future. In a sense, we do not know who we are or how to live until we understand our place in the story." McKnight and Barringer, *Church Called Tov*, 55. The authors continue by pointing out that not all of the stories we tell are true: toxic churches tell false narratives to protect the pastor and the church amidst sexual violence or other moral issues.

10. Siegel, *Developing Mind*, 364.

11. Rimé, "Mental Rumination," 274.

12. Siegel, *Developing Mind*, 364.

Neuroscience posits that our brains are designed to make sense out of our experiences. Siegel cites research that focuses "on the specialized functions of the brain's two hemispheres" to convey how the organ, the brain, seeks to understand its experiences. In the study, pictures were independently shown to each of the hemispheres of split-brain patients,[13] demonstrating how each hemisphere attempts to make sense of the images in its own way. The isolated right hemisphere seemed "to be able to make sense of the essential meaning of what it" saw and heard even though it was unable to communicate it verbally. It got the overall essence of what was happening. The isolated left hemisphere also sought to "make[s] sense" out of what it saw or heard, but it did so verbally—it told a story. The story that was concocted, however, either ignored or neglected to notice certain details, such as facial expressions, which were significant for explaining what was transpiring overall in the picture. Siegel concludes that "the interpreter function" of the left hemisphere appeared to be "driven . . . by a need to reason about cause-effect relationships."[14] It sought to make sense out of events or others' behavior through the use of narrative.[15]

Gottschall draws from another study to illustrate how our minds naturally yearn for order in our surroundings that are imbued with meaning and purpose. He describes a 1944 short-animated film by Fritz Heider and Marianne Simmel (which is available on YouTube)[16] that contains geometric shapes: a big square, a big triangle, a small triangle, and a small circle. After Heider and Simmel showed the film to 114 research participants, only three described seeing geometric shapes moving around the screen while the remainder of the participants recounted a melodrama composed of tantrums, romance, and a predator who was

---

13. Split-brain patients were frequently individuals "in whom the corpus callosum has been cut for the alleviation of medically intractable epilepsy." de Haan et al., "Split Brain," 224. The corpus callosum is "the massive tract of nerve fibers that is the communication cable of the cerebral hemispheres." Connors and Stein, "Michael Gazzaniga," *Omni*, 99.

14. Siegel, *Developing Mind*, 367.

15. Siegel also points out that the right hemisphere seemed unable to see the cause-effect relationships. Siegel goes on to summarize the differences of the left and right hemispheres' abilities to make sense: "The left hemisphere tries to create explanations for the information it receives, but it lacks the ability to process the context of this information . . . The right hemisphere processes the overall gist of a scene and creates a context rich representational 'understanding.'" Siegel, *Developing Mind*, 367–68.

16. For example, see Heider and Simmel, "Heider and Simmel Movie."

deceived.[17] This study points to how we are geared to tell stories in an attempt to make sense or meaning of life's experiences.

As humans, we also develop a story in order to fashion and mold our identity, to make sense of who we are. Researchers assert that persons will create a *narrative identity*, which is "the internalized, evolving story of the self that each person crafts to provide his or her life with a sense of purpose and unity."[18] The narrative identity brings order and structure to our lives through the use of a life story. According to Dan McAdams, the person's identity is shaped into a story that entails all the story elements of "setting, scenes, character, plot, and theme," a process that begins in "late adolescence and young adulthood."[19] Individuals start by drawing from their basic life history (e.g., their parents, siblings, where they were raised, etc.) and extend beyond that by incorporating portions of their experiences from their past and present while including their plans for the future. The stories are not shaped and molded in isolation. Instead, they reflect a person's culture, mirroring its morals, principles, and convictions, which a culture implicitly and explicitly champions. This implies that life stories are both uniquely personal and public as they are told in a way that makes sense both to the storyteller and the audience. It is this formation of our life stories that plays a necessary part in experiencing more fully integrated, meaningful lives.[20]

Using story to claim one's identity may also make a significant statement that is distinct from the dominating culture for some people groups. Adrienne Chan perceives that among indigenous peoples, storytelling is a significant methodology. It "is a process of reclaiming the story, to own the story, rather than be defined or storied by others."[21] It becomes a way for indigenous peoples to declare their own voice and identity rather than succumbing to the voice and identity placed upon them "by hegemonic forces."[22] Colonialism disconnected indigenous people groups from their "land, language, and community," resulting in "social and political alienation and turmoil." Therefore, as the indigenous peoples employ

---

17. Gottschall, *Storytelling Animal*, 104–6.
18. Adler, "Living into the Story," 367.
19. McAdams, "Psychology of Life Stories," 101.
20. McAdams, "Psychology of Life Stories," 101. See also Adler and McAdams, "Time, Culture, and Stories of the Self," 97–9; McAdams, "Narrative Identity," 359–72.
21. Chan, "Chapter 11: Storytelling, Culture, and Indigenous Methodology," 171.
22. Chan, "Chapter 11: Storytelling, Culture, and Indigenous Methodology," 172.

storytelling, they are reclaiming their identity, and in this process, they are also cultivating their own healing,[23] a subject to which I now turn.

HEALING NATURE OF STORIES

As highlighted above, we live, sleep, and breathe stories. Funny. Sad. Long. Short. Simple. Complicated. Fiction. Non-fiction. We like stories. We are persons with stories. We have familiar stories from our culture, nation, and/or region. We know stories about our church, our family, and our own personal experiences. We are storied people. But telling or listening to stories is not only for our enjoyment. Stories may also contain healing qualities that have the potential to produce beneficial effects in the teller and/or the listener.[24] I underscore in this section samples of qualitative and quantitative research to emphasize the healing nature of stories, first for the teller and then for the listener.

Healing Nature of Storytelling

Researcher 'Seun Bamidele writes, "Storytelling is one of the most fundamental means of making meaning. As such, it is an activity that pervades all aspects of healing. When storytelling becomes overt and is given expression in words, the resulting stories are one of the most effective ways of making one's own interpretation of events and ideas available to others. Through the exchange of stories people involved can share their understanding of a topic and bring their mental modes of the world into closer alignment."[25] Various kinds of psychotherapies are built on this foundation that telling one's story has a healing impact. In narrative therapy, for instance, research demonstrates that transformation occurs,

---

23. Chan, "Chapter 11: Storytelling, Culture, and Indigenous Methodology," 172.

24. There are other studies that indicate sharing a story of a negative experience could reactivate, not ameliorate it. Bernard Rimé notes this research: "Other psychologists suggested that communicating a major negative personal experience could reactivate the emotional disruption rather than resolve it (e.g., Tait & Silver, 1989). Indeed, the need to confide in others about a major life event is frequently unmet (e.g., Dunkel-Schetter & Wortman, 1982), and social responses to the expression of difficulties or distress are often negative (Lazarus, 1985; Strack & Coyne, 1983)." See Rimé, "Mental Rumination," 280.

25. Bamidele, "'There's No Thing as a Whole Story,'" 40.

particularly the speedy, amelioration of clients' symptoms, when clients actively strive toward making meaning through the use of narrative.[26]

Healing among women of color occurred through the sharing of stories in an exploratory research project conducted by Starks et al. It was reported among the "28 women of color social work educators" who participated in this project that the women experienced "personal and collective healing." During the course of the study, "[s]ome women recalled, for the first time, traumatic incidents in their lives, while others were not even aware of how inoculated they were from discomfort and humiliation."[27] This corresponds with Bamidele, who writes, "Telling one's story brings to consciousness experiences that may have been buried in the pursuit of forgetting. Forgetting is a passive experience. The experience of intrusive memories might also be classified as passive. But both are often experienced as a loss of control. To counter this, narrative in a supportive context becomes an active decision. Narrative can be empowering when the individual decides how and where they are willing to share memories."[28] While on one level the women in the study spoke of "re-traumatization," they came out of the study "with a sense of being supported, sustained, and validated throughout the process." This led to a commitment to assist "the next generation of women of color as social work educators."[29] This study conveys, then, how storytelling is healing, resulting in an empathic future action toward others.

Other studies have demonstrated that writing about a trauma may have health benefits. Social psychologist James Pennebaker became curious about persons who regularly described having physical symptoms and learned that these individuals had sustained trauma during their youth, which they had kept hidden.[30] In response, Pennebaker oversaw a lab experiment in 1986 among students in which one group wrote about a substantial trauma that they had experienced but had concealed from others, and the other group wrote about less significant subjects. All the participants were required to write for fifteen minutes a day for four days. The study showed that for the next four to six months, the group, who wrote about their secret traumas, visited school health services about

26. Adler et al., "Narrative Meaning Making Is Associated with Sudden Gains," 839–45.
27. Starks et al., "Gathering, Telling, Preparing the Stories," 7–9.
28. Bamidele, "'There's No Thing as a Whole Story,'" 42.
29. Starks et al., "Gathering, Telling, Preparing the Stories," 12.
30. Pennebaker, "James Pennebaker."

their symptoms at approximately half the rate as the other group.[31] Pennebaker later conducted a similar study among students in which he had the participants' blood drawn three times: (1) before the participants had engaged in the writing process; (2) after the participants wrote for four days; and (3) six weeks after the completion of the study. The blood was then examined for immune functioning. This study revealed that those who wrote about their trauma demonstrated improved immune functioning, and they also visited school health services less frequently in the months following the study.[32]

Pennebaker concludes that writing about a traumatic event causes two things to transpire immediately. First, people are admitting to themselves that a wound has occurred in their lives, which I see as a form of self-empathy. Second, when people put this experience into words, they are creating order within themselves. For Pennebaker, this is when persons begin to grasp how traumatic experiences are connected to other parts of their lives; therefore, it is a way to bring understanding or make meaning out of it. In contrast, when persons have a traumatic incident that they are not processing or are attempting to keep at arm's length, this incident tends to return to their minds again and again. They may ruminate on it, or new events may trigger memories of it. According to Pennebaker, these people have not assimilated the original traumatic experience, causing it to resurface repetitively. However, if people communicate about an emotional wound, such as through writing, they are quieting their minds as they are no longer trying to find meaning in it. Pennebaker believes this leads to other benefits. If one is not fixated on it, the person's sleeping patterns improve, which generates other health benefits, both mentally and physically. He cautions, however, that while expressive writing is healthier than not giving voice to one's trauma, it is not a cure-all.[33]

The Healing Nature of Storylistening

But it is not only telling a story that may have an ameliorative effect. Storylistening may also produce transformation in the one who is hearing the story. A study conducted by Guilherme Brockington et al. indicates

---

31. Pennebaker and Beall, "Confronting a Traumatic Event," 274–81.
32. Pennebaker, et al., "Disclosure of Traumas and Immune Function," 239–45.
33. Pennebaker, "James Pennebaker."

that listening to a story may benefit humans both psychologically and physiologically. The researchers sought to see the impact of storylistening on hormone levels by conducting a study involving eighty-one children who were hospitalized in ICUs with similar respiratory issues. (The fundamental background for this study is that levels of the hormone cortisol are higher during stress, and levels of the hormone oxytocin increase amidst social bonding and empathy.) The children were randomly placed into one of two groups: Children in the storylistening group were read a light-hearted or amusing story, and children in the riddle-solving group were "to solve an amusing question posed by the storyteller" (e.g., "What is it?"). Just prior to and immediately after this 25-to-30-minute activity, a saliva sample was taken from each child, and each child rated their pain levels. Additionally, after the activity, the children participated in "a free-association word quiz" in which they viewed seven illustrations of a "nurse, hospital, doctor, sick person, book, pain, and medicine" and gave words that they associated with each picture.[34]

The results of the above study indicate that listening to a story may be beneficial. While the cortisol levels of both groups were lower after the completion of their activities,[35] the storylistening group fared better. The storylistening group had reduced pain levels and cortisol levels in comparison to the riddle-solving group, and their oxytocin levels were also greater, pointing toward a higher level of attachment.[36] In addition, the storylistening group indicated a higher use of positive emotions in comparison to the riddle-solving group after viewing pictures of a nurse, doctor, hospital, etc. For example, a response in the riddle-solving group to an image of a nurse was, "a crabby lady who gives me nasty-tasting medicine," whereas a response in the storytelling group was, "a person who helps us get well and go home."[37]

The study's results also illustrate how listening to stories contains more benefits than mere "entertainment value." As the authors state, the

---

34. Brockington et al., "Storytelling Increases Oxytocin and Positive Emotions," 1–2.

35. Brockington et al., "Storytelling Increases Oxytocin and Positive Emotions," 2.

36. Brockington et al., "Storytelling Increases Oxytocin and Positive Emotions," 3. The authors write, "Our results revealed that both interventions involving positive social interactions were associated with increased oxytocin levels in hospitalized children. However, those assigned to the [storylistening] group presented an increase in oxytocin levels twice as large as children in the Riddle group while also reporting marked decreases in subjective pain scores." See Brockington et al., "Storytelling Increases Oxytocin and Positive Emotions," 4.

37. Brockington et al., "Storytelling Increases Oxytocin and Positive Emotions," 4.

study points to how stories permit persons to "identify with the main characters"; offer an opportunity to "become emotionally invested" in others; mentally mimic different worlds; and allow persons to relocate themselves in another time. As such, the authors argue that stories contribute to individuals' learning in how to adapt both psychologically and behaviorally in the face of difficult situations.[38] It helps to explain why many movie-goers may exit from a rom-com smiling, feeling better than when they entered. It parallels with survivor-participant Jackson's experience of healing movement as he read and listened to the stories of others. Jackson not only read various biographies of individuals who walked through horrible situations, but he also periodically listened to a call-in Christian counseling show. He acknowledged that deep and extended counseling did not transpire on the show since callers only received five minutes of the counselor's time. Still, Jackson found it helpful to hear the stories of others as well as the advice of the counselor. If he listens today, he is encouraged as he is now able to answer some of those same questions that he held previously on his healing journey, indicating his own growth and change. As Sunwolf comments, "Storytellers have long recognized the power of narratives to move listeners from the pain of the moment to a happier-ever-after with powerful narratives provoking intense flashes of insight for listeners who are ill (insights that may be invisible to a healthcare provider). Trauma, illness and grief create frightening forests of pain, with unfamiliar roads; in such a context, listening to stories suggests myriad pathways out of dark forests."[39]

A story may also teach others, thereby producing a necessary change. Valerie Wieskamp demonstrates how telling a story of violence can create awareness, prompting changes both in an organization and in individuals. According to Wieskamp, the issue of sexual violence in the military was addressed after survivors from the military told their stories. Their courage to recount their stories was a major factor in modifying an institutional system.[40] Such stories may also shift people's perspective about sexual violence and the survivors. The stories may instruct others how "institutional and cultural norms create an atmosphere that enables sexual violence," particularly when these stories avoid depicting victims as "inherently vulnerable."[41] If stories emphasize the potentiality of sur-

---

38. Brockington et al., "Storytelling Increases Oxytocin and Positive Emotions," 5.
39. Sunwolf, "Rx Storysharing, prn," 3.
40. Wieskamp, "'I'm Going Out There and I'm Telling This Story,'" 134.
41. Wieskamp, "'I'm Going Out There and I'm Telling This Story,'" 146.

vivors' strength and healing, they can inform listeners that survivors are experts in their healing process, indicating the strength of the survivors, and challenge the recurring theme "that sexual violence happens" to those who are "inherently vulnerable."[42] In other words, stories, even ones of trauma, have the capacity to challenge others by increasing others' sensitivity and understanding, thereby generating transformation. By maintaining this focus on stories of trauma and their potentially being transformative in nature, I now turn towards how the retelling of Christ's trauma story may hold transformative healing for survivors.

THE RETELLING OF A TRAUMA STORY AS HEALING

I have reviewed how stories of all kinds, both fiction and nonfiction, potentially produce change for the teller or the listener. More specifically, I have illustrated how the telling of a story of a deep wound or trauma may have healing, transformative qualities. In order to consider how the retelling of Christ's trauma may be healing, I return to the earlier discussion on the effects of trauma, particularly underlining the effect of shame. I related how the body tells the story of trauma and how the Lord's Supper is an embodied retelling of Christ's trauma. I continue this conversation on the Lord's Supper by building on this chapter's exploration of the healing nature of telling (and retelling) a story. I will show how survivors may experience healing benefits by participating in the Eucharist through the repeated retelling of Christ's story of trauma with an emphasis placed on shame.

Common Stories of the Cross

We have just seen that stories matter, and the way in which we tell a story again and again also matters, as indicated in the foregoing chapter. In Corinth, the message that was retold by way of embodiment during communion was shaming those with nothing while elevating those with status. Admittedly, today's churches in the United States and Canada are more than likely not being accused of partaking of the Eucharist in the exact manner as those in the house churches at Corinth; nevertheless, the repeated word-story presented about the cross at the time of communion leaves a distinguishing mark, be it negative or positive. The question

---

42. Wieskamp, "'I'm Going Out There and I'm Telling This Story,'" 147.

becomes, "What type of story is being told during the Lord's Supper?" In my experience, the word-story, which is recounted among contemporary pentecostals at the Lord's Table, is frequently drawn from one of two atonement views: satisfaction theory and/or penal substitution theory.[43]

Satisfaction theory emphasizes Christ's death satisfying, or paying, a debt that humans owe to God (this is different from the *Christus Victor* theory in which a payment is made to the devil). Having originated during the medieval era, it is based on an understanding of reciprocity between lords and vassals. A lord protected the vassals under him, and the vassals, in turn, honored the lord. When vassals failed to remain loyal to their lord who was over them, the vassals were required to give something to satisfy the lord. Both the gravity of the crime and the level of rank determined the degree of punishment: the more grievous the crime and the higher the rank, the greater the punishment. Gazing through this lens, the story of the cross centers on how human sin is a demonstration that humans have failed to bestow the honor to God that God is owed; therefore, in order for their sin to be forgiven, it must be punished so that God maintains God's honor. This penalty or debt, however, can only be paid by a human who is without sin while also being divine. As a result, out of God's love for humanity, God directed Christ to die on humanity's behalf (it is important to note that God did not force Christ to die), and Christ chose to honor God by dying to save us.[44]

The second atonement theory that serves as a backdrop when participating in the Lord's Table is the penal substitution theory. This understanding, emerging out of a legal system foreign to the medieval period, stresses that Christ's death satisfies God's wrath rather than satisfying a debt that humans owe. The theory is based on God's justice, connoting that God can neither engage in a relationship with those who are sinful, nor can God merely pardon sin. Instead, God's justice demands that the guilty be punished while the blameless are rewarded. With Romans 6:23 and Galatians 3:13 as a foundation, this mode emphasizes that our sin, which puts us under God's wrath, is punishable by death, but God's wrath

---

43. For the discussion on these two atonement theories, I am drawing from Green and Baker, *Recovering the Scandal of the Cross*, 116–52. I am not alone in my assessment. Green and Baker note that the penal substitution theory dominates among evangelical theologians. See *Recovering the Scandal of the Cross*, 142n38.

44. Green and Baker, *Recovering the Scandal of the Cross*, 126–31.

is satisfied through Christ's death on the cross. Christ, then, is a substitute for our punishment—he is accursed for us.[45]

While advocates of either theory may directly or indirectly paint their theory as being the complete explanation of the cross, neither theory comprises the cross's entire message. Both theories offer aspects about the meaning of the cross that are founded on Scripture while simultaneously reflecting their individual time periods and culture. As Joel Green and Mark Baker perceive, the former may produce a picture of God as an unforgiving, exacting medieval lord, and the latter may generate a vision of God who does not relate to humans because of love for them but because of a law that exists outside of God to which God is subjected.[46] Such theories may imply to pentecostal survivors that they are bad, indicating their shame, and that God is a harsh, punishing god (a view of God that is addressed in chapter 5). If the survivors fail to triumph over trauma's impact on their lives (e.g., depression, dissociation, fear, etc.) and flounder in their efforts to live victoriously, their perception of being bad and God's disappointment in them may intensify. This may, in turn, heighten a sense of God's anger towards them, increasing their fear of God. The retelling of these views of the cross alongside the partaking of the Eucharist may deepen the shame of survivors while bolstering barriers in their relationship with God rather than healing it,[47] particularly when instructed to examine themselves to see if they are worthy to participate.

An Alternate Story of the Cross

In contrast, a repeated retelling of a word-story of the cross that views the cross as an act of solidarity, rather than an act only of punishment and justice, may contain more healing movement for survivors when at the Lord's Table. An act of solidarity heals through validation and identification. By looking through the lens of solidarity, Mennonite theologian C. Norman Kraus asserts, "God accepts fully his [God's] responsibility for creation. He [God] is not a cynical or insincere Creator who created human beings vulnerable to evil and death and then placed sole

---

45. Green and Baker, *Recovering the Scandal of the Cross*, 140–50.

46. Green and Baker, *Recovering the Scandal of the Cross*, 134–47.

47. To see a pentecostal approach to atonement, trauma, and healing, see van Horne's work, such as "Atonement for Sexual Abuse Survivors"; van Horne and Claiborne, "Trauma, Atonement + Healing."

responsibility on them when they failed."[48] As Paul writes to the Corinthians, "God made the one who did not know sin to be sin for us" (2 Cor 5:21). Kraus posits both the cross and the incarnation testify of "God's solidarity" with sinful humanity.[49] One way the incarnation and the cross are in solidarity with humanity, which is vital for survivors, is in Jesus's shame.

Unlike Western culture in which an unawareness exists about the prevalence of shame, ancient Greco-Roman and Jewish cultures placed a heavy emphasis on both honor and shame. Thus, the Corinthians understood the lack of honor, the shame, that was seen in the incarnation and especially on the cross. In one sense, one could state that the subtext of Jesus's story of his life and death was shame. Throughout his life, as Kraus writes, Jesus "identified with the socially excluded and despised and shared the stigma of their inferiority,"[50] such as being referred to as "the son of Mary" (Mk 6:3), implying he is an illegitimate son. He was from Nazareth, causing Nathanael to wonder if anything good could come from there (John 1:46). He was poor as indicated when he stated, "the Son of Man has no place to lay his head" (Mt 8:20; Lk 9:58). New Testament scholar Green reminds readers that during Jesus's life, he ministered to the poor; however, "poor" is not to be understood only as a low economic status; instead, it embraces those who "for any number of socio-religious reasons" are reduced in importance to a status outside the realm of belonging to God. By ministering to the poor, Jesus portrays that no one is outside of God's grace.[51] Therefore, by not living a life of cultural honor, he defied the cultural systems of honor and shame, seeking to bring honor to those who were dishonored.

Yet it was not only Jesus's life but also his death that identified with those of a lower status. Kraus points out that Western theories of the cross place a heavy emphasis on guilt, not shame.[52] This means that Westerners overlook the shamefulness of the crucifixion as an aspect with which survivors may identify. However, Kraus declares, "*The cross is the epitome of this identification with us in shame*" (italics in original).[53] Kraus describes a crucifixion as "the most shameful execution imaginable"

48. Kraus, *Jesus Christ Our Lord*, 157.
49. Kraus, *Jesus Christ Our Lord*, 157.
50. Kraus, *Jesus Christ Our Lord*, 217.
51. Green, *Gospel of Luke*, 211.
52. Kraus, *Jesus Christ Our Lord*, 207.
53. Kraus, *Jesus Christ Our Lord*, 217.

on the account that he "died naked, in bloody sweat, helpless to control body excretions or to brush away the swarming flies."[54] Jerome H. Neyrey writes how purposely exposing one's loins was viewed as an insult, but even more so was "the involuntary stripping of clothing" off of others, which humiliated and shamed them, as in the case of those who were crucified.[55] Kraus depicts the crowd at the cross, jeering and mocking Jesus, as he becomes "a spectacle of disgrace." Rather than being stoned as a "heretical prophet," the religious leaders called for Jesus to be crucified as a "blaspheming messianic pretender." This was stressed by their heckling words, "He saved others, but cannot save himself," which dishonored him by portraying him as feeble, ineffective, and a failure.[56]

Green indicates the shame of the crucifixion when he writes of how it was perceived by both the Romans and the Jews. For the former, "death by crucifixion" was not a type of death that Roman citizens normally endured, and for the latter, being crucified came to mean one is "under the curse of God" (Dt 21:22–23).[57] Kraus explains that being cursed of God is in contrast to experiencing God's blessing. It expresses God's fierce disapproval and abandonment to the depraved repercussions of those cursed actions. Paul connects this Deuteronomic text to the shame of Christ's death in his writing to the Galatians (3:13). Rather than referring to a legal penalty because of one's guilt, together these passages convey that the accused was a "defilement of the land." This comes to the fore when Israel was directed not to engender shame "on the land" by hanging "the 'accursed body'" out in the open on display overnight. With this in mind, Kraus concludes that we should connect the curse of the law to the "shame of defilement and ostracism," not guilt and legal penalty.[58] The Deuteronomic and Galatian texts remind readers about a characteristic of shame: it fears abandonment and rejection and brings about a separation from the community. Christ being crucified outside the city walls illustrates that Christ identifies with being shamefully banished, including identifying with those without status in the Corinthian church.

54. Kraus, *Jesus Christ Our Lord*, 216.

55. Neyrey, *Honor and Shame in the Gospel of Matthew*, 25. Neyrey gives an example of the humiliation and shame through the involuntary removal of clothes, which occurred with those who were defeated in war. The captives were forced to be nude as they were led in a procession, which is quoted in Isa 20:4.

56. Kraus, *Jesus Christ Our Lord*, 216.

57. Green, "Death of Jesus," 148.

58. Kraus, *Jesus Christ Our Lord*, 217n13.

Because shame and honor were such a major part of the ancient world, the Corinthians would be aware they are proclaiming Christ's shameful death when Paul reminds them that as they eat the bread and drink the cup that they are proclaiming Christ's death (11:26). Both the experiences of the poor in the Corinthian church and Jesus's life and death indicate that the experience of shame is connected to relationality.[59] Shame transpires in association with others; thus, it isolates.[60] The Corinthians' jostling for position during the Lord's Supper suggests how humans believe that they are capable of defeating shame by exerting power over it; however, *power over* is a sign of shame. Shame eats away at the *imago Dei*, swallowing humanity up into its void. The more humans attempt to extricate themselves from shame through powerful speech, a higher status, or the praise of people (or in our contemporary world of the accumulation of *likes*), the more shame dominates. We, as humans, make futile attempts to banish shame through accomplishments, but there will always be another human better than you or I. Shame, then, is a void, out of which we cannot wrest ourselves. However, when the Eucharist links believers to Christ's history,[61] his shameful death experience, it has a healing effect—this event of trauma has the eternal impact of rescuing us.

The story told through the Lord's Supper, a meal, informs us that while no one is better or greater than God, God does not cling to this status. Instead, God lays it aside by joining humanity in their void, their never-ending impossibility of trying to be better than the other. By becoming shame or by moving into humanity's shame, which has been a part of humanity since the marring at the Garden of Eden, God overcomes it. God enters into the depths of the darkness of shame. God does not come to us with brilliance and flashy tactics but quietly comes as one of us. God does not enter into humanity by preaching on a glitzy stage but unpretentiously reaches us by participating in our death of shame as the human-divine one. While humanity competes with one another, using each other as a measuring stick, cruciformity moves unostentatiously by joining us in our impossibility of the death of shame, thereby

---

59. DeYoung states, "[S]hame in all its forms is relational. Shame is the experience of self-in-relation when 'in-relation' is ruptured or disconnected." DeYoung, *Understanding and Treating Chronic Shame*, 18.

60. Green and Baker write, "Shame can potentially disrupt relationships more than guilt . . . Shame . . . is an isolating, alienating experience." Green and Baker, *Recovering the Scandal of the Cross*, 158.

61. Green, *Toward a Pentecostal Theology of the Lord's Supper*, 254–55.

broadcasting, "I love you." More than a social media *like*, the cross communicates boldly, "You matter." More than the brilliancy of praise, it more loudly states, "You are valued."

Both contemporary and Corinthian believers, who participate in the Lord's Supper, may identify with Christ's death experience, his shame, and find validation by knowing Christ is with them. Survivor-participant Frances relayed how significant the cross was for her as it spoke of how Christ took her shame on the cross. Partaking of the Lord's Supper could allow a survivor, like Frances, to participate in God's story in a similar manner that God has participated in hers. It could speak profoundly to survivors that as God became present to their death experience (i.e., physical death and shame), particularly their experience with death via trauma, they become present to his death experience through the Lord's Supper. This locates them in God's story, even at a place that typically isolates—their shame.

A Pentecostal Story of Healing

Being placed in God's story through the repeated retelling of Christ's trauma story is particularly significant for pentecostals. As storytelling and storylistening beings, pentecostals have always valued the telling of stories.[62] As a child, I recall hearing and reading testimonies, whether it was about the salvation of a former prostitute or a person who was miraculously healed. My parents frequently attended the public monthly meetings of Full Gospel Business Men's Fellowship where the focal point of the gathering was to listen to the testimony of the speaker. Biblical stories have also been emphasized in pentecostal circles. Pentecostal sermons have included a broad range of Scripture from the stories of the Israelites to the stories of Jesus in the four Gospels and of the early church in Acts. From stories of contemporary people to stories of the Bible, the stories changed us, challenged us, and comforted us. As listeners, stories have inspired, influenced, and inspected us. They depicted a different response to life's challenges than what was common in a fallen world. They pulled us into the life of another time, place, or person, and it was there that the stories opened our eyes to another way of being, causing us to catch a glimpse of healing as God envisioned it for the whole world.

62. I explain this more in *Who Is Present in Absence*, particularly in the section on testimony, 82–85.

Storytelling in pentecostalism formed communities and in turn molded the theology of these communities. When persons told their stories of being baptized in the Spirit as evidenced by speaking in tongues, the people hungered and thirsted for a corresponding experience. When people heard stories of a miraculous physical healing, the sick yearned for healing in their bodies, too. Their faith was bolstered as they walked to the front, seeking prayer that their bodies may also be whole. Through the telling of stories, many people also identified with each other as they shared similar experiences. Parallel stories connoted a place to belong. Individuals had found their people. These stories resonated with them, carrying more of a punch because the modern teller's story overlapped both with the stories of Scripture and the listener's experience. Voices shouted "Amen!" when the stories internally rang true with the hearers. From the stories of the lives from Scripture and from the stories of contemporary lives, there emerged a pentecostal theology—a theology of encounters with God. A theology of healing for us and for our world.

These stories of healing encounters with God continue to place today's pentecostals in God's story. Typically, complete healing experiences are the ones that are worthy of testimonies as they provide the means by which pentecostals find themselves in God's story. If their story is similar to the stories of Jesus or the early church in Acts, they become part of God's story. Pentecostals have traditionally identified themselves within the story of God by proclaiming that what occurred in Acts occurs in the church today. In other words, the healings through the apostles in Acts have become a paradigm of healing for contemporary pentecostals. They have envisioned a way to experience God's presence in this world.

But as I have portrayed above, the story of Christ's shame may also place persons within God's story. As believers continue to tell the story of the cross of Christ until he comes, we are telling a story that places us in Christ's story and he in ours. As a story of identification, it heals; thus, Jesus's story of shameful trauma is healing. Additionally, the fact that we repeatedly tell this story of shame and trauma until Jesus returns indicates that there is hope for complete healing for all, particularly survivors. While Christ's story is a story of shame, it is also a story that is a testimony of future healing for the world, for each person and each survivor. We as believers will continue to tell it by partaking in the Lord's Supper until the world is completely whole. To repeatedly retell the story of Christ's shameful trauma until God is all in all is to retell a healing story, a story of healing in our future.

CONCLUSION

This chapter has considered how stories may yield healing effects by drawing from the experiences of the participants; by demonstrating how humans are storied people who heal through storytelling and storylistening; and by portraying how retelling Christ's shameful trauma is a healing identification. The participants told and retold their stories of trauma at some point in their healing journeys. This type of storytelling is a natural part of our humanity because stories matter to us. When we tell or listen to a story, changes transpire in us, be it psychologically and/or physiologically. Similarly, when we retell or listen to the story of Christ's shameful trauma, we humans move towards healing. As we identify with Christ through the retelling of Jesus's shame, we are inserting ourselves into Jesus Christ's story—God's story of healing for the world. This story, Christ's story of trauma, is a story that tells of an act of solidarity. By placing ourselves in Christ's story, which is a form of identification and validation, we experience healing. As believers, we will tell and retell Christ's story until the arrival of the eschaton, the time when God's healing ministry is complete throughout the world. I continue this theme of stories in the next chapter by noting that the telling of each survivor's story of healing is one of uniqueness.

4

Telling the Unique Story

How it looks for everyone is a little different, a little unique.

—Kiley, a counselor-participant

We cannot look to another person for any kind of comparison because no two people heal the same way.

—Megan, a counselor-participant

Dominique was laying inside a room with concrete walls. She was eighteen years old, strapped to a gurney in a mental hospital. Having been placed there because she tried to harm herself, it was evident that she was out of control. She had attempted suicide five times, and the week was not yet over. She said, "I got so where I did not feel like I had a relationship with God at all." Alone in this room, she wondered if God loved her.

And then someone entered the room . . .

☙

Dominique had been raised in a home with a physically and emotionally abusive father but with a mother who was a pentecostal believer. As such, her mother was determined that her children would attend church. It was at a church meeting at age thirteen that Dominique decided to follow Jesus. Although Dominique had forcibly put a stop to the sexual abuse that she had been experiencing at the hand of a different relative, the impact of the abuse continued to rage on three years later. Now, wearing a paper gown in a psychiatric hospital, she was being medicated, having been diagnosed with post-traumatic syndrome with anxiety.

At such a low point in her life, Dominique believed that God had been taken away from her. She yearned to have God back, but to her, God was gone. Encompassed by shame, she asked God if she even mattered. Dominique told God that if she had done something wrong that had caused God to leave her, she was sorry. She desperately prayed, "God, have you ever loved me? If you love me, please let me know . . . I know you're not supposed to ask for a sign, but I really need a sign." Amidst this very dark hour, Dominique felt the peace of God come over her whole being, as if two arms were holding her.

And that is when a nurse came into the room.

The nurse's entrance was unusual because no one was permitted to enter until the doctor released the patient from that concrete room. The nurse called Dominique by name, stroked her head, and said, "I just want you to know that Jesus loves you, and he's here with you. Please don't try to kill yourself anymore." At that moment, Dominique realized that God did love her; no one had taken God from her.

It was here, in a concrete room in a psychiatric hospital, Dominique's healing journey from sexual violence began.

⌁

While listening to Dominique's story, I had become a student. Absent were the wooden desks with a child's initials carved in the surface. Gone was the grayed-haired teacher, with facial lines from years of instructing small children and chalk on her hands after lecturing on the finer rules of fractions. Missing were the quizzes to test my understanding or the unending exercises for homework. Only two persons were present: Dominique was the instructor, and I was her student. Instead of a lecture, Dominique taught me about trauma and her unique healing journey by way of story.

Dominique's story is unique. It is one of a kind. It cannot be copied since she alone owns all the rights and privileges to the original. Not even a family member may duplicate it. The story's uniqueness is a consequence of multiple factors. Dominique's personality is singular. Her relationship with God is unlike any other. Her familial history is distinct. No one may authentically say to her, "I know just how you feel" because her feelings are her own. Her experiences belong only to her. To borrow from an old television advertisement, "Her healing story is priceless."

Such uniqueness may be said of all the participants' stories that are contained within these pages. Consider trauma's impact on the participants described in the second chapter. Their experiences convey not only similarities but also differences. As previously discussed, the body tells the story of trauma, and this also implies that no two bodies tell the story exactly the same way since each body is unique. Thusly, if only one body tells a particular story of trauma's repercussions, it is substantial in and of itself. This is a pattern that continues throughout this book as the participants also verbally communicate their stories: the oral telling of their stories illuminates, both tacitly and explicitly, the similarities and dissimilarities of their experiences.

The entirety of this book is a nod toward uniqueness since it is based on qualitative rather than quantitative research. Qualitative research highlights the experiences of each person, prioritizing the importance of each participant's story. In this light, the hearing of a story becomes an opportunity to learn. The hearers are students being taught about trauma and the person's experience. The distinctiveness of each story tutors its students about the concept of uniqueness and the uniqueness of the story, such as the start of Dominique's healing journey. I am asserting that recognition of individual stories is an essential aspect of learning about sexual violence, sexual trauma, and healing from it. As such, I am centering on the paradoxical commonality of uniqueness and its significance (1) by lifting up nine influential factors that contribute to the uniqueness of the healing journeys of the participants and (2) by highlighting diversity in unity within the body of Christ as portrayed in 1 Corinthians 12. It is to be noted that this chapter differs from other chapters as it relies heavily on the experiences of the participants. In this way, it embraces the concept of uniqueness, allowing the participants to speak for themselves.

THE STORY'S UNIQUE FEATURES

Prior to outlining the nine unique features of the healing journeys of the participants, I turn toward why it is necessary to consider this topic of uniqueness.[1] Discussing the subject of uniqueness in a culture that

1. Root points out that Western culture has shifted in its understanding of the self. Previously, the focus was on sacrificing the self for something or someone bigger than oneself. For instance, one sacrificed for the church, country, and family. The implication

champions individuality may seem optional at best and needless at worst. Those who are old enough may sheepishly admit to loudly crooning the lyrics of "My Way" with Frank or Elvis (but only when they were alone in their car). Those who are young enough cannot recall a time when they could not choose personal ringtones and create individual playlists on their phones. Advertisements, too, have unceasingly catered to our individuality with slogans like "have it your way" or "the best coffee for the best you." In light of the pervasiveness of our cultural trait of individuality, it may seem that the subject is rather banal. However, I believe there are other cultural hallmarks that give rise to the necessity for this conversation. And being pragmatic is one of them.

The Significance of Uniqueness

Those from the United States are apt to be practically-minded people. An underlining question in our culture is, "What works?" Some American readers may approach this book with this very question (see the preface). When we find *what works*, we will often sing its praises to the world. Companies, of course, rely on this type of word-of-mouth advertising. Such reliance is typically demonstrated when taking a survey after buying or using a particular product or service: *On a scale from 0 to 10, how likely is it that you would recommend [X] to a friend or colleague?* Companies and individuals know: Whether it is a brand of truck, computer, or phone, we inform others of how it is efficient and well-constructed. If it is a surgeon, a counselor, or a massage therapist, we will testify about that person's compassionate personality and exceptional skill. If it is a self-help book, a particular neuropsychological therapy, or a specific meditation, we will bear witness to others of how it changed our lives. The implication is: *If it worked for me, it* will *work for you.* Pentecostals, too, are characterized as being pragmatic by preferring a theology that works. If the teachings and/or prayers of a particular faith healer or deliverance ministry produced a miracle, we urge others to pursue their miracle by attending that same meeting or seminar.

---

is that which was bigger than the self helped to direct the self, but in present day culture that which is bigger than the self is to "affirm" the self. The country, church, and family are to affirm the unique self, not direct it. As Root notes, we now live in an era of an "ethic of authenticity." No one is to tell someone else what it means for a person to be authentically, creatively, uniquely human. See Root, *Church after Innovation*, particularly see chapter 8.

With this type of practical bent in a culture, both with those in the United States in general and pentecostals in particular, it stands to reason that potential companions to survivors may be tempted to map out healing journeys for them. *Read this book. See this minister. Practice this prayer ritual.* This kind of delineation not only impacts the type of journey a survivor is being prescribed to walk but also its duration. As counselor-participant Megan has observed, would-be-church-helpers may seek to place a survivor's healing journey on a specific timeline rather than recognizing how a survivor's journey may differ from their preconceived notions or experiences. Megan put it this way: "We don't let people suffer well. We decide a timeline on somebody's grief." That is, people decide "how long something should bother" another person. Megan, however, believes that there is more "complexity" involved in that everyone has their own story. She offers an example of a person who was sexually assaulted both as a child and as an adult. That person's journey is very different from an adult-survivor who did not experience childhood sexual abuse. The survivor of childhood sexual abuse "already [has] come to believe that anybody and everybody" cannot be trusted while the adult-survivor without the "lineage of trauma" has "places of safety and goodness in other relationships." The internal war of the mind also varies: The adult-survivor experiences the absence of a script that was written as a consequence of childhood sexual abuse, which has been playing in the mind of a survivor of childhood sexual trauma prior to the start of the counseling sessions. Even if survivors share a common trait, a magical formula that encompasses the path toward healing for every survivor is nonexistent. Counselor-participant Joel implied as much when he spoke of needing God's wisdom on how to navigate each individual's reticence to talk about the sexual trauma in the counseling session. In short, there is not a one-size-fits-all healing plan.

Being human involves complexities. Being human entails comparable and contrasting characteristics, like those that emerged in the participants' stories. Such similarities and dissimilarities correspond to pastoral theologian Emmanuel Lartey's intercultural approach to pastoral counseling, casting light on uniqueness's importance. Utilizing a quote from the 1948 work of Clyde Kluckholn and Henry Murray, this approach's basic rule of conduct is: "*Every human person is in some respects (a) like all others (b) like some others (c) like no others*" (italics in original).[2]

---

2. Lartey, "Pastoral Counseling in Multi-Cultural Contexts," 327.

This statement underlines both the aspects of sameness and difference within humanity. As Lartey explains, all of us are *like all others* in that there are "human characteristics" that "all humans as humans share." Being *like some others* points toward "cultural" aspects that "we receive through the socialization processes" that we experience "in our social groupings," such as traditions, morals, and dialects. We are also *like no other*, which refers to the "individual" elements that "are unique to" each person.[3] Adapting from Lartey, I propose that this project is cognizant of three perspectives. First, it alludes to the details that all survivors share in their healing journeys. It assumes that there will be evidence of common humanity in each story, despite the differences. Second, it notes characteristics that more than one survivor shares but not all of them. Some will draw from identical resources during their healing journeys, but others will not. Third, it highlights aspects that appear "to be uniquely attributable to the personal characteristics" of a survivor's healing journey.[4] This chapter calls attention to the latter two by emphasizing the paradoxical commonality shared by all the survivor-participants: their unique healing journeys. In the words of counselor-participant Kiley when she was asked to name the key factors of a healing journey: "Oh my gosh, it's just so different and individualistic."

It was this characteristic of uniqueness that more than one counselor-participant wanted pentecostals to understand about healing from sexual violence. Megan, recognizing humanity's propensity to compare, sought to tell survivors: "No two people's journeys are the same." Kiley aimed to empower pentecostal survivors by informing them that "healing means what you want it to mean. What that looks like is what you want it to look like." This implies "that there are options." By underscoring the survivor's choices, Kiley is purposefully attempting to hand the "wheel back" to the survivors since their "autonomy has been disrespected" through their experience with sexual violence. She assures them that there are "many options" and "many ways to heal," such as making use of therapists, psychiatrists, pastors, or support groups. She has heard how some survivors heal by volunteering at a domestic abuse shelter. Others have used EMDR (Eye Movement Desensitization and Reprocessing);[5]

---

3. Lartey, "Pastoral Counseling in Multi-Cultural Contexts," 327.
4. Lartey, "Pastoral Counseling in Multi-Cultural Contexts," 327–28.
5. The original idea of EMDR was formed by psychologist Francine Shapiro in 1987 while she was walking and reflecting on painful memories and realized that "rapid eye movements produced a dramatic relief from her distress." After more research

some have drawn from narrative therapy by telling the story; and some have benefited from medications. Regarding survivors, Kiley believes there is "no wrong stop" on the ongoing journey towards healing. But in regard to pentecostals who are not survivors, she wants them to know that the "healing journey . . . looks . . . unique and different for each person." Survivor-participant Jackson seemed to agree when he said, "I try to encourage people to take whatever that step is for them for their healing journey. I think it could be different for some people than it was for me." With this in mind, I now turn toward some of the unique features of the participants' stories of healing.

---

and experimentation, Shapiro eventually developed a procedure that was taught and used by others. Originally, therapists asked clients to recall the details of the trauma by bringing the images to mind, including sounds and thoughts the person experienced. The therapist then requested that clients follow the therapist's index finger with their eyes as the therapist "moved it slowly back and forth about twelve inches" from the client's right eye. The clients talked about the feelings and images that surfaced while watching the therapist's finger move back and forth. Clients continued to talk as different experiences emerged that may have previously seemed unrelated to the original incident (research now indicates that these experiences are somehow connected in the mind). As each memory and/or feeling surfaced, clients described what came to mind while watching the back-and-forth movement of the therapist's index finger (see van der Kolk, *Body Keeps the Score*, chapter 15). While today's clients still describe their feelings, thoughts, and images during an EMDR session, therapists now use various devices, such as small hand-held devices that generate rhythmic pulses and/or audio sounds. According to the website of the EMDR Institute Inc., clients center on external stimuli while telling their painful memories, feelings, and thoughts. That is, a network of traumatic memories (be it little "t" trauma or big "T" trauma) are connected in the brain and accessed during EMDR so that the information is processed, and new associations are made. EMDR has been shown to relieve "affective distress," reformulate "negative beliefs," and reduce "physiological arousal." (See EMDR Institute Inc., "What Is EMDR?") Counselor-participant Joel, who is trained in EMDR, describes it as the "core" of his therapy. He asserts, "[EMDR] dovetails so well with how the Spirit of God works with us. It's so beautiful how the Holy Spirit takes that modality and, for the client who's open to it, just unpacks it." Joel describes EMDR as being based on "a memory network that is ensconced over time." For him, "a negative belief" comes from "an early wound," which in his experience is often a wound that occurs prior to age ten unless there is a big-T trauma later in life. He perceives that the "Enemy, the accuser of the brethren," pounds that negative belief into the person, such as "I'm not good enough; I'm responsible; I'm not safe; I'm powerless; I'm helpless; I'm trapped; I'm not in control." Joel sees that the problem, which has carried forward from the trauma, "is the belief that came out of that." He says, "For me, that's where the healing needs to take place whether it's a spiritual healing or whether it's emotional-psychological healing or both at the same time. That has to happen." He states that "this early negative belief" snowballs over time due to its "compounding effect." Thus, if that trauma is not released, it is necessary to return to where it entered. For Joel, this what EMDR accomplishes.

Telling the Unique Story: The Participants

I am drawing from Wolfelt by outlining nine generalized aspects that engender differences in healing from sexual violence while also underscoring a few specific factors from the participants' stories. Although Wolfelt focuses on the unique journey of a mourner who is grieving a person's death, I have adapted his list of influences for my purposes by including, excluding, and adding to the factors of his original list.[6] As Wolfelt admonishes, this general list is not a comprehensive one; there are other factors that may impact the reasons a person's healing journey "is what it is."[7]

Influential Factor 1: The Nature of the Relationship with the Perpetrator

Research demonstrates that a majority of the survivors are acquainted with the person who sexually assaults them. In the case of sexual abuse, 93 percent of youth who were victims knew their perpetrator.[8] In another study of 991 women in Scotland, over 90 percent of rape and sexual assault survivors knew their attackers.[9] In line with this trend, all the participants in this qualitative study knew their perpetrators, but the nature of each relationship was distinct. For some of them, the perpetrator was a close family member, such as a parent, a sibling, or another relative. For others, it was a neighbor, a church congregant, or a trusted professional. By adapting from Wolfelt, it could be said that each survivor-participant's journey was influenced "by [a] prior attachment" or trust that existed in the relationship and by "the function [that] the relationship served" for the survivor.[10] As Wolfelt recommends, the key to this influential factor is to view the relationship and its effects from the survivor's point of view.[11]

Mackenzie, who experienced sexual abuse on multiple occasions, taught me about the ambivalent feelings of being sexually abused at age

---

6. For more information, see Wolfelt, *Companioning the Bereaved*, 109–25.

7. Wolfelt, *Companioning the Bereaved*, 109.

8. RAINN reports that "of sexual abuse cases reported to law enforcement, 93 percent of juvenile victims knew the perpetrator." RAINN, "Perpetrators of Sexual Violence: Statistics."

9. Adams, "Sex Attack Victims Usually Know Attacker," lines 1–3.

10. Wolfelt, *Companioning the Bereaved*, 109.

11. Wolfelt, *Companioning the Bereaved*, 110.

ten by a sister, who was her best friend, and also by a cousin, with whom she had fallen in love. As with Mackenzie, children are often confused: they like the attention, but they dislike what is transpiring. Jade showed me the complexities of the relationships with her abusers. She often said to people: "The people that I love the most, hurt me the worst." Jade described the abuse as being "so devastating" when she realized that the people that she had "looked up to" had sexually abused her. She illustrated this by drawing from her relationship with her brother: "I just thought the world's sun really set on him. He knew everything, and yet he sexually abused me for several years and for many, many years denied it afterwards. I'd confronted him as I got stronger, and he denied it."

Since the participants were acquainted with those who abused them, Jade was not the only participant to consider confronting others in their healing journeys. Prior to seeing a counselor, Mackenzie had read in a book that it was necessary for survivors to confront their abusers. Mackenzie admitted that such advice was unhelpful for her at that time. It was later in her journey, after she had summoned up enough courage, that Mackenzie decided to confront her cousins with the help of her counselor. However, her counselor recommended that it was better for Mackenzie to wait because she was not yet healthy enough, particularly if the cousins responded by denying the abuse or throwing it back on her by saying she liked it. At the time of the interview, Mackenzie did not believe she would ever confront them.

Confronting the abuser is a decision that may surface during a survivor's unique journey. Confrontations can empower survivors who have had power stolen from them, but they also can backfire, sending the survivor into an emotional downward spiral. The potential companion to survivors, then, is invited to see the survivors' perspectives about their past, present, and future relationships with their perpetrators.

Influential Factor 2: Circumstances of the Sexual Violence

The circumstances surrounding the incident(s) of sexual violence have a huge effect on the healing journey of a survivor. A major aspect of this influential factor is the age of the survivor, such as if the survivor was a child or an adult when the sexual violence occurred. As noted earlier, children may dissociate from the sexual violence until later in life, which influences how a person heals. The number of times the person has experienced sexual violence also has a unique impact on the healing journey. A potential companion to survivors may be tempted to judge and compare a healing journey involving multiple incidents of sexual violence to a journey involving one incident. The companion may automatically assume that the fewer number of incidents signals a lessening of the impact of sexual violence on the survivor. An attentive companion, however, perceives the journeys as simply different and avoids judging one as more complicated than the other. Elizabeth taught me about the shock of experiencing sexual assault as an adult without any prior history of sexual violence. During her journey, she was forced to reckon with the reality that sexual violence happens and can happen to her. Some circumstances of sexual violence may involve wrestling with the issue of preventability during the healing journey, such as survivors believing they could have averted the abuse. Frances implied as much when she taught me about working through the shame in relation to her ability to make different choices as a teen when she was sexually abused by her stepfather.

Some circumstances of sexual violence include issues beyond the survivor's control. Destiny showed me how a fundamental, unmet need for a growing child had a hand in her experiencing sexual abuse. She was raised in a very poor family, which resulted in her not having enough food to eat. Her neighbor, however, had a tree that produced apples, but to receive an apple, Destiny had to sit on his lap. One of her struggles is to resist heaping blame on the little girl inside of her. Destiny explained, "When I blame her, I really back myself up and say, 'Can you honestly blame her for being hungry? Can you honestly blame her for being so hungry that she just wanted an apple from that tree?'" I learned from Sutton how a fear of not submitting to authority played into the circumstances of his sexual abuse. Sutton was in middle school when he was hired to work in a recording studio of a Sunday School teacher, who asserted his spiritual authority over Sutton to inflict sexual abuse.[12] Drawing from Wolfelt, the potential companion to a survivor is aware that

---

12. Raine and Kent demonstrate how characteristics of religious institutions, including evangelicals and pentecostals, cultivate grooming of youth and adults for acts of sexual violence. This includes not questioning spiritual authority, having patriarchal structure, teaching about a hedge of protection, and the emphasis on power. Raine and Kent, "Grooming of Children for Sexual Abuse in Religious Settings," 180–89.

there are an infinite number of circumstances that may influence the survivor and mold the survivor's "why" of the healing journey.[13]

Influential Factor 3: The Unique Personality of the Survivor

Many of us rush to categories like introvert/extrovert, optimist/pessimist, idealist/realist, etc. when asked to describe our personalities. These general categories help us to label our distinctiveness while also identifying with a particular group of people. In other words, the categories normalize our uniqueness. This is perhaps the appeal of personality tests, like the Myers-Briggs with its sixteen types or an enneagram test with nine. But, the unique personality of the survivor is not merely about personality tests, which categorize the survivor as a certain type. It also is about viewing beyond the categories to the uniqueness of each person. As Wolfelt suggests, this factor includes how they formerly handled difficulties, such as whether or not they previously fled or faced crises directly. It also recognizes the person's "self-esteem, values," worldview, and feelings, and needs.[14] Survivor-participant Jackson was self-described as having "a very high emotional quotient" rather than being "a numbers person," and he also professed to being a questioner. He told me how he liked "to be challenged and to challenge people about why" they "do certain things." This has influenced his relationship with God and his questioning about the nature of healing. During his journey, he wondered, "Why did Person A get healed, and Person B didn't? Why does Person A immediately quit drugs, never has to go through withdrawal, and then Person B seems like they [continue to] suffer . . . [by] going back into it for forty years or for the rest of their lives?" He then revealed, "I haven't quite figured out why that happens."

I learned from Destiny about the differences between siblings even though they were sexually abused by the same person. The reader may recall Destiny's issues of trust and abandonment. In the interview, she contrasted these issues with that of her sister's desire to have control of her life, including her sister's attempts to control God. Destiny also highlighted how her sister "has a lot of arthritis in her body," which Destiny connects to her sister's refusal to deal with issues in relation to the sexual abuse. For Destiny, when people internalize their anger or have bitterness

---

13. Wolfelt, *Companioning the Bereaved*, 112.
14. Wolfelt, *Companioning the Bereaved*, 115–16.

in their hearts, it will come out in their bodies in one way or another. Both the unique stories of Jackson and Destiny illustrate how, to paraphrase Wolfelt, the personality of the survivor has an immense impact on the way healing from sexual violence is distinctively experienced. Thus, potential companions are to be "very careful about generalizing" the ways in which people heal from sexual violence.[15]

Influential Factor 4: The Family System of the Survivor

I also learned from several of the participants about their families and how their families influenced their healing journeys, which references how a family system helps or exacerbates a problem. When we were born, we were dropped into a multi-generational family system that had been operating for years. Patterns existed on how to relate. Roles were established. Spoken and unspoken rules were to be obeyed. As a growing baby within this family system, we slowly began to learn about these patterns, the rules, and our role within the system as these are the elements that help the family run smoothly—that is, maintain balance and resist change.[16] This balance is called *homeostasis*, and it provides predictability, normalcy, and a sense of control within the family system. Keep in mind, however, a homeostatic state does not suggest that the family system is healthy. It may be (and often will be) quite the opposite. In such a case, the family system's dysfunction becomes normalized and predictable, providing a sense of control for that system.[17]

Rules of a family system assist in maintaining this balance and control. These rules may be spoken, such as a parent who says to a child, "Big boys and girls don't cry," or unspoken, such as being silent about the ongoing abuse transpiring within the family. When homeostasis is disrupted by a perceived threat, members experience anxiety, which is called *emotional reactivity*. For example, when the son or daughter becomes an adult and openly cries or talks about the abuse that happened,

---

15. Wolfelt, *Companioning the Bereaved*, 116.

16. This is adapted from my blog, Engelbert, "Powerful Reality of a System."

17. The theory of family systems posits that the family is an emotional unit in which the members influence each other. Thus, the theory explores how the parts relate to each other rather than analyzing the individual parts to determine the whole. It asks about the relationships within the system, or about the patterns or rules of the family system that keep it in balance. This presentation of family systems is drawn from Murray Bowen's perspective, who is considered the father of family systems theory.

other members of the family may become anxious. They are emotionally reacting to the one who dared to break the family rule and disturb the family system's balance. Family members may distance themselves from the one who broke the rule or attempt to move closer by joining with that one who broke the rule. They may fight with the wayward breaker of the rule or rebel by doing the opposite of what is being asked of them, which occurred in Mackenzie's family.[18] When Mackenzie attempted to discuss with her sisters about the physical and emotional abuse of their father, they rebelled by defending him: "Dad was a wonderful father." Mackenzie shared with me about her unmet expectations: "I thought after my dad died and he was buried, that I could talk to my other siblings about the physical abuse that he did. That was a mistake."

I learned from Jackson, Dominique, and Elizabeth about multigenerational patterns within family systems. Jackson discovered about being conditioned by his family when he was participating in a three-day intensive with a life coach as part of his healing journey. He came to understand that his thinking and behaviors were by and large conditioned by, or patterned after, his mom. Jackson told me how these learned patterns are like roots that require cutting, or trimming. His life coach utilized an analogy of a vineyard in which experienced growers on occasion cut some of the roots to improve the quality of the fruit. Others with less experience either cut all the roots or fail to cut any roots, resulting in an average or a poor crop. In like manner, within families, some people fail to understand which roots to cut. Some cut all the roots by withdrawing from life because of the pain that they experienced.[19] Dominique explicitly referenced cycles of abuse within her family system as she spoke of her mother being abused by her father and, as mentioned above, Dominique was emotionally and physically abused by her father. Not all patterns in a family system are abusive, however. Some patterns are occupational. For example, a ministerial pattern existed in Elizabeth's family as her great-grandmother was a church planter, and her father was a minister.

Both Jade and Mackenzie showed me how sometimes cutting yourself off from the family is necessary to protect either others and/or yourself. In addition to reporting that she had confronted her brother about

---

18. Richardson lists four symptoms of anxiety, which tend to surface when someone is uncomfortable with the differences between family members: complying, fighting, distancing (cutting off), or rebelling. Richardson, *Family Ties That Bind*, 26.

19. While root pruning does occur occasionally, it is more common to cut the vines annually.

the sexual abuse, which he denied, Jade relayed how her brother eventually apologized. He admitted that the reason he was finally apologizing was because he could "no longer live with the guilt of it." Jade asked him, "Have you told anyone else in the family?" to which he emphatically said, "No." She retorted, "I still look like the bad person because I cut off all relationships in the family because I wanted to make sure that you didn't sexually abuse my children. But I'm still the bad person in the family because nobody will ever know why I cut off the relationship." Unfortunately, this brother-sister exchange was discouraging for Jade rather than being what could have been a time of encouragement.

Mackenzie spoke of cutting herself off from family members for her own emotional health. Several weeks prior to the interview, Mackenzie had cut herself off from her sisters by no longer responding to the family thread of texts, which Mackenzie's counselor affirmed; previously, the counselor repeatedly saw signs of healing until Mackenzie engaged the family texts, at which time she was "sucked back down into this whole toxic family system." Similar to Mackenzie's counselor, the thoughtful companion to survivors takes notice of the references to the family system as they help to explain how survivors respond to those outside the family; how the survivors respond to pain; the extent of the familial support; and how the system impacts the healing journey.

Influential Factor 5: Gender and the Conditioning of Gender Roles

Gender also is an influential factor on a survivor's healing journey in two ways: (1) the conditioning of gender roles for both the perpetrator and the survivor; and (2) the gender of the perpetrator and the survivor. An important principle for companions to survivors to follow is to avoid generalizations about gender roles. While a tendency exists to refer to all survivors as "she" and all perpetrators as "he," the stories of the participants demonstrate this is not accurate. As counselor-participant Megan asserted, "It's not like it's exclusive: all males are perpetrators, and all females are victims. Absolutely not."[20] Megan spoke of counseling men

---

20. This traditionally has been the position of the church as they have instructed male ministers to safeguard themselves by refusing to counsel a woman alone, which has been referred to as the Billy Graham rule. Such a rule may form a false sense of security as it overlooks that females may sexually violate females, and males may sexually violate males. As such, the rule ignores the necessity for boundaries and accountability in all relationships.

who were sexually assaulted by women, and those who have experienced sexual violence by a person of the same sex, which, for her, forms "a different kind of complexity." To borrow from Wolfelt, the capacity for sexual violence "transcends gender."[21]

The conditioning of gender roles in both the church and culture influences the survivors' healing journeys through the messages communicated about both women and men. Megan expressed the power of the church's messages to girls and women when she described the possible consequences of girls who were told, "You are a temptation." That message is, to quote Megan, "so brutally assaultive to a young girl." She explains that if the girl's father is sexually abusing her while she is hearing that message, she may think, "I'm the reason why my dad is doing this." This, of course, tends to lengthen the healing process for the survivor.

Some messages of conditioning of gender roles dove-tail into each other. If women hear, "She was asking for it" or "If you wouldn't have dressed like that, this wouldn't have happened," it supports messages about men, such as "Men are animalistic" and "Boys will be boys." Through these messages, as Megan pointedly states, it becomes the job of the woman to ensure she is modest. Megan believes that modesty is not wrong, but when it is placed on the woman to manage the sin or sexuality of the man, it is an issue long before a girl or a woman is sexually assaulted. Megan illustrates her point by drawing from a survivor's perspective: "When you already hold, 'It's my job,' or 'I'm the object,' or 'I'm the seducer,' [or] 'I'm the seductress of the situation,' you're already thinking, 'What did I do to bring this on?'" Megan insists that it is not the woman's job to be the keeper of a man's lust. Instead, it is important for the church to instruct men to engage their own story of lust and arousal. She continues, "Women, [we] shouldn't feel like it's our job to tend to a man's integrity. It's madness to me . . . We all individually stand before God. So why do I have to keep a trail of men intact as part of my journey? No!" The reflective companion to survivors acknowledges this problematic conditioning of gender roles in both the church and culture and how this type of conditioning can influence, even extend, the healing journey.

Furthermore, a helpful companion to a survivor is cognizant that the gender of both the perpetrator and the survivor have repercussions on a survivor's healing journey. Megan discussed how a female, who was sexually violated by a male, may formulate the "vow [that] all men

---

21. Wolfelt, *Companioning the Bereaved*, 122.

are bad." As such, the woman's view of God may be affected as she may believe she cannot trust God if God is viewed as male. It influences her "capacity to trust." Megan believes that if one cannot trust, one cannot hope. When counseling such a survivor, Megan refuses to skip over this issue entirely because doing so results in "leav[ing] out a piece of the healing journey that needs to be engaged" for it will have an impact on how a person relates to God.

Influential Factor 6: Religious/Spiritual Background

As Wolfelt points out, "the personal belief systems" of the survivor "have a tremendous impact" on the healing journey, which was the case for the survivor-participants.[22] For the survivor-participants, their spiritual journeys have been an integral part of their healing from sexual violence. Each survivor-participant had evidence of a positive shift in their relationship with God within their story. This will be developed more fully in the next chapter since this is a crucial piece of the survivor-participants' stories, deserving more coverage than will be allotted in this section. With that being said, one spiritual characteristic that calls for discussion, which surfaced in some of the participants' stories, is forgiveness.

Although a few participants mentioned the subject of forgiveness in their healing journeys, it was Jackson and Destiny who taught me that forgiveness was how they embarked on their healing journeys. As told in the opening story of the last chapter, Jackson began his "forgiveness journey" at age sixteen, which he equated to his healing journey from sexual violence. Jackson is quick to underscore that forgiveness is both a decision and a journey. While he had to decide to forgive, all the feelings of animosity did not disappear. Jackson elaborated, "I had to make that decision and then it's kind of a continual thing" where he had to say in the beginning, "No. No. I forgave that, and I need to heal from it and not go down that route again." Jackson provided an example of how his forgiveness journey was a process. When social media emerged on the scene, the perpetrator's daughter connected with Jackson. This connection fueled questions in Jackson's mind on how he would respond if the perpetrator "asked for a friend request." This prompted further speculation on how Jackson would respond if the man appeared at the door and said, "Can you forgive me? I realize what I did was wrong." Jackson decided at the

---

22. Wolfelt, *Companioning the Bereaved*, 119.

time that (A) he would not accept a friend request, and (B) he would say, "Yeah, I forgive you. Now, get off my front porch." While he was unwilling in those days to have a lengthy discussion with his abuser, Jackson assured me that hatred did not reside in his heart toward his abuser. As Jackson has continued in the process of forgiveness, he has now reached a place where he is more inclined "to sit down and have a conversation with him."

Destiny, too, believed that her healing journey from sexual violence began with forgiveness. After she was married and the memories of the sexual abuse surfaced, Destiny experienced strong feelings of anger toward the perpetrator, the neighbor with the apple tree. Reacting in her fury, she had a plaque created that said, "This man is a pedophile and rapist. I hope he rots in hell." With the finished plaque in her possession, she drove to the cemetery, where the perpetrator was buried, to insert her own testament about his life in the ground. As she walked around the cemetery, Destiny eyed a woman, who approached the perpetrator's grave to tend to it. When the woman had completed her task, she turned and said to Destiny, "He was a good father," and Destiny thought, "Maybe he was to you, but he didn't leave the neighbor girls alone." Once the woman had departed, Destiny walked up to the grave and thought, "I hope you're in hell. I hope you're in hell," and shoved the little pegs of the plaque into the ground and left, never to return again.

Years later, Destiny experienced either a dream or a vision, in which she and God had been discussing heaven. God asked her, "But can you forgive him? What if he is here? What if he is the thief on the cross? Can you forgive him?" Destiny said, "I knew in that heartbeat that I had to forgive him." She understood that if she arrived in heaven and her abuser was present, she had to be all right with it. In fact, his being in heaven became acceptable to her in that moment. She knew that if she did not let go, she "would never have life." Destiny clarified, "I would never find any peace, and I would never be free of what the past had done to me. But he couldn't have my future. I was not going to give that to him." Upon saying, "Yes, I do forgive him," she instantly experienced "an overwhelming sense of peace and calm." She explained, "It was a peace that I had never known until that point. For so many years, I felt like I had been running, and it was kind of like if the memories had caught up to me, I would probably die. I knew that I would attempt suicide." But for Destiny, this "was a peace and a feeling of 'I want to live. I have so much to live for. I have a future.'" She understood that the neighbor with the apple tree may have stolen from her in the past, but he could not rob her of her future.

Prior to leaving the subject of forgiveness, I offer a couple of comments about this important topic. Some potential companions may insist that the survivor forgives and reconciles with the abuser. Pentecostal theologian Lisa Stephenson affirms how this is often a tendency among believers. Unfortunately, Christians have routinely asserted that it is the survivor's duty to reconcile with the perpetrator, not the perpetrator's responsibility to take the first step. Stephenson, however, offers pentecostals a path that resists diminishing the importance of forgiveness while also considering the survivor's needs. This path involves moving and expanding the theological "framework from" being only "one of forgiveness" to being "one of healing." In this way, Stephenson portrays healing as the whole process and forgiveness as one part of that process. It may even be one of the final steps rather than one of the first, like with Jackson and Destiny.[23]

Influential Factor 7: Survivor's Support System

The very essence of sexual violence is that it is relational. Thus, it is vital for the healing of such an intimate, relational act to transpire within a relational support system, which is why a companion for survivors is essential. As Wolfelt writes, "The lack of consistent, compassionate support systems makes for a naturally complicated" healing experience. Healing from sexual violence necessitates the involvement of supportive, empathic, hopeful individuals.[24] Drawing from Wolfelt, some survivors may seem to have support, but it eventually comes to light that their environment lacks "patience, compassion, and extended support." Others may "have support early" in the healing journey, but it wanes over the long haul. Still, other survivors may have an accessible support system, but they struggle to avail themselves of it. But there are some who have ongoing support and purposely receive that help from others. These individuals seem to comprehend that healing from sexual violence "is not something they can do by themselves."[25]

---

23. Stephenson, "Toxic Spirituality," 42.
24. Wolfelt, *Companioning the Bereaved*, 113.
25. Wolfelt, *Companioning the Bereaved*, 113–14.

This was the case for Elizabeth. I learned from Elizabeth that her journey began at "a point of desperation" as she was faced with the fact that she could not walk this path on her own. She openly shared about her struggle: "I just hated that because I think for me the most challenging part of this healing journey has been needing the help of other people. And a lot of conversations with God were [about] the fact that this violation was so painful, and I am so private that sharing it in exchange for help and finding a new way forward was just incredibly difficult." Elizabeth has relied heavily on prayer warriors during the dark times of questioning and doubt. When she is unable to find hope on her own, she is "really quick now to just reach out to the warriors" by saying, "I need you to pray because of . . ." She has come to understand that the prayer warriors are not required to know "the specific, gory details" since God knows. It does not matter in Elizabeth's mind if she supplies them with "a little bit of information," "a lot of information," or no information as she can "still ask for help." She strongly believes that God has somebody to give her the support she needs. Of course, she would be thrilled if God placed the hope within her so that she could keep her struggle private—just between God and her. But she acknowledged that "it's not how he [God] chose to do it."

Mackenzie, too, perceives prayer warriors as essential for the healing journey. Mackenzie sent me the following in an email several months after the interview: "I just want to emphasize once again the importance of having a group of Prayer Warriors who have been praying for me as I journey to healing. This is spiritual warfare, and their prayers are necessary."

Jackson's support involved mentors and friends that he sought out who were transparent about their own struggles. Jackson delineated the type of support he found to be helpful and unhelpful: "It's kind of a dichotomy because the individual men would be very helpful, but the church as a whole, not so much." Frances also had friends in whom she could confide for support, and Jade had one particular confidant that prayed with and listened to her. Sutton, Destiny, Dominique, and Mackenzie additionally described how their spouses were an integral part of their healing journeys, whether by listening, being understanding, being faithful, and/or praying. This theme of support will be addressed again in part two when I outline the helpful ways that the church may supply a safe place for survivors.

Influential Factor 8: The Utilization of Various Resources

As Kiley mentioned earlier, each survivor has many healing options from which to choose for the healing journey, and this emerged in the stories of the participants. The various resources used by the survivor-participants are as different as their personalities. Furthermore, each survivor-participant drew from more than one modality, with some being helpful while others were not so helpful. This implies that a prescribed one-size-fits-all healing journey is simply not a feasible option. Instead, a companion walks alongside the survivors, following their lead, because they, not the companion, are the experts in their healing journeys. Companions are to realize there is no program to follow, but they follow the person, the survivor. To help explain this factor of drawing from various resources, I highlight some of the similar resources used by some survivor-participants, which is followed by noting two unique modalities described by two participants.

Keeping in mind that every human person is in some respects like some others, I call attention to a few of the resources shared by some of the participants. Some, but not all, spoke of completing various Bible studies and/or reading particular books throughout their healing journeys. More than one survivor-participant attended support groups for survivors; however, the reviews were mixed as to their effectiveness or whether or not the groups were appropriate for them. Several participants sought help from professional licensed counselors or therapists during their healing journeys. Jackson's regret in this regard was that he had not seen a counselor earlier in his journey. More than one experienced EMDR, and in addition to that, Mackenzie received help from Dialectical Behavior Therapy (DBT). DBT taught her to embrace the *acceptance of reality*, which is: *pain plus an acceptance of reality is equal to ordinary pain*. This is different from: *pain plus a non-acceptance of reality is equal to suffering*. In the latter, the person works hard to make the pain not real by denying that it happened or by trying to find the reason it occurred. These strategies keep a person from embracing what actually transpired. For Mackenzie, DBT taught her to accept her reality. When she accepted what had happened, she gave herself permission to move on and to receive the help that she needed by processing the memories instead of trying to make what had happened magically disappear or blame herself for it. Other survivor-participants spoke of receiving help from other professionals such as a spiritual director, a life coach, a pastoral counselor, and/or clergy. As seen in Dominique's story above, some survivor-participants talked of integrating prayer and Scripture reading and/or memorization throughout their healing journeys.

Survivor-participant Jade specifically highlighted the singularity of her journey when she described the resources for her healing journey as probably being "outside of the box of traditional, regular counseling." Her journey particularly prioritized the use of *theophastic healing prayer* by receiving help from counselors who were trained in this method of inner healing. Theophastic healing prayer, which is also called Transformation Prayer Ministry (TPM), was started by Baptist minister Ed Smith. Smith teaches that the Spirit is at work in all Christ-followers, renewing their minds and purifying their faith, to bring about transformation; thus, theophastic healing prayer underscores what Jesus is doing in the life of every disciple. For Smith, the Spirit is endeavoring to transform believers by identifying those beliefs to which they hold that are the opposite of the truth. The question is: How may believers participate in what God is doing?[26] According to Jade, it involves bringing Jesus into the memory. She illustrated this by relating a memory of her laying and crying in her bed after she had been sexually violated. When the counselor and Jade prayed to see where Jesus was in that memory, Jade saw Jesus coming and sitting on her bed, stroking her hair, and singing to her. She described a beautiful, empathic, healing scene: "He's got tears running down his face as I've got tears running down my face, and he begins to sing to me in a language that I don't know. I didn't know the language at all, but it was so beautiful." This touched her so deeply that she said for many, many years, "I'd go back to that memory of him sitting on the bed with me, and that would just bring me such comfort. That also helped to heal a lot of the anger and the pain because the pain was just so great."

Elizabeth indirectly accentuated her unique journey when she spoke about realizing through a vision that her healing journey would involve more than one modality. In the vision, she was inside a sandcastle, which was as large as she was, that had walls that kept her inside while they simultaneously kept others outside. The vision revealed to Elizabeth that God's plan was not to remove the walls instantaneously because it would have been too much for her since she was inside the sandcastle. In contrast, it showed her that God was washing away the sand from the bottom up so that the sandcastle incrementally became smaller and smaller, gradually exposing her to the outside. Eventually, the sand would

---

26. Smith, "Transformational Prayer Ministry."

be completely washed away, giving her a foundation on which she could firmly stand. She understood that God was going to orchestrate her healing by sending individuals to her who played either a big or a small part in her healing journey. Therefore, she has drawn from a wide assortment of resources, such as a psychiatrist, an acupuncturist, a nutritionist, functional medicine providers, and regular medical providers. Elizabeth identified her journey as "a complete makeover." She emphasized that "all of our body is integrated, and so I didn't know which helpers were going to be in my life. I didn't realize how this would affect every system, but he's [God has] provided the helpers."

In conjunction with the vision, Elizabeth drew from the expressive arts when she eloquently painted through words two analogies that depicted her multi-faceted healing journey. First, she described a mosaic in which various broken pieces are used by an artist to create a picture. She told me that these pieces are not placed randomly but are put in place by an artist who has a specific vision. Second, I learned from her about the Japanese art of Kintsugi, which she characterized as "broken pottery that is repaired by using lacquer that's mixed with powdered gold or silver or platinum." This analogy signifies for Elizabeth that the rich elements, which she associates with fine jewelry, are being used to recreate broken pottery. In this image, God is the Potter who is recreating her, the clay, by using the precious metal to reinforce her broken pieces. Through these analogies, she taught me how the expressive arts have been instrumental in her healing journey.

Influential Factor 9: Miscellaneous

For the final influential factor, I have combined several miscellaneous influential factors under one heading in order to abbreviate the list of factors that may contribute to a survivor's journey being unique. This does not indicate the end of an all-inclusive list, and neither does it mean that these factors are less important. Instead, it conveys that in the qualitative interviews that I conducted, these factors were not as strongly represented as others. One such factor is the ethnic and cultural background. While this has a significant influence on one's healing journey, it was not overtly evident in the face-to-face interviews since each participant was of a White, European descent and from Canada and/or the United States. Companions are not only to note the ethnic and cultural backgrounds of survivors, but they also are to be self-aware concerning their own backgrounds. As Wolfelt suggests, such self-examination becomes necessary to avoid projecting their own cultural experiences onto survivors.[27]

Other losses, such as deaths of significant attachments or divorce, may also impact the healing journey. Frances relayed about her divorce and the death of her mother, both of which affected the beginning of her journey. Finances may additionally play a part in the healing journey. Mackenzie recognized that her family's insurance and financial security enabled her to continue seeing a counselor during her journey whereas others may not be as fortunate. Further important factors may include physical health, job security, or the human developmental stage of the survivor (e.g., young adult, middle-age, elderly, etc.). An implication of these miscellaneous factors is to be attuned to how a factor may be beneficial (such as financial security), may generate additional stress (e.g., death), or be neither helpful nor unhelpful (such as cultural aspects) during a healing journey. It is important, as Wolfelt mentions, that the companion remains "sensitive" in order to assist survivors in their understanding of how an added intense situation or strain "may naturally slow down, inhibit, and complicate" the healing journey.[28]

THE CORINTHIAN STORY OF DIVERSITY WITH UNITY

Having outlined nine influential factors that contribute to the singularity of a survivor's healing journey, I turn towards how uniqueness is also emphasized in Paul's letter to the Corinthians, specifically the accentuation on diversity with unity in the body of Christ (1 Cor 12). Since I was raised as a Classical Pentecostal during the mid-sixties and into the mid-eighties, I recall numerous pentecostal ministers preaching and teaching from 1 Corinthians 12 and 14 with an emphasis on the gifts of the Spirit and speaking in tongues. Typically, a pentecostal exhortation involved instruction on the usage of each gift with an insistence on not to forbid speaking in tongues (14:39). It was an era when pentecostals were not yet accepted in the Christian mainstream, so scholars and ministers were placed in a position to defend their theological beliefs and practices. My approach here seeks to take a more panoramic view of this epistle, calling attention to the numerous types of divisions within the Corinthian church, including divisions about spiritual gifts. I agree with Fee who

---

27. Wolfelt, *Companioning the Bereaved*, 119.
28. Wolfelt, *Companioning the Bereaved*, 122.

believes that it was normal for believers in the early church, rather than the exception, to pray in tongues, causing Paul to address the abuses in Corinth.[29] In this light, chapter 12 is similar to chapter 11 of this epistle as it also focuses on the divisions that appear during the church's worship gathering. While chapter 11 centered on the unacceptable social stratification evidenced during the partaking of the Lord's Supper, chapters 12 through 14 revolve around those who deem themselves as more spiritual than others in the body of Christ. Fee defines "being 'spiritual' as "to edify the community in worship."[30] For my purposes, I am underscoring chapter 12 in this section where the apostle concentrates both on unity and diversity, being one as a body while honoring every person's gift within the body.

At the beginning of chapter 12 (vv. 1–3), the apostle speaks of the past life of the Corinthian believers. Scholars, such as Craig Blomberg, Craig Keener, and Fee, point out that more than likely ecstatic utterances occurred not only in Christian gatherings but also in pagan religions; thus, it is possible that some of the members had previously prophesied and/or spoken in tongues in pagan religious services.[31] Fee perceives that Paul is contrasting the Corinthians' prior pagan "experience" to their current Christian "experience."[32] The fact that they prophesied and/or spoke in tongues as pagans demonstrates that "inspired speech" is not necessarily "evidence of the Spirit" nor of being spiritual.[33] Instead, as Fee surmises, "the ultimate criterion of the Spirit's activity is the exaltation of Jesus as Lord," not simply the operation of the gifts.[34] It is the message, not the utterance, that is the definitive test.[35] In other words, they are to

---

29. Fee, *God's Empowering Presence*, 585. Fee is explaining the reasons he holds that Romans 8:26–27 refers to praying in tongues. Fee states, "[F]ew NT scholars . . . would believe that the Lord's Table was celebrated in the Pauline churches were it not for the *abuse* of it in Corinth. This text seems to suggest the same was generally true about speaking in tongues, namely, that it was the common, everyday experience of the early churches to pray in this manner, which we learn about chiefly because it was abused in the gatherings of God's people in Corinth" (italics in original).

30. Fee, *First Epistle to the Corinthians*, 570.

31. Blomberg, *1 Corinthians*, 243; Fee, *First Epistle to the Corinthians*, 577–81; Keener, *The IVP Bible Background Commentary: New Testament*, 492.

32. Fee, *God's Empowering Presence*, 151.

33. Fee, *First Epistle to the Corinthians*, 578.

34. Fee, *First Epistle to the Corinthians*, 582; see also Fee's *God's Empowering Presence*, 157–58.

35. Fee, *God's Empowering Presence*, 152. Keener seems to agree: "Because some boast in their gifts, Paul points out that giftedness does not reveal which spirit inspires one . . . The true test was thus not inspiration but content, especially the message of

exalt Jesus Christ, not themselves, through the gifts of the Spirit. They are to be unified in their seeking to glorify God, not divided by a competitive attitude. Paul underlines in the remainder of this chapter how both diversity and unity are to be mirrored in the church by drawing from the triune God as the giver, or patron, and by employing an analogy of the human body.

The next three verses highlight both diversity and unity by Paul's implementation of a trinitarian reference:

- different gifts . . . same Spirit (v. 4);
- different ministries . . . same Lord (v. 5);
- different results . . . same God (v. 6).

Such differences do not indicate that God fails to be at work. Neither do the differences point to the superiority, the spirituality, or the giftedness of the person. Instead, it is the same God who gives the gifts to each one for the benefit of everyone in the body (v. 7), not merely to benefit the individual members. Diversity is not for increasing a member's status. Keener rightly states, "[G]ifts are expressions of God's generosity, not of human merit. To boast in a gift as if it were merit insults the patron or giver."[36]

This trinitarian reference (vv. 4–6) is evidence that God is a God of unity and diversity, not uniformity. This is God's very essence. Since members within the triune God are distinguished by both diversity and unity, it stands to reason there is to be diversity in the body of Christ with a call for unity, not uniformity. As Fee writes, God is manifested as "diversity in unity," hence, the church is also to be characterized in a similar manner.[37] Not only is unity with diversity to appear in this present age, but unity with diversity will also be in the future—the eschaton—when the God of unity and diversity is all in all (1 Cor 15:28). That which God calls good in Genesis 1 with its diversity of plants and trees, birds of the air, creatures of the sea, and land animals with hooves and those without will remain distinct, but each one will be filled with the presence of their Creator. Neither will humans be uniform but both male and female will retain their uniqueness while being imbued with God's presence, being like their Savior, Jesus Christ. This is the future toward which the church

---

Christ." Keener, *1–2 Corinthians*, 100.

36. Keener, *1–2 Corinthians*, 101.

37. Fee, *God's Empowering Presence*, 159.

of today is being pulled as it seeks to live out unity now—with diversity. Fee comments about the Corinthian church, which is also applicable for the contemporary church: "Thus in the present they must cultivate loving, responsible relationships in the body of Christ; and their times of public worship must be for mutual edification, not for heightened individualistic spirituality."[38] The emphasis on diversity continues in verses 4 through 7 in the listing of nine diverse manifestations of the Spirit (vv. 8–10). This is followed by a notation summarizing what Paul has already stated: the giver is the Spirit who distributes as the Spirit "decides to each person" (12:11).[39] In case the reader missed it, this underscores once again that the gifts are not based on merit, rank, status, or a level of spirituality; they are gifts, given by the Spirit.

The apostle then seeks to fortify the concept of diversity in unity by turning to the analogy of a body with many members. Prior to this, Paul references Christ's body when discussing the church's partaking of the Eucharist (11:23–24) and when speaking of the Corinthians being one body (10:17), and it is to this that Paul now returns. Using this analogy, Paul underscores diversity over and above uniformity by saying, "the body is not a single member, but many" (12:14). B. J. Oropeza notes that although the apostle uses an analogy to speak of the various congregants, "their connection with Christ is real because they all share the same Spirit of God who dwells with them as with the risen Christ."[40] Ethnicity or class of a member does not matter for they "were all made to drink of the one Spirit" (v. 13).

When Paul draws from an analogy of the human body, it was more than likely not the first time the Corinthians had heard such an analogy; however, his usage may have surprised the Corinthians. In a well-known speech, a chief magistrate of the Roman Republic was seeking to persuade the lower class to cease rebelling against the ruling class by using an analogy of the human body. The story depicted parts of a human body revolting against the body's belly, complaining that they were being forced to serve the belly. To them, the belly contributed nothing but was only taking pleasure in the food that it was given. As a result, the parts desired to set themselves free from the belly's rule. The hand was to withhold food from the body's mouth, and the mouth was to refuse to open

---

38. Fee, *First Epistle to the Corinthians*, 573.
39. Fee, *God's Empowering Presence*, 174.
40. Oropeza, *1 Corinthians*, 165.

if food was given. Of course, the outcome of such a rebellion was death.[41] But instead of championing its original meaning of upper and lower social classes, Paul flips the meaning. Keener explains that the apostle is underscoring "equality" in contrast to affirming society's ranking.[42] Thus, as Roy Ciampa and Brian Rosner note, Paul is supporting the converse of the culture: it is the "strong" who are to hold the "weak" in higher esteem, not the other way around.[43] This reversal exposes again how a life of cruciformity is contrary to an endorsement of power, merit, and status. The Corinthian church's embodiment of culture was not the embodiment of the way of Jesus Christ. God's way uses what the world views as foolish to shame those considered wise in the world (1:27). God's way uses the "low and despised in the world" (1:28) over those with a higher status. Likewise, the Corinthians were being called to embody these ways of God within the body of Christ.

Not only does the apostle reverse culture's ranking, Paul's analogy also clearly points toward the necessity for diversity over uniformity. He does not diminish diversity but champions it. A foot is not a hand. An ear, an eye, and the nose also are dissimilar in function. An eye differs from a hand, and a head varies from a foot. Just because a foot is not a hand does not mean it is no longer a part of the human body. If the whole body were an eye, how could one hear? The body of Christ reminds us that each person is like no other while being like some others and like all others.

Our awareness of such differences occurs by means of comparison. As a person, I am unaware of my uniqueness until I encounter the other. That is, it is through my comparing who I am with another person that I discover the distinctiveness of both the other and me. This type of comparing grants me the opportunity to gain more clarity about who I am. However, when comparison moves toward judgment and competition, it disrupts how I relate to others and to myself. The Corinthians had seemingly moved from simply noticing differences and celebrating them to judging and competing with each other. Competition is often based on merit, resulting in the hierarchical ranking of the differences by classifying some members as inferior (and even unnecessary), and others as superior (and more necessary). This resulted in belittling and boasting among some of the members. Such attitudes and actions become

---

41. I am drawing from the quotation of Menenius Agrippa's analogy and usage as found in Ciampa and Rosner, *First Letter to the Corinthians*, 597–98.

42. Keener, *1–2 Corinthians*, 103.

43. Ciampa and Rosner, *First Letter to the Corinthians*, 598.

irrelevant when it is recognized that God, not persons, has decided the placement of each part of the body (v. 18). S. J. Hafemann points out, "Paul's approach is to make it clear that true spirituality and giftedness are not compatible with arrogant boasting and competition based on one's place in the body of Christ or in society, or with parading one's gifts before others."[44]

Such differences do not negate caring equally for each member of the body of Christ. Paul instructs the church to rejoice with those who rejoice and suffer with those who suffer (12:26), no matter if the members are exceedingly visible or hardly visible to others. This instruction implies Fee's above definition of what it is to be spiritual: to edify the community. In other words, Paul is calling for the church to normalize, or empathize, with each member's life experiences. No matter if the experience is exceedingly unique or quite ordinary, members of Christ's body are to enter into those experiences as Christ has entered into the experiences of all of humanity—poor, rich, unremarkable, notable, Jew, Gentile, slave, free, male, female, etc.[45] That is to say, a person who is spiritual enters into the life of others in the body of Christ via empathy, no matter who they are. A spiritual person embraces cruciformity by being with the other, not only those who are of a higher or the same status. A spiritual person is one who edifies the body of Christ by suffering with all who suffer and rejoicing with all who rejoice. Unlike the Corinthians' connotation of one who is spiritual, a spiritual person embodies a life of cruciformity, not competitiveness.

CONCLUSION

This chapter has lifted up the unique healing journeys of survivors of sexual violence. It has reminded the church that each human is (a) like all others; (b) like some others; and (c) like no others. With this in mind, it

---

44. Hafemann, "Corinthians, Letters to the," 166.

45. This type of issue may appear in pentecostal and evangelical churches as churches gravitate toward strong, captivating leaders, perceiving them as more spiritual. McKnight and Barringer describe qualities of a "gift- or grace-filled" church culture that is in contrast to a culture in which pastors or church leaders are deemed more important than other congregants. The authors write, "The gift of grace does not establish a hierarchy of power relationships, in which some people are deemed superior to others. It makes us all siblings of one another. The gracious gift of God's *tov* makes us all equally loved and valued members of the body of Christ" (italics in original). McKnight and Barringer, *Church Called Tov*, 117.

has invited the church to consider that healing journeys are unique with some similar and dissimilar aspects; therefore, even though a modality may produce healing for one person, it may or may not generate healing for the other. Such diverse healing journeys reflect the diversity in unity in the very essence of the triune God as well as in the body of Christ. In 1 Corinthians 12, Paul accentuates that God is a God of equality and diversity. The church is called to embrace equality and diversity in unity by empathically entering into the stories of *all* who suffer and *all* who rejoice. Such diversity dispels the idea that modalities of healing must be uniform. Therefore, those who walk alongside other members of Christ's body are invited to join with others, including survivors, on their unique healing journeys. They are invited to honor diversity as God honors diversity and to see the beauty in the difference.

5

Telling the Story of False Gods

They're here [in counseling] because God didn't work.

—JOEL, A COUNSELOR-PARTICIPANT

[Pentecostal beliefs and/or practices] were unhelpful initially in that spiritual authority is so emphasized that the abuse could continue, and I felt fear of not submitting to authority. This has been a long journey of dealing with spiritual leadership and a sensitivity to abuses.

—SUTTON, A SURVIVOR-PARTICIPANT

I also learned that God was willing to come and be with me in it.

—JADE, A SURVIVOR-PARTICIPANT

DESTINY DESCRIBED HER NON-PENTECOSTAL church upbringing as being "very rule driven," centering on a "very Old Testament God" who was "vengeful, wrathful." She had learned, "If you do this, this will happen; if you don't do this, this will happen."[1] She received very little instruction about Jesus except for "he was the guy who hung on the cross," and she had "put him there"—it was her sin. Even being told she had a guardian angel contributed to her sense of blame, particularly after the sexual abuse began by the neighbor with the apple tree. Destiny explained, "I knew that I had done something horribly wrong because my guardian angel

---

1. This is what psychologist Melvin Lerner calls the *just world theory*.

was not protecting me. My guardian angel had left, and I was alone." She had understood "from a very early age" that if these kinds of things were happening to her, it must be because she had performed some bad deed. "It was [her] fault. The guilt was at [her] door."

For Destiny, she and God travelled on divergent paths because God "really wanted nothing to do with" her. God was aloof and apathetic about her decisions, her day, or how she treated others. This view came to the fore when her mom gave her a book that spoke of a person's name being written on God's hand. Destiny thought, "Oh, Mom, if you only knew what four-letter word was probably written on his [God's] hand for my name." Eventually, she realized that her name was inscribed on God's hand, but it was not what she had thought.

Her notion of God began to be revised after she started attending a nondenominational church, having departed from both the denomination of her upbringing and a similar denomination she attended as an adult. It was at this point Destiny decided to embark on a search as to who God really was. By doing so, she was resisting the idea that God was the harsh and distant taskmaster about whom she had learned in her youth. Although she had been taught not to read the Bible because it was beyond her comprehension, Destiny embarked on a journey of reading the Word at her sister's urging in order to uncover God's genuine character.

As illustrated through Destiny's story, an aspect of the survivor-participants' healing journeys includes healing (reconciling) their experiential-relational views of God. Psychologists refer to these views as *God images* as the attention is on how individuals relationally and emotionally experience God. I learned from the survivor-participants that their experiential-theological understandings (their God images or God representations) changed as they moved towards experiencing God as more loving. God became seen as the God who was joining with them rather than towering over them. Such healing occurred as God united with the survivors in their God representations, thereby transforming them.

This chapter is a continuation of the second chapter's introductory presentation of identifying God as the God who enters into our death experiences, our impossibilities. That chapter discussed how this divine characteristic was vividly displayed in Christ's crucifixion. I recounted the backstory of Paul's ministry in Corinth in which he had a mystical experience as God entered into the apostle's hostile, impossible circumstance. God's identity was revealed to Paul through God's act of ministry by joining with the apostle in his void, his abyss of death. I now continue this theme by exploring how God joins survivors in their void and heals their experiential-theological understandings of God. This will be accomplished in three movements: (1) by outlining the psychological theory involving God concepts, God images, and attachment; (2) by drawing from pentecostalism's mystical leanings to demonstrate how God heals the God images and the survivor-participants' images of the self; and (3) by examining how God enters human impossibilities through the Spirit, as seen in 1 Corinthians 12 and 14.

GOD CONCEPT, GOD IMAGE, AND ATTACHMENT

Life has a way of impacting our understanding of God. Sometimes spiritual and theological changes occur gradually as holistic healing transpires through our ongoing human development. These incremental changes may silently pass us by, being largely unnoticed until something causes us to reflect and realize our experiential-relational beliefs about God have shifted. On other occasions, change may involve theological turbulence as our understanding about God may undergo radical, crucial shifts amidst adversity. Hardship may upend our solid theological moorings, turning our beliefs about God and how God functions in the world inside out and upside down. Our prior certainty about the operations of God may metamorphose into a confusing disarray as certainty devolves into uncertainty, and theological order turns into doctrinal chaos. I bore witness to both types of healing transformations in the stories of the survivor-participants.[2] By drawing from the survivor-participants' experiences, this chapter explores this experiential-theological healing, which will also be referred to as experiential-relational healing. After calling attention to comments by the counselor-participants about the theological revisions of survivors, I briefly explain in this section the psychological theory of God concept and God image as it relates to how persons are

---

2. Kennedy et al. discovered that 60 percent of survivors of sexual violence surveyed among predominately inner-city minority women placed a higher priority on spirituality after the assault. Kennedy et al., "Changes in Spirituality and Well-Being among Victims of Sexual Assault," 322–28.

attached to caregivers while integrating it with some experiences of the survivor-participants.

Insights from the Counselor-Participants

I was first invited to learn about survivors' experiential-theological changes when more than one counselor-participant emphasized this shift as a regular part of a survivor's healing journey. When I inquired about the general characteristics of the healing journey of pentecostal survivors, Megan was of the opinion that "it will largely depend on how they were educated on their view of God." She perceives that if believers are genuinely honest, they must address who they believe God is. According to Megan, some survivors attempt to avoid this subject by stating, "God will heal me." However, Megan refuses to allow survivors to gloss over the issue in this way but pushes them to wrestle with this question. For example, she may ask, "What do you make of a god if your view [of God] is that he [God] was sitting there, watching? How does that impact your relationship with Jesus?" Megan frequently invites believers to "rage," resisting the urge to exclude God "from honest conversations." She admits that expressing such anger is very challenging for pentecostals. Many pentecostal survivors interpret such fury as being "sacrilegious," "disobedient," or "not trusting." Some may say, "How could I question God when he's [God's] omnipresent [and] omniscient?" But Megan invites her clients to embrace their humanity by thinking like King David, who praises and worships God one minute, but in the next minute he criticizes God for abandoning him.

Counselor-participant Dayton seemed to elaborate on this same issue when I asked how pentecostals experience God during their healing journey. He frequently focuses on healing "the kind of image" counselees "hold of God." Dayton surmises that "the pain of sexual violation is the catalyst to help them to do that because they eventually find" that their beliefs about God and their experiences of God are insufficient. This is mainly because the struggle has "been so enduring" (as indicated by Joel in the above epigraph). Dayton detects an incongruity between what pentecostal survivors believe about God and how they experience God in which one or both "may not be true or accurate." As a result, he commonly sees survivors' beliefs about God being disrupted. Dayton responds by coaching them through an integrative process in which their cognitive knowledge of God agrees more with their experiences of God. For instance, survivors may cognitively believe that since God is all powerful, they simply need to pray, and God will remove their suffering. For Dayton, this is incongruent with how believers theologically embrace suffering; thus, he is frequently helping survivors in their development of "a theology of suffering" in which their experience of God is "rooted in their pain and suffering," not in a surface sensation of feeling "good." Namely, he is helping survivors move towards congruency in which what they "know about God" on a cognitive level is integrated with how they are "known by God on experiential-affective level."

Counselor-participant Shauna spoke similarly when she described in general the healing journey of pentecostal survivors. She often initially sees an "over spiritualization," which she discerns "as a defense response against the vulnerability, shame, fear, etc. attached to the sexual trauma." She witnesses many survivors who cling to their cognitive beliefs of God (God concept) "while their unconscious attachment with God" (God image) is frequently "negatively impacted," such as when persons "may unconsciously perceive God as distant, unavailable, or punishing them." Such a perception engenders survivors to respond in one of two ways: They may "engage in works" as they make an unconscious attempt to "prove their worth to God," or they may "pull away from God," which may include attending church while "feel[ing] empty, numb, [or] disconnected from God." When asked what was most challenging for pentecostals during their healing journey, Shauna replied, "For many, the hardest part is reconciling their faith—believing the goodness of God amidst atrocities, injustices, and trying to recenter to a felt sense of security and trust in God when their faith is profoundly shaken." By following Shauna's lead, I now look to the psychological theory of God concept and God image.

Theory of God Concept and God Image

Distinguishing the terms of God concept and God image is essential in exploring the development and change of the survivor-participants' experiential-relational views of God. Louis Hoffman defines God concept as "a person's cognitive or theological understanding of God."[3] Individuals generally draw from their God concept, such as the information they

---

3. Hoffman, "Cultural Constructs of the God Image and God Concept," 3.

learned in Sunday School, catechism, church, or doctrinal texts, when they are asked to name three characteristics that describe God.[4] Without much thought, they may turn to doctrinal teachings from their church when they proclaim that God is loving, faithful, and omnipresent. These doctrinal descriptors may differ from their God images, which Hoffman defines as "a person's emotional experience of God."[5] Believers may perceive that God has abandoned them when trouble enters their lives. This may lead to multiple attempts to convince God to draw near to them again by repeating the phrase "I'm sorry" or re-confessing old sins. As Jacqueline Rasar et al. explain, God images not only involve persons' feelings toward God but also their sense of God's feelings toward them.[6]

According to Glendon Moriarty, feelings about and experiences with God are particularly evident when people do something wrong.[7] Such feelings appeared not only in Destiny's story above but also in the story of Frances. Similar to Destiny, Frances experienced a message from the church that generated an intense fear of God.[8] Unlike Destiny, she heard this message from her pentecostal church while she was growing up. Upon hearing sermons that threatened her with hell, she became too fearful to make a commitment to Jesus Christ because she "was just so scared of getting it wrong." When her childhood image of Jesus remained unchanged, Frances's fear of Jesus continued into adulthood as she saw Jesus as the one "who was gonna chase me down with a flaming sword at the end of time." Not only was God presented to her as scary, but her fear of connecting with God also emerged because she considered herself to be impure since she had been sexually abused as a child. In her mind, this lack of purity explained why she was unable to speak in tongues even though she had sincerely sought the baptism of the Holy Spirit.

---

4. Hoffman writes, "The God Concept is the more dominant factor in conscious thought. When a person is asked about God, they are likely to talk about their God Concept, or what they believe about God." Hoffman, "Cultural Constructs of the God Image and God Concept," 4.

5. Hoffman, "Cultural Constructs of the God Image and God Concept," 2–3.

6. Rasar et al., "Efficacy of a Manualized Group Treatment Protocol," 268.

7. Moriarty, *Pastoral Care of Depression*, 43.

8. McKnight and Barringer, in discussing how to change a toxic church culture to a good (*tov*) church culture, write, "How we understand and *feel* about our relationship with God is formed and fostered by the culture of the church we're in. We tend to equate how we stand with the leaders of the church, and how we stand with the congregation—that is, our conformity to what they approve and disapprove—with how we stand with God" (italics in original). McKnight and Barringer, *Church Called Tov*, 83.

Edward B. Davis et al. provide a helpful contrast between God concept and God image: the former is "learned chiefly via explicit and intentional learning" while the latter is "learned chiefly via implicit, emotional, and incidental learning."[9] These distinctions underscore how persons are usually unaware of their God image. Although persons may not explicitly be able to identify their God image, they routinely operate out of it.[10] It is often more evident when persons experience a life event that is psychologically crippling. For some believers, their God concept cognitively declares that God is sovereign and in control, even if hardship comes. However, when hardship inexplicably does come, their unconscious God image may be seen operating when they experience feelings of despair as they wonder what they have done wrong for God to be punishing them. Survivor-participant Elizabeth seemed to hint at both her God concept and God image when she said that at the beginning of her healing journey from sexual violence, one of her questions was, "Where was God?" She "knew intellectually" that God was present "but living that out and having that as [a] discovery" was still being worked out with God at the time of the interview. Yet Davis et al. also caution that the contrasts are not as distinct as described here but are provided to underscore the primary characteristics of each of them.[11] This could be said of Destiny's story who learned from her church about a god who was distant, which merged with her early God image.

God Images, Attachment, and the Self

When considering how individuals develop their God images, various theorists draw from how securely or insecurely persons are attached to their caregivers.[12] Our interactions with our primary caregivers form a

---

9. Davis et al., "God Images and God Concepts," 52.

10. This is indicated in the writing of Merle Jordan who refers to the God image as *operational theology* and the God concept as *professed theology*. He goes on to define operational theology as "the implicit religious story by which one is living, including unconscious material." See Jordan, *Taking on the Gods*, 29.

11. Davis et al., "God Images and God Concepts," 52.

12. To explain how God images evolve, various researchers draw from the psychological theory of attachment. Attachment theory was developed by psychologist John Bowlby, who held that people operate from an innate attachment behavioral system, which is activated when persons feel threatened. Upon activation, persons seek out a secure base, an attachment figure who is wiser and stronger, for support and protection. As a child, I recall being awakened in the night by a thunderstorm and feeling

type of "blueprint" that supplies direction on how to interrelate or "what to expect in social interactions."[13] This suggests that a kind of internal guidance system was being formed within us through our relationships with those who were watching over us. Like a GPS, it now guides us in how we think about ourselves (whether we think we are intelligent or stupid); how we perceive others think about us (whether we believe they see us as fascinating or boring) and interact with us (whether they appear interested or disinterested); and what we think about ourselves in relation to others (whether we see ourselves as attentively listening or talking too much). Therefore, if our primary caregivers were unavailable and not attuned to us, which created our insecure attachment with them, we may now believe that others are unavailable, and we may not be attuned to ourselves by being unaware of our own feelings and needs. However, if our caregivers were attuned to us and available when we needed a sense of safety, which formed a secure attachment with them, we may presently believe that others are available, and we may be more in tune with what is happening inside of us.

With this in mind, it is believed that the type of attachment, be it secure or insecure, that persons have with their primary caregivers influences their relational experience with God. Moriarty notes research

---

afraid; thus, I either cried until my parents arrived or I ran into my parents' bedroom for support. If my parents soothed me, I could eventually relax, having experienced a felt sense of security. This in turn deactivated my innate attachment behavioral system, and I could go back to sleep. Depending on how the parents habitually respond to a child's sense of threat, the child will develop one of two overarching categories of attachment, a secure or an insecure attachment style, which are divided into four *internal working models*. Jay Belsky describes the *internal working model* as being similar to "an internal guidance system" that both filters and assesses a person's experiences of social encounters, which directs one's behavior (see Belsky, "Developmental Origins of Attachment Styles," 166). Siegel notes that a secure attachment with a secure working model is developed when parents are consistent in offering a safe haven by: responding in a timely manner; being in tune to the child's needs and inner world; and being emotionally at hand (see Siegel, *Developing Mind*, 100). If, however, attachment figures respond in such a way that an insecure attachment is formed, persons may develop an insecure working model. An insecure working model is formed in individuals when attachment figures are: inconsistently emotionally at hand or regularly emotionally unavailable; erratically fulfilling or consistently not meeting the internal/external needs of the child; and unpredictably responsive or constantly unresponsive to the child's needs [see Siegel, *Developing Mind*, 99–139]. Moriarty et al. write that a therapist may assume "that a client's attachment style and God image will parallel. It follows that changing a person's internal working model will also change their God image." See Moriarty et al., "Understanding the God Image through Attachment Theory," 49.

13. Davis et al., "God Images and God Concepts," 53.

that reveals that individuals, who were securely attached to their caregivers, may now "have a positive relationship with God" and self.[14] In this qualitative study, I was taught by more than one survivor-participant that parents may negatively influence a person's view of God when there is an insecure attachment with the caregivers. Elizabeth discussed being a wanted child while also being an unexpected child who was neglected. She recognized that her parents may not have fully reflected the parenting of God, so a major turning point in her healing journey was realizing that the Heavenly Father was not like her earthly father. Her Heavenly Father can always be trusted. She came to see that if God the Father was alongside her during her earlier difficulties, then God the Father would remain faithful and with her during the darkest times, even amidst her healing from sexual violence.

Survivor-participant Mackenzie discussed her negative God image due to her physically and emotionally abusive father. She spoke of this to Jesus: "Jesus, I trust you, and I trust your Holy Spirit. But I don't think I could trust your Heavenly Father if he is anything like my father, and I don't want to have anything to do with him." But when the Spirit showed her John 14:9, in which Jesus says, "The person who has seen me has seen the Father," she was surprised: "You mean to tell me that your Father is like you, Jesus?" For Mackenzie, this was a "revelation. It was like being born again all [over] again." For the first time she comprehended that it was her relationship with her earthly father that had caused her to be quite fearful of God the Father. She confessed that she thought that she had known who God the Father was, but she now realizes that she had not. Mackenzie's story is supported by Alice Kosarkova et al. in their quantitative study of surveying 1,800 Czechs who were over the age of fifteen. The researchers found that those who experienced childhood trauma were "less likely to report positive images of God" by describing God with "terms such as critical or angry" rather than as loving or forgiving.[15]

While primary attachment figures are commonly the parental caregivers who influence an individual's God image, such as Mackenzie's father, others in a person's life may also be attachment figures, being viewed as the wiser and stronger ones, as seen in Jade's story. Jade was approximately thirteen years of age when she discovered that God loved her. This

---

14. Moriarty, *Pastoral Care of Depression*, 59.
15. Kosarkova et al., "Childhood Trauma and Experience in Close Relationships," 8.

insight was very moving for her, so she became quite emotional when she announced it to her older brother. Unfortunately, he burst her bubble when he said, "That can't be true, Jade. Go [and] look in the mirror, and you'll know that God doesn't love you." Jade had a birth defect: she had been born blind in her left eye. Her brother indicated that since she had a disability, God could not love her. This left a costly impression on Jade as she thought, "He's my older brother. He knows everything. He must be right. The church must be wrong." Therefore, she basically turned her back on the church and walked away until after she was married.

However, caution is to be observed when automatically assigning individuals as being insecurely attached to God when they had insecure relationships with their caregivers. Moriarty writes that some individuals, who were insecurely attached to their primary caregivers, appear to be securely attached to God. Some researchers theorize this may be because individuals compensate for their unmet "needs through a highly personal relationship with God." Other researchers speculate that such individuals are simply mimicking "a secure relationship with God" by overtly displaying "religious behaviors," which covers up their actual insecurity with God.[16]

As seen thus far, humanity's attempts to relate to God have often generated incorrect God representations, or God images. Our striving to experience God can form faux God images, images frequently based on our human attachments. These images are described as "idols" by Merle Jordan, which are formed from our experiences with parents or parental-type figures and "are projected onto God."[17] Our faulty image of God is connected to a faulty image of self. Jordan explains that our God images, which he refers to as *operational theology*, reveal how we believe we are "defined or valued" by God.[18] Survivor-participant Destiny perceived God was uninterested in her; thus, her self-esteem was low. But when she began to believe that God held her dear to God's heart, her self-esteem became higher. In this way, one's self-concept is tightly braided with one's God image.[19] As Jordan writes, "[T]he doctrine of personhood is always

---

16. Moriarty, *Pastoral Care of Depression*, 59.
17. Jordan, *Taking on the Gods*, 30.
18. Jordan, *Taking on the Gods*, 22.
19. Jordan, *Taking on the Gods*, 24.

related to the doctrine of God."[20] Thus, for Jordan, the "self is always defined in terms of Other," no matter if it is a faux Other or not.[21]

Moriarty agrees that the self has an emotional impact on how we experience God. He draws from research that demonstrates that a strong self-image indicates a positive view of God, and a poor self-image suggests a negative view of God. The former "feel that God loves them" while the latter does not.[22] This leads Moriarty to surmise, "When the self changes, the God image will change along with it."[23] Moriarty explains that the self is a lens that we use "to focus on information that confirms our self-understanding and to ignore information that is contrary to our sense of identity."[24] He illustrates that if children are not experiencing love and care from their primary caregivers, they will not have a sense of safety. This results in their becoming angry at themselves and being convinced that "they are 'damaged' or 'bad,'" which provides the children with a rationale for their caregivers' actions. Such a response helps the children to continue to view their parental figures as "'good'" while offering them a path to gain their parents' love and approval by "fix[ing] themselves."[25] They, in turn, create a false idol of God by projecting their parents' lack of care onto God. As with their parents, they believe that they must do everything perfectly in order for God to love them. This forms a false image of self as they become their own savior. According to Jordan, creating such a false image of self is often "an attempt to provide one's own rescue" in the light of their false image of God. If one cannot trust in a loving God who takes the initiative by providing the atoning work for humankind, then one must form "self-atoning strategies" to survive.[26]

For those of us who have been a part of the Western church for a number of years, we possibly have glossed over the commands not to worship any false gods or graven images. Commandments One and Two of the Ten Commandments (Ex 20:3–4) may have seemed to be irrelevant to us. We have not put on display or even owned any physical idols . . . ever. We have not bowed down to any golden images or erected any statues. However, as this section suggests, false gods are not always clothed

20. Jordan, *Taking on the Gods*, 22.
21. Jordan, *Taking on the Gods*, 22.
22. Moriarty, *Pastoral Care of Depression*, 57–58.
23. Moriarty, *Pastoral Care of Depression*, 58.
24. Moriarty, *Pastoral Care of Depression*, 60.
25. Moriarty, *Pastoral Care of Depression*, 60–61.
26. Jordan, *Taking on the Gods*, 30–31.

in gold, stone, or wood, but they may come to us in a familiar form—a form with which we are most comfortable—our attachment figures. As a result, instead of trusting in a God of mystery, our operational faith is in a God who is more predictable, bearing the image of those who watched over us as children. Our God image may be the kind that nurtures anxiety and shame as we strive to be perfect or pleasing to God so that we may procure God's favor. Our God image may be a God who is distant, a God who is not overly involved in our lives. Our theological-experiential image of God may portray God's love as being no greater than our own. It is a love that is fickle, shifting like the sand. With such unconscious, ingrained perceptions, how are we to emotionally experience God differently? To paraphrase the apostle Paul, who will save us from this death? Thanks be to Jesus Christ our Lord who enters into our impossibilities, our certain death!

CHRISTIAN MYSTICISM, PENTECOSTALISM, AND SURVIVORS

The previous section pointed out how God images are based on our emotional, relational experiences with God. We tend to transfer the secure or insecure attachment we had with our primary caregivers onto the transcendent Caregiver. This influences how we perceive ourselves and God. The self is likened to a pair of sunglasses that is used to help us focus on information that supports our understanding while screening out those things that may hinder or confuse it. This creates an impossibility for us to see God and the self differently, or even more authentically, when our understanding is based on faux images of self and God. God, however, seeks to reveal God's self to us and to reconcile (heal) our God images. God reveals God's self as one who enters into our impossibilities, our deaths, while simultaneously healing our God images. God is the God-joiner with humanity, changing our image from a God who is far, far away to a God who is truly alongside us. Drawing from Andrew Root's *The Church after Innovation*, this section will explain how God's entering into humanity's impossibilities is linked to Christian mysticism, which is connected to pentecostalism and the stories of the survivor-participants.

Christian Mysticism Linked to God in Nothingness

According to Root, there is what is called *the thin tradition*, which "seeks God where God seems unable to be found. It claims . . . that God can be found only in the places that appear to be Godforsaken."[27] That is, God is found in nothingness. Root relates how nothingness currently exists in American culture and describes how finding God in nothingness is a path followed by mystics, such as Meister Eckhart, John Tauler, and the unknown author of *Theologia Germanica* from whom Root draws.[28] Root details how current culture has moved away from an emphasis on standardization and conformity to difference and uniqueness. From companies and churches to individuals, stress is now placed on identifying your niche, your distinctiveness, or your uniqueness. Previously, churches sought to conform to their denomination's standard. Churches had a common hymnal, Sunday School curriculum, devotionals, and magazines, engendering a sense of togetherness and common culture. I could travel out of town and be assured that a church within my pentecostal denomination sang similar songs and used the same Sunday School lessons as my home church. However, as Root points out, today the death of a company, church, or an individual influencer is the lack of originality and uniqueness. Those who stand out are not those who adhere to convention, but those who sing their own song, who swim against the stream. For individuals, the self, too, continually seeks to be seen, to stand out from among the rest rather than be a traditionalist by conforming. Pressure mounts as the self competes with others to be extraordinary and singular, making the uniqueness of the self the center for creativity and innovation rather than an organization or the transcendent Caregiver.[29] Social media contributes to the competitiveness when members are gauged as unique based on the number of *likes* that their posts receive. The rules of exceptionality and singularity dictate that individuals create a unique brand and are to increase the number of followers through their innovation and creativity.[30] In short, it is up to the unique self.

---

27. Root, *Church after Innovation*, 210.

28. See Root, *Church after Innovation*, chapter 10.

29. We now live in an immanent frame in which our lives are completely framed within a natural order, not a supernatural one. I am drawing from Smith's definition of *immanent frame* in *How (Not) to Be Secular*, 141.

30. See Root, *Church after Innovation*, chapter 8. Root is specifically addressing churches in this work. He asserts that the perspective that the self needs to be exceptional is spilling over into the church as each church is pressured to find its particular

Being steeped within a culture that accentuates and relies on the self implies that survivor-participants are faced with the challenge to heal themselves of their sexual trauma. However, they are often unable to overcome trauma's grip through the Western can-do attitude. Since they are frequently marked with psychological disorders, dissociation, repercussions, and emotional intensity, they are commonly incapable of measuring up to the competitive powerhouses that define the parameters of Western success or to the ideal image of a pentecostal who lives triumphantly. Instead, their experience of sexual trauma holds them fast in the talons of shame, and this becomes their impossibility, their death. The more they attempt to extricate themselves out of the black hole of shame through their attempts to be good, the more the walls of shame cave in around them. The more good deeds that they try to do and the better they attempt to be, the more shame whispers, "It's not enough." They may read their Bible and pray every day, relying on their own abilities, but shame, unabated, scoffs in hushed tones at their pathetic endeavors. Since shame remains forever dissatisfied, many survivors cannot find wholeness through such self-effort. This portrays shame as a harsh, demanding taskmaster. Like a hamster running on a wheel, they cannot free themselves from shame's clutches. Nothing is ever enough for shame's insatiable appetite. They will never be deemed good enough. This keeps the self trapped in its inability to gain freedom from the bondage of shame. It is incapable of obtaining liberation from the implicit, emotional false images of God and self. It longs for God but remains incapacitated to achieve a divine encounter and heal the self.

For Root, the freeing of the self is found on the path of Christian mysticism. If one is to follow the path of mysticism, it involves the need for the self to embrace the futility of having the skill to initiate an encounter with God. As pentecostal theologian Daniel Castelo writes, it is necessary that the initiative to know God comes from God. This is because "human striving cannot bridge the gap between Creator and creation" since "knowing God is not a human achievement but a kind of participation in grace."[31] Christian mysticism accepts that the self can-

---

niche and thereby grow. A church's certain death is perceived to be the result of the church not growing, which flows from a lack of innovation. This places more pressure on a church to avoid death through their own creativity and innovation. While creativity and innovation are not evil in and of themselves, nevertheless, dependence is being placed on the self and the self's creativity rather than leaning on God and God's creativity. Root, *Church after Innovation*.

31. Castelo, *Pentecostalism as a Christian Mystical Tradition*, 40.

not accomplish enough to permit the self to know God. Root explains, "[T]here is nothing inherent within the self that allows the self to produce its own good. There is nothing in the self that permits the self to know, understand, and encounter a God who is truly God. Selves are not constituted to know either their own selves or the God who made them. A self who wants to know God must first embrace that they cannot know God (and cannot know the self). This is the negative way."[32]

The above discovery is liberating for the self. Upon realizing how incapable the self is to know God and the self, the self is free to be the finite clay it was created to be instead of continually striving to be the Infinite Potter. Paradoxically, individual freedom may be discovered when the limitations of the self are realized. No longer must the self be something the self is not, but the authentic self (in contrast to the false self) can be accepted as the finite, created being the self truly is. As Root explains, "The self can be loved by embracing the self's limit, by confessing that the self has no power in itself to know God. The self is freely allowed to be a creature again."[33] Liberation may emerge upon accepting the self's incapacity to be the agent in producing an encounter with God. It is in the welcoming of this impossibility that the self becomes ready to encounter God. It is in this place of nothingness that God appears. Root writes, "When the self acknowledges that it cannot know God, the path opens to receiving a true encounter with God, who is outside and beyond the self. God comes to the self; God reaches out to us. The negative way relativizes the self so that the self can be a creature able to receive the gift of the real presence of God."[34]

God, then, enters into the nothingness of our incapacity to force God to encounter us. God's coming into this void was the case for Dominique, who spoke frankly about her previous views of God and how desperate she was for God's love. Earlier in her journey, she did not believe that God could just love her. Since she was "a bad girl" and "a dirty girl," she perceived that she did not "deserve God's love." She felt too much shame to approach God, demonstrating how shame holds people captive. She decided that if God was to love her, it was necessary for her to *make* God love her. But this created an impossibility for her as she said, "This is God. How do you force him [God] to do something he [God] doesn't want to do?" Yet, God entered her impossibility on multiple occasions, such as

32. Root, *Church after Innovation*, 214.
33. Root, *Church after Innovation*, 215.
34. Root, *Church after Innovation*, 215.

related in the last chapter. Sometimes God freely expressed God's love for her by sending people into her path who would speak a word to her, such as, "Hey, God loves you. God cares about you," or "God's on your side."

Linking Christian Mysticism to Pentecostalism and the Survivors

Turning to Christian mysticism is pertinent to this discussion because pentecostal scholars have made connections between it and pentecostalism, and because multiple survivor-participants had mystical experiences.[35] I mainly draw from Castelo, who notes that unlike evangelicals, pentecostals' knowledge of God emerges from experiences rather than through a rationalist, intellectual method.[36] Castelo focuses on three themes that are shared by pentecostalism and Christian mysticism:

(1) *Purgation and sanctification.* Castelo underscores the connection between the Holiness movement in the 1800s and pentecostalism in the 1900s, both which emphasized sanctification. While pentecostalism historically spoke of power, it did so in conjunction with purity; one was to undergo "a period and a process of consecration and purgation" to be ready to receive the power of God.[37] It is this desire for purity that links pentecostalism to Christian mysticism.

(2) *Illumination and maturation.* As Castelo mentions, both pentecostalism and Christian mysticism have placed a high priority on attending to one's spiritual formation. Spirituality is seen as vibrant, requiring humans to be vigilant in their devotion. By participating in communal activities, e.g., worshipping God, testifying, waiting and praying at the altar, anointing with oil, etc., persons are shaped in their spirituality. It is participation in these collective church activities that is essential in instilling a spirituality that incorporates

---

35. Some examples include: Coulter, "Spirit and the Bride Revisited," 298–319; Nel, "African Pentecostal Spirituality as a Mystical Tradition," 1–10; Poloma, *Mainstreet Mystics*.

36. Margaret Poloma describes in her research project of the Toronto Blessing how the experiences of pentecostals connect to Christian mysticism: they embrace mystery and miracles; they have mystical experiences containing a different type of awareness beyond their five senses; they experience what pentecostals perceive as what is "ultimately real"; they hear familiar Christian terminology amidst their experiences; they undergo various affects during their experiences; and their experiences contain "literal and metaphorical" insight. Poloma, *Mainstreet Mystics*, 24–32.

37. Castelo, *Pentecostalism as a Christian Mystical Tradition*, 51.

both being and knowing, a narrowing of any gap between what I know and who I am. Participation then is key to embracing what Castelo calls "a God-drenched reality."[38]

(3) *Union and transformation.* Castelo holds that the most dominating theme that connects pentecostalism to Christian mysticism is the emphasis on divine encounter.[39] He writes that "[b]eholding God, sensing God, feeling God" is a way of knowing in pentecostalism.[40] It may even be said that a desire for an encounter with God is the focus of a pentecostal worship service.[41] During a worship service, as Castelo comments, pentecostals assume "that God is available and in turn can act and surprise through a kind of 'event' in which one's creaturehood is overwhelmed by the sheer glory of the Creator."[42]

If pentecostalism is of the Christian mystic tradition as Castelo claims, then it is to be expected that many of the survivor-participants discovered healing of their God images and sense of self via mystical encounters with God. God entered into the impossibility of their self, their attempts to satisfy God and to change their perceptions of God. Broadly speaking, the survivor-participants had two types of encounters with God when they spoke of changes in their understanding of and relationship with God. The first emerged from a more natural development, such as completing a Bible study, reading God's Word, or evolving as the person aged. The second was a result of a supernatural encounter with God, such as a vision or mental image.

As demonstrated by Destiny and other survivor-participants, a God image is malleable over time. Destiny no longer regards God as a remote deity who seeks to "zap" people when they engage in sin. Neither does she maintain that God is a deity who records in "the Book of Life" each offense she commits, obligating her to pay the price for each wrongdoing on Judgment Day. Instead, Destiny has discovered an interactive relationship. She interrelates with God by admitting, "Yes, I did that wrong. Yes, I sinned," and turns to God and asks, "How do we do this?" She presently refuses to make any decisions without first talking to God, and she regularly hears God's voice in response. She describes herself as "running

---

38. Castelo, *Pentecostalism as a Christian Mystical Tradition*, 52.
39. Castelo, *Pentecostalism as a Christian Mystical Tradition*, 53.
40. Castelo, *Pentecostalism as a Christian Mystical Tradition*, 52.
41. Engelbert, *Who Is Present in Absence?*, chapter 3.
42. Castelo, *Pentecostalism as a Christian Mystical Tradition*, 53.

hard after" God because she resists "mak[ing] that move without" God. This is evident in her healing journey from sexual violence as it has involved gentle nudges from the Spirit, saying, "Go this way. Do this." This is how God has "very slowly healed [her] heart."

Destiny illustrated the Spirit's healing work by recounting an incident that had transpired just prior to the interview. The previous weekend had begun with Destiny's being in the company of some "really thin, pretty people," and it continued the following day when she attended a bridal shower in a beautiful, well-appointed house that contained "a dream kitchen." In one weekend, Destiny experienced two kinds of glamour: One entailed the ideal body while the other was the picture-perfect home. It was the combination of the two social gatherings that was demoralizing for Destiny, causing her to feel "really down" during the bridal shower. While she was making her way to the powder room amidst her despondency, she uttered under her breath, "I wish." She instantly heard a voice say, "Someday I hope that you see what I see. That you are beautiful, and that I love you, and someday I hope that matters more to you." Immediately, she received what the Spirit was whispering in her ear, which altered her demeanor. As she walked out of the bathroom, she held her head high and thought, "Enjoy the day. You are his [God's] creation. You are loved, and you are beautiful."

When I asked her how she is different today in contrast to twenty years ago, she stated, "I'm a woman who is loved, loved unconditionally, and forgiven, and I know where I'm going." She explained that previously her basic philosophy was: "I don't care how good you are. I don't care what you've done. I don't care what you believe. You're going to hell." Therefore, it is of major significance for her to be able to say, "I'm redeemed and forgiven," and to acknowledge, "I'm loved no matter what. It doesn't matter what I do or don't do. It doesn't matter if I miss." She readily confessed that she sometimes misses God's voice and fails to do what God instructs her to do; nonetheless, she is confident that God "still loves" her. She self-assuredly proclaimed, "Nobody can take that away anymore." Destiny is no longer convinced that God's love is capricious. Instead, she confidently asserted, "It's just there no matter what."

Jackson also relayed about his growing awareness of his gradual transformation. He mentioned attending a Bible study on the book of Daniel, which centered on Daniel's three years of training. The take-away for the group was an invitation to view their lives in three-year spans. Jackson realized, "When I look at three-year spans, I can always see growth." In his viewing of the beginning and the ending of any three-year span, Jackson becomes amazed in how his "faith has increased," how he is "stronger, closer to God," and how he is "learning to rely on the Spirit more."

When I asked Jackson how he experienced God on his healing journey, Jackson spoke of how he shifted in his understanding of God as he has matured. He mentioned that his father was abusive toward his mother, so it was justifiable that as a teenager, he viewed God as "a judge who was ready to zap us if we did something wrong." However, as he has gained more experiences in life, becoming a father and then a grandfather, his God image has changed. He first moved toward an increased understanding of "the father heart of God" to now seeing God more like a grandfather who is more patient. Such a shift in his perception led Jackson to issue a caution to pentecostals. He urged pentecostals to be careful in how they hold holiness and moral living to such a high level. While this quality is good, it also seems to suggest that if pentecostals are not walking exactly like they are called to walk, they will lose their salvation. In light of the discussion on God images, this conveys a danger of a faux God image and a false self that may surface within pentecostalism—one in which God is a vindictive God, and we are our own savior. Melissa Fuller's work supports Jackson's experience when she writes that a person's "distinct perception of God continues to develop" as the person ages. The person is "continually being molded and influenced by old experiences in combination with new experiences that are on the spectrum of either positive or negative; such experiences can reconcile or undermine previously held perceptions."[43]

Like Destiny, sometimes healing movement in a God image occurs through reading Scripture or completing a Bible study. Earlier I spoke of how Mackenzie's understanding of God the Father shifted by the reading the Scripture that states when she sees Jesus, she has seen the Father. The change in her relationship with God the Father arose more than once in my interview with Mackenzie. It surfaced in what Mackenzie called her "life verse," in which she paraphrased Zephaniah 3:17: "My Daddy is always with me. My Daddy is mighty to save me. My Daddy greatly delights in me. My Daddy quiets me with his love. My Daddy rejoices over me with singing." It also appeared in the acronym *L-A-C-K*, which Mackenzie learned from a Christian speaker/author, reminding her that

---

43. Fuller, "Female Sexual Assault Survivors' Perceived God-Image," 4.

in Christ she lacks nothing: *I am **L**oved; I'm **A**ccepted; I'm **C**omplete; I'm **K**nown.*

Besides the gradual changes by God's Spirit who molded and shaped the survivors, more than one survivor experienced mystical divine encounters that generated healing of their God representations. God's unfailing love became more real to Mackenzie in a mystical experience during therapy. Mackenzie frequently struggled with mental images such as being chained naked in a barn and sexually tortured. As she recalled this scenario during an EMDR session, she saw that Jesus was standing outside the door of the barn. While Mackenzie desired to invite Jesus into the barn to rescue her, she was too engulfed in shame to make the request, illustrating shame's relentless grip. Jesus, however, entered the barn, whereupon she began to cry because Jesus was so holy while she was so sinful. Mackenzie witnessed Jesus approaching and tenderly removing the shackles from her wrists and ankles and placing her gently on the barn floor. She then watched in astonishment as Jesus put the shackles on his own wrists and ankles and hung in the barn naked. She audibly cried out amidst her tears: "Jesus took my place!" This was followed by immediately falling to "the floor in a heap, crying tears of gratitude," becoming overwhelmed by Jesus's love for her. After she eventually returned to her chair, she lifted her arms in worship as Jesus gently covered her with his robe of righteousness.

Jade also experienced a gradual shift as well as mystical divine encounters, which helped to reconcile her God image. Her God concept, which she received from the pentecostal church, was "that God knows everything, and God is in control of everything." This was challenged during her healing journey as she became enraged at God and asked, "Why did you put me in this family? Why did you put me in a family where there's been abuse for seventeen years by multiple people in my family?" This view of God was reconciled in three ways during her healing journey. First, the pastor, to whom she had first approached, said, "It is okay that you are angry with God. God's shoulders are broad enough for you to pound on his [God's] chest, and he's [God is] okay with that." Second, she heard from another person that when she was angry with God, she was still in communication with God. She was still in a relationship with God because she was talking to God about her anger. Third, she realized that God was speaking to her mother, but her mother was not listening. This realization came when Jade had a mystical experience of seeing Jesus sobbing and sobbing while keeping his back to her mother when she committed inappropriate sexual acts. He informed Jade, "Many times my Spirit tells her not to do these things to her children, but she chooses to not listen to me, just like many times when my Spirit talks to you, and you choose not to listen." This allowed Jade to see that God was not sitting on God's hands, so to speak, but God was acting while respecting her mother's free will. Jade now perceives that God is no longer completely in charge, but rather God is in charge only to a degree because of humanity's free will. She believes that God honors free will as seen with the individuals who sexually violated her.

Frances, too, recounted a mystical experience, which generated a healing of her God image. Although Frances remained scared of Jesus due to her church upbringing, she continued to be attentive to her spirituality. As an adult, she believed in "multiple ways to the divine," as was evidenced in her worshipping the Goddess and owning a statue of Ganesh. However, she eventually sensed the call of Jesus to follow him amidst her healing journey; even so, her fear of Jesus persisted, causing her to be too frightened to make a commitment to him. When she had a third intense experience of Jesus calling her to follow him, she decided it was time to talk to the Goddess since that was her "closest representation of the divine." She described herself as being very agitated as she went into her meditative state in which she conversed with the Goddess at a bench by a well. The Goddess typically wore a hood during these meditative experiences, so Frances had never glimpsed her face. When Frances informed the Goddess that she did not know what to do about the call to follow Jesus, the Goddess responded by pulling back the hood, revealing the face of Jesus. Upon seeing Jesus's face, she immediately fell into Jesus's lap and cried. For me, this implied that all her fears and agitation were erased as Jesus joined her in her fear and began the healing of her faux God image. Jesus then took her to the well, poured water over her, and baptized her for the very first time in her life. Later in the interview, I asked her what was most surprising during her healing journey, and without hesitation she said, "Having Jesus show up and then baptize me."

Dominique was feeling down one night when God entered her nothingness through a mystical encounter. While driving to work, she asked God: "God, do you ever think of me? Do I ever cross your mind?" As she gazed into the night sky, she was unprepared for what she saw: a giant blood moon. Its immense size captured her attention, prompting her to pull over to stare at it for thirty minutes. When she discovered that neither her husband nor her co-workers had seen it, she understood her blood-moon experience as being from God just for her. Dominique felt as if God was saying to her, "I love you, and I'm thinking about you, and I'm here with you." She said, "After that, [it] was like a whole different relationship between me and God." She described it as "a me-and-him-thing" that caused her to "feel very special" and "very loved."

The above transformations of the survivor-participants' false images of God and self explain how God ministers through God's very presence to the survivors, doing what they cannot do for themselves, which is provide an encounter with the living God.[44] God reveals God's character to them by uniting with them in their darkness, their futile attempts to genuinely see and completely satisfy God. The shifts in the survivor-participants' God images supports Moriarty's beliefs that history is rich with occurrences "of God breaking through and drastically affecting the lives of many individuals." Moriarty admits it is not easy to distinguish "between the effects of the real God image and the real God," but we still believe that God ministers to humanity in direct ways and changes us.[45] That is, as Jesus entered into humanity's inability to encounter God and joined humanity in their death, so Jesus continues to enter into persons' impossibilities today through the power of the Spirit. I believe that the way in which God ministers to humanity by accompanying humanity in their void was partially overlooked by the Corinthian church (and sometimes by those in today's pentecostal church) when the Spirit's gifts became tools to assert power over the other, which I explore in the next section.

THE SPIRIT ENTERS OUR IMPOSSIBILITIES

The preceding chapter's discussion of 1 Corinthians 12 concentrated on the elements of unity and diversity. I continue to explore 1 Corinthians 12 and 14, but I center on a characteristic of the Spirit by focusing on Paul's corrective of the Corinthians' practice of the manifestations of the Spirit. Previously, I recounted that the divisions relating to the spiritual gifts in the Corinthian church revolved around some believing they were

---

44. Root writes, "Out of this impossibility, which God shares completely, God gives God's sure presence to minister directly to the self, giving to the self what the self cannot find within itself. The self is given a direct and real encounter with the true God who comes into the weakness and impossibility of the self to redeem and save the self from its drive for singularity." Root, *Church after Innovation*, 211.

45. Moriarty, *Pastoral Care of Depression*, 59.

more spiritual than others. I remind the readers that being spiritual involves *edifying the community in worship*. An element of edification is being morally or spiritually uplifting or, as Fee writes, the building up of others, which is also a characteristic of love (8:1).[46] Fee sees that the apostle's concern about the gifts in chapters 12 and 14 is that they "are for the building up of the community as a whole" and not mainly for edifying "the individual believer."[47] That being said, Paul does not exclude how the gifts may benefit the individual (14:4).[48] My goal in this section is to demonstrate how edification includes entering into the nothingness of others, which is a characteristic of the persons of the triune Godhead; thus, I emphasize here the person of the Spirit as seen in the manifestations of the Spirit (1 Cor 12, 14) and in pentecostal beliefs.

The Spirit Joins the Corinthians in their Impossibilities

The phrase "manifestations of the Spirit" (v. 7) may denote divine encounters, or in accordance with this chapter, signal Christian mystical experiences. While Paul uses three separate words (*gifts*, v. 4, *ministries*, v. 5, or *results*, v. 6) to note the "individual activities" of the persons of the Trinity, Fee sees these as "simply three different ways" to point toward the "'manifestations' of the Spirit."[49] Fee comments that by switching to the word "manifestations," it is probably Paul's way of expressing his desire to focus on the Spirit, not the gift nor (I would add) an individual who is being used in the gift. Fee continues, "Thus each 'gift' is a 'manifestation,' a disclosure of the *Spirit's* activity in their midst" (italics in original).[50] That is, a manifestation of the Spirit is an encounter with God, the very presence of God. The focus is on *God's* coming to them. As such, I perceive that the Corinthians may be some of the church's earliest mystics.

Yet, as promoted by the mystical tradition and illustrated by the survivor-participants, such divine encounters are not accomplished through meritocracy, which is in contrast to Roman culture (as discussed in chapter 2), or by being good (see above). Oropeza affirms that the manifestations are not like magic, allowing believers to manipulate God.

---

46. Fee, *First Epistle to the Corinthians*, 657–58.
47. Fee, *First Epistle to the Corinthians*, 589.
48. Fee, *First Epistle to the Corinthians*, 589–90n32.
49. Fee, *First Epistle to the Corinthians*, 586–67.
50. Fee, *First Epistle to the Corinthians*, 589.

He continues, "God's Spirit has the ultimate authority to permit or deny the human experience of what we today might identify as supernatural occurrences."[51] As pentecostals, we are in danger of being misguided if we implicitly believe that we are capable of conjuring up an encounter with God through our praise and worship since our worship services tend to be framed in this fashion. As will be presented (chapter 7), pentecostals believe God is still God. It is God's nature and God's grace that compels God to enter into our nothingness by way of the manifestations of the Spirit. It is not through our self-effort since God's presence is a gift.

In discussing the manifestations of the Spirit, pentecostals have typically viewed verses 8–10 as being significant as they list the nine gifts of the Spirit, which they believe remain active in the church today. While some pentecostal ministers may teach that these verses contain a complete list of the gifts of the Spirit, Keener disagrees. Keener compares this list with other Pauline lists (Rom 12:4–8; 1 Cor 12:28; 12:29–30; 13:1–2, 8–9; 14:26; Eph 4:11) and concludes that Paul's "lists are ad hoc—that is, he is making them up 'on the spot'—and vary considerably."[52] Keener sees the list in 1 Corinthians as the apostle's way of paying attention to those "gifts that are most relevant to his readers' situation." The culture of Corinth championed rhetoric and "reasoning abilities"; therefore, the Corinthians "prized gifts such as 'wise speech' and 'knowledgeable speech,'" and they also cherished speaking in tongues (1 Cor 14). This list, then, underscores those manifestations that particularly connect to the church at Corinth.[53] Rather than a verse-by-verse exegesis, I am highlighting in this section the aforementioned manifestations of word of wisdom, word of knowledge, and speaking in tongues.

At the top of Paul's list are the manifestations of *word of wisdom* and *word of knowledge*. These two manifestations stress two activities that were exceedingly valued in the Greco-Roman world: oratory and philosophy. Keener notes that the Greek term frequently translated "word" may also be translated "utterance" or "rhetoric," signaling the Corinthians' emphasis on oratory, a reflection of the culture. The ancient Greco-Roman athletic competitive games are renowned today, which also included the Isthmian Games near Corinth; however, less familiar is that these games involved not only physical prowess but also oratory competition.[54]

51. Oropeza, *1 Corinthians*, 162.
52. Keener, *Gift Giver*, 81.
53. Keener, *Gift Giver*, 81–82.
54. Keener, *Gift Giver*, 81–82. Gorman comments that "the biennial Isthmian

The Corinthian church's own competitiveness appears in a multitude of ways in this letter, but it is visible in 1 Corinthians 1 in how they embrace antiquity's notions of "wisdom" and "power." As Keener highlights, the word for "wisdom" may also include rhetoric, which is implied when the apostle refers to "clever speech" (1:17), "debaters" (1:20), and "superior eloquence" or "persuasive words" that were based on "human wisdom" (2:1, 4–5).[55] The apparent influence of the culture's championing of such speech-making is seen in Keener's comments on how some Corinthian believers preferred Apollos over Paul because he was more skilled as an orator (1 Cor 1–4).[56] Gifted orators were highly prized, allowing them to accrue (merit) more power because of their abilities. They were the winners.

Keener continues by highlighting how Paul's emphasis on *wisdom* and *knowledge* points towards the culture's priority placed on the words of philosophers and sophists.[57] As Fee notices, the phrase "word of wisdom" was referencing an issue that was confronted in the opening of the epistle (1:17—2:16), "where in the name of wisdom the Corinthians were rejecting both Paul and his gospel."[58] Fee perceives that the apostle in 1 Corinthians 12 is now refashioning the idea of wisdom by taking into account the Spirit's activity.[59] This presents wisdom in quite a dissimilar fashion from that of the Corinthians, in which having wisdom in the Roman culture translates into power, prestige, and praise. However, according to Fee, Paul is accentuating the manifestation of the word of wisdom as being from the Spirit, not from the individual. He is also emphasizing that it is an utterance spoken by those who preach Christ crucified (the genuine wisdom of God), not by those who cling to power and prestige.[60] A connection, then, exists between the one who preaches and lives a cruciformed life and who speaks a word of wisdom from the Spirit.

Similarly, word of knowledge refers back to an earlier discussion in the letter. Keener writes of how Paul reprimanded the Corinthians

---

Games" were "[s]econd only to the Olympiad." The games were hosted by the "neighboring Isthmia" and included competition among athletes, musicians, dramatists, and rhetoricians. Gorman, *Apostle of the Crucified Lord*, 278.

55. Keener, *1-2 Corinthians*, 28.
56. Keener, *Gift Giver*, 81–82.
57. Keener, *Gift Giver*, 82–83.
58. Fee, *First Epistle to the Corinthians*, 591.
59. Fee, *First Epistle to the Corinthians*, 592.
60. Fee, *First Epistle to the Corinthians*, 592.

when some declared "to have special doctrinal knowledge from God that they assumed made them better than Christians who did not possess it (8:1–3)"; thus, Paul reminded them of two aspects about their knowledge: it will be set aside (13:8) and is characterized by being "incomplete" (13:9).[61] As Oropeza comments, Paul was both de-emphasizing the "skill" of believers while emphasizing their "enablement" by the Spirit; hence, there was no room for boasting (8:1–3) as these manifestations were from the Spirit.[62] They were not a matter of merit nor of being good enough, both of which focused on the person rather than the Spirit.

Concerning the Corinthians' emphasis on speaking in tongues, I turn to 1 Corinthians 14. Fee views that 1 Corinthians 14 combined the previous two chapters (1 Cor 12, 13). He sees that Paul is asserting that the Corinthians' only objective when they meet together was to be love, which was to build one another up—edification (vv. 1–3, 12, 17, 26).[63] This was in contrast to the influence of the Greco-Roman culture, which engendered attitudes of building up themselves. Paul's specific reproof conveyed that the Corinthians were possibly speaking in tongues in order to present themselves as more spiritual. If so, speaking in tongues became a vehicle to accumulate more power—more status or a higher position in the eyes of other believers. Tongues had become a status symbol, a way to boost themselves. As such, the assembly lacked mutual edification, intelligibility, and order. As Oropeza writes, the summary of 1 Corinthians 12, 13, and 14 is the maintaining of order and doing all things appropriately, which "will foster the building up rather than disruption of solidarity among congregation members" (14:26, 33, 40).[64]

In response to the Corinthians' unrestricted speaking in tongues during their meetings, the apostle does not forbid speaking in tongues. Instead, he stresses the manifestation of prophecy when they gather together, which emphasizes the building up of the body. Keener writes, "[P]rophecy serves one's spiritual colleagues directly (14:3); the difference is between self-edification and edifying others (14:4). Although both purposes may be commendable, the former can be done privately (cf. 14:18–19) rather than at the rest of the assembly's expense."[65] Keener explains that the apostle believes speaking in tongues is "desirable," but

61. Keener, *Gift Giver*, 83. See also Fee, *First Epistle to the Corinthians*, 593.
62. Oropeza, *1 Corinthians*, 162–63.
63. Fee, *First Epistle to the Corinthians*, 652.
64. Oropeza, *1 Corinthians*, 195.
65. Keener, *1–2 Corinthians*, 113.

prophecy is "even more desirable" as it attends to more than just the self (14:5, 18–19).[66] In other words, the goal is edifying, strengthening, comforting, and consoling members of the assembly by entering into the suffering of others (12:26), which is also healing. This is the way of the Spirit.

The Spirit Joins Pentecostals in their Impossibilities

This characteristic of the Spirit, as one who enters into our impossibilities, was portrayed above in the lives of the survivor-participants when they had encounters with the divine. This same characteristic of God's Spirit's joining with or entering into the survivor-participants' healing journeys also came to the fore in my conversation with counselor-participant Joel. Joel believes God is deeply involved in the healing process of both Christian and non-Christian survivors. As a pentecostal, Joel highly values "the work of the altar in people's lives." However, he accentuated that the altar experience is not all that is necessary for healing, but both the altar and discipleship are needed. Joel defines the altar as "that moment of emotion and experience where we are empowered to walk" the path "of discipleship, both alone and with other people." This means that he defines discipleship as being "systematic in accountability and in training and in truth." He asserts that without the altar, motivation is lost, and without discipleship, the person lacks "the information for change." Joel acknowledges that those who are mandated by the courts to attend counseling may lack the altar experience; however, for those who call him on the phone, that in and of itself *is* the altar experience. He believes that frequently the healing process of pentecostals begins with an altar experience in which the Spirit is "tugging at them and loving on them in the pew or wherever they might be reading or . . . listening to worship music." This becomes "a safe place to begin to have an inner dialogue with the Spirit," which is where "God begins to soften the soil" of pentecostal survivors. For Joel, God is behind the survivors' calling him on the phone. It is when they have reached "such a difficult spot" that they phone "a total stranger" and will pay him money to tell him "their deepest secrets." As Joel says, "That takes a lot." Destiny confirmed the involvement of God's Spirit when she told me that "the presence of the Holy Spirit" had made the biggest difference in her healing journey.

66. Keener, *1–2 Corinthians*, 113.

As indicated in Joel's experience of being called by strangers, believers now have the opportunity to participate in this healing ministry of the Spirit. Contemporary pentecostals often remind each other that the spiritual manifestations are a sign of God's coming kingdom, a glimpse of our future of a new heaven and a new earth. They see the gifts as a demonstration of an inbreaking of the eschaton into today's world. It is a proleptic experience of the now-but-not-yet, which signifies an eschatological hope (eschatology is a theme in 1 Corinthians, which is discussed more fully in chapter 7). In addition to this, however, I believe that the gifts of the Spirit are simultaneously exhibiting cruciformity by dying to self's ambitions of *power over* the other and entering into the other's impossibilities. Earlier (chapter 2), I depicted how participating in the Lord's Supper (1 Cor 11) is a reenactment of God's being a minister through the incarnation by joining us in our death while simultaneously healing us. Jesus Christ reveals God and heals sinners within his very being as divinity ministers to humanity in the person of Jesus.[67] Here I am centering on the Spirit, the third person of the Trinity, as the one who enters into humanity's impossibilities through the Spirit's manifestations through believers (1 Cor 12, 14). As with Jesus Christ, I perceive that two aspects are concurrently transpiring through believers' participation in the manifestations of the Spirit: believers are joining in the Spirit's healing ministry by participating in Christ's future reign where all of creation will be whole, and believers are joining the Spirit in the black holes of others. The latter is an act of cruciformity, a partaking in Christ's past—the cross. The manifestations of the Spirit are a means by which followers of Jesus participate in Christ's healing ministry by joining others in their death through the power and the presence of the Spirit.

The Spirit's accompaniment of others into their darkness while moving with them toward a future of wholeness is not a foreign understanding of the Spirit within pentecostalism. Cheryl Peterson employs Rambo's understanding of the "middle Spirit" and Holy Saturday, which is that space between the cross and the resurrection, to demonstrate how the Spirit joins survivors in their suffering. By joining with survivors, the Spirit bears witness and gives voice to the trauma and its repercussions throughout the winding, twisting journey of healing toward new life. This means that the Spirit not only bears witness to the suffering which

---

67. I am referring to the hypostatic union in which Jesus is both fully divine and fully human; therefore, within the very being of Jesus the divine is ministering to humanity. See Engelbert, *Who Is Present in Absence?*.

"'remains' from trauma" but also accompanies survivors "into the promise of new life on the other side of Holy Saturday."[68] Cheryl Bridges Johns also sees a coming alongside in suffering as a characteristic of the Spirit. For Johns, a pentecostal feminist reading of Scripture views difficult scriptural passages of women being abused and killed as spaces in which "the Spirit [is] brooding over the world throughout the Ages; taking under her wings its slavery, abuse, and patriarchy.'"[69] Therefore, Johns perceives that when women "are brought low within the biblical narrative," so too is "*Shekinah*" present, "lying in the dust, and anguished by human suffering" (italics in original).[70] We then are invited "to participate in this work of brooding" as we read the biblical text, to wait in the pain and suffering and be attentive to the Spirit's healing work.[71] Likewise, the Corinthians are invited to join the healing ministry of the Spirit by being alongside those who are suffering rather than asserting power over others. Oropeza seems to agree when he writes about 1 Corinthians 12:4–11: "Our apostle challenges the Corinthians to turn from a status-seeking orientation to one of voluntary self-giving for the edification of others."[72]

The manifestations of the Spirit are not for the exaltation of a human being, creating or striving to be a spiritual celebrity (an oxymoron if ever there was one). Neither are they about becoming persons with positions of power and influence in the eyes of others, thereby avoiding the uniting in the suffering or honoring of the other (12:26). Glorification of the individual disempowers the other rather than edifies. The manifestations of the Spirit are not for taking power or status away from others but for joining with others in their void, thereby healing them. The Spirit's portrayal of power is a means of entering into the other's death, such as:

- The *message of wisdom* and the *message of knowledge* join others by providing a revelation of some kind;[73]
- The gift of *faith* unites with others, providing "a particular endowment of faith, the sort that moves mountains," or do "what was virtually impossible";[74]

68. Peterson, "Pneumatology in the Time of #MeToo," 30.
69. Johns, "Grieving, Brooding, and Transforming," 18.
70. Johns, "Grieving, Brooding, and Transforming," 17.
71. Johns, "Grieving, Brooding, and Transforming," 18.
72. Oropeza, *1 Corinthians*, 162.
73. Fee, *First Epistle to the Corinthians*, 593.
74. Keener, *Gift Giver*, 83.

- The *gifts of healing* focus on entering into others' sicknesses;
- The *performance of miracles* seeks to partake in others' impossibilities.

This is the way of the Spirit. It is the way of love.

The next part of the book continues this chapter's emphasis on participating in Christ's ministry by centering on pentecostal praxes of healing in order to offer a safe place for survivors. The themes of healing praxes that emerged from the participants include: listening, waiting, and learning.

PART TWO

Providing a Safe Place for Survivors

6

Listen to My Story

Listen without judgment or without accusations or trying to fix people.
　　　　　　　　　—Sutton, a survivor-participant

We need to learn how to listen better.
　　　　　　　　　—Megan, a counselor-participant

I find churches just are ill equipped to provide the kind of support that people need . . . People are not trained in just holding presence, listening, and holding space, and that's what people need.
　　　　　　　　　—Dayton, a counselor-participant

Jade taught me how pentecostals listen to and wait on God. She spoke of a repeated mystical experience that transpired over an extended period during the Sunday evening worship service of her pentecostal church in which she saw herself as a little girl of approximately five years of age. In this repeated experience, Jesus approached the little girl and said, "I want to take you to meet my Father," to which she responded, "Okay." However, after they had taken three or four steps, the little girl announced, "Oh, I've changed my mind. I want to go play in the park," to which he replied, "OK. Let's go play in the park." Over and over again, Jade envisioned the two of them going to the park and swinging in the swings together instead of going to the Father. After several months of this repeated scenario, on one particular Sunday evening, the little girl did not ask to play in the park, but she accompanied Jesus to meet the Father. Jade believed this change in her response signaled her having experienced sufficient relational healing regarding fathers, affording her a readiness to encounter Jesus's Father.

As Jesus and Jade continued walking along a pathway, they came to a doorway, and Jesus said, "This is as far as I can go. You can go in, and the Father is sitting in there on a chair." When Jade went through the doorway, she entered into a brightly lit room in which she saw God the Father without clearly seeing the Father's face. As she walked over to the Father, the Father picked her up and placed her on his lap. The Father then lifted her high above his head, moving her around a little while simultaneously tickling her so that the two of them laughed together. After the Father put the little girl down, they began to play hide-and-seek in which she peeked around the Father's chair and looked at the Father, generating laughter first from the Father and then from her. When she returned to the front of the chair, the Father picked her up and again placed her on his lap and said, "I'm your dad, you know." The shock of this realization caused her to cry as this was quite exciting for the five-year-old-emotional part of her heart. Amidst her excitement, she went to the far corner of the room and pulled on a huge angel's robe, saying, "He's my dad, you know," and the angel nodded. She then walked over to Jesus, pulled on Jesus's garment, and said, "He's my dad, you know," and Jesus replied, "I've been trying to tell you that for a long time."

It was not until after she had repeatedly experienced this mystical encounter that she realized its significance. When she was almost six years of age, she learned that her stepfather was not her biological father. Her older sister informed her that what Jade believed to be her surname was not actually hers. Her sister warned her: "If you're bad, my dad is gonna send you to your dad, and your dad doesn't want you." Such news shattered Jade's world as she no longer knew where she belonged. The five-year-old Jade realized in that moment: "Everyone else belongs in this family but me." But God saw and heard and continued to be aware of her need for healing even when she remained unaware as an adult. As she stood in a worship service, being open and listening during these divine-initiated encounters, Jade's unknown needs for identity and belonging were being healed.

Part one emphasized aspects about the healing journeys of survivors of sexual violence by seeking to answer the question, "In what manner is healing demonstrated in the lives of pentecostals who have experienced physical sexual violence?" Chapter 1 underscored the prevalence of sexual violence and the importance of seeing, hearing, and believing the survivors. However, if pentecostals are to be supportive throughout the healing journey, it is necessary that they be informed about the characteristics of sexual trauma. Hence, chapter 2 stressed how trauma impacts the whole person so that the body remembers the trauma throughout a survivor's life. Chapter 3 underlined the significance of telling and retelling the story during the healing process as the survivor-participants told others about their experiences of sexual violence. Chapter 4 highlighted that while healing journeys share similar characteristics, each healing journey is unique. Chapter 5 focused on the healing of the survivors' false images of God as they journeyed towards a more harmonized experiential-theological understanding of God.

Jade's story above introduces part two of this book in which I am answering the question, "How may pentecostals provide a safe haven for survivors who are healing from sexual violence?" My focus is on developing pentecostal healing responses to survivors who are part of our pentecostal communities.[1] Because this section centers on pentecostal theological praxes, it offers responses that incorporate pentecostal theology and/or Scripture in order to further a survivor's healing. The elements of praxes contained in this section are listening, waiting, and learning, each of which are visible in Jade's story as she listened to God, waited for God, and learned from God. Her story becomes evidence that each of these elements has historically been a part of pentecostalism. This chapter begins this exploration by taking up the pentecostal characteristic of listening.

Jade's above experience of listening to and waiting for God is in stark contrast to her experience with another pentecostal. When disturbing memories had begun to surface at the beginning of her healing journey,

---

1. If we are to change from a community who plugs its ears and closes its eyes to sexual violence to a community who listens to survivors, we need to change our story. McKnight and Barringer make this point in their discussion on changing a church culture from toxic to compassionate: "Because it all begins with a narrative, with the stories we tell, the way to begin forming a new culture of empathy and compassion is by learning to tell a new story." McKnight and Barringer, *Church Called Tov*, 107.

Jade had gone to the altar on a Sunday night and told the pastor she was feeling quite depressed. He replied, "I was depressed once . . . But then I learned how to just snap out of it. You've nothing to be depressed about. You have four children. You've got a roof over your head. You've got a car in your driveway. You're married. You're with your husband. You have no reason to be depressed. You just have to choose not to be depressed." As Jade departed from that place, she thought to herself: "I'll never go forward again for prayer because you're not hearing me, and you don't understand the full magnitude of depression and what's going on inside for me."

This above pentecostal response is in line with a culture that stresses speaking, not listening. The Western perception of listening is like the American treatment of a traffic light. When someone else is talking, we behave as if it's a red light, being impatient while we wait for that moment when we have the green light to speak again. Here, listening may be regarded as that interval or space in a conversation that becomes an opportunity to complete other tasks since I am *doing nothing else but listening*.[2] We may act as if listening is like a competitive game of chess in which during my opponent's turn I construct my next move, my argument, in which I seek to take over and win.[3]

While listening may be underrated, being perceived as a necessary steppingstone to state one's views, I assert that listening is an essential ethical, embodied action for the church that enhances the pentecostal church's theology of healing. I emphasized in chapter 3 that the telling of the story was of great importance for the survivors in their healing journeys. While that chapter touched on the healing properties of both storytelling and storylistening, I placed a priority on the *telling* aspect. Now I return to this theme of storytelling, but my prime concern is storylistening. I argue that it matters how companions listen to the stories of survivors of sexual violence. Drawing from the concept of embodied

---

2. As Lisbeth Lipari explains, listening then becomes "the absence of speech, a gap, a lacuna, a fissure. It is the red light I wait at until I may speak again. It is 'killing time,' 'doing nothing,' or contrarily, it is rigorously goal oriented: when is he going to get to the point already?" Lipari, *Listening, Thinking, Being*, 13.

3. Lipari writes about listening in our culture: "In legislatures, on talk radio and television shows, verbal wrestling matches masquerade as dialogue, and listening occurs only, if at all, as a means of preparing one's next move in the spectacle. And even when listening is addressed in classrooms, courtrooms, or television studios, it is done primarily with the aim of conquest and control. We either listen to our adversary's arguments so we may defeat them, or we listen in order to 'master' some material, facts, or theories." Lipari, *Listening, Thinking, Being*, 12.

listening, my purpose is to augment a pentecostal theological praxis of healing by (1) demonstrating that listening is already a characteristic of pentecostalism that includes the whole body; (2) describing how listening involves one's whole being, which is also an ethical response as presented by Lisbeth Lipari; (3) exploring Paul's ethical call to the body of Christ in 1 Corinthians by drawing from Gorman; and (4) concluding that listening is a necessary sign of a Spirit-filled church, living out Paul's ethical kenotic model.[4]

LISTENING AS A PENTECOSTAL

As suggested in the last chapter, a church community that has traditionally identified as Spirit-filled has frequently been characterized as having supernatural experiences with God. These communities have commonly claimed to have the *full gospel* as they have typically emphasized and experienced the manifestations of the Spirit and have theologically supported this emphasis by drawing from 1 Corinthians 12 and 14 (see this book's chapters 4 and 5). Since I was raised as a Classical Pentecostal, the most recurring manifestations that I have personally experienced in a service have been speaking in tongues, interpretation of tongues, and prophecy, customarily referred to as the *vocal gifts*. Some of these communities have held that speaking in tongues is the initial physical evidence of the baptism of the Spirit with an accompanying mission to make disciples among men and women. This means their theological focus has underscored speaking and telling: speaking in a language of the Spirit (*glossolalia*) and telling others about the gospel of Jesus Christ. Through this lens, one may conclude that pentecostals are mainly known for various kinds of speech, be it the operation of the vocal gifts, the baptism of the Spirit with the evidence of speaking in tongues, or the proclamation of the gospel.

Despite this attention given to speaking, others have not overlooked that listening is also deeply embedded in pentecostalism. I recall being instructed as a youth that hearing God is similar to listening to a radio: I simply need to turn the dial and tune into God's voice, which is constantly broadcasting.[5] T. M. Luhrmann, an anthropologist, investigates

---

4. Portions of this chapter were presented at SPS. See Engelbert, "Not Tongues but Listening."

5. T. M. Luhrmann also discovers similar instruction in Luhrmann, *When God Talks Back*, 45.

the emphasis on listening in her research among Vineyard pentecostals. When Luhrmann paraphrases from *Dialogue with God*, she writes, "God is always speaking to you . . . The Christian just needs to learn how to listen."[6] And listening is what pentecostals strive to do. Tania Harris, in her qualitative study that involved 204 revelatory experiences from 89 Australian pentecostals, indicates that people hear from God through a variety of means, including visions and internal messages.[7] Harris also relates her own experiences of listening to and hearing from God, employing these experiences alongside Scripture as a way to instruct others to expect and recognize the voice of God in *God Conversations*.[8] Survivor-participant Elizabeth seems to agree with Harris's research and experiences as she spoke of needing to listen to God during her healing journey: "His sheep know his voice. With all the noise in the church, I had to learn to listen for him. I knew his voice, but I had to learn to listen again. 'Is what they're saying what you want me to do? Is this the way you want healing to look like?' I didn't know when I started this journey. I'd never been on a journey like this. I never walked with anybody because I couldn't."

As a pentecostal, I have frequently experienced worship services in which pentecostals pause and listen when a holy hush descends on the congregation. The whole congregation waits in silence, hoping for a word from God. When a person gives a message in and interpretation of tongues or a prophecy, pentecostals continue to be attentive, listening to words by the Spirit spoken through a member of Christ's body. Poloma bears this out in her writing about prophecies among pentecostals of the 1970s when she writes how a gathering becomes completely quiet when God's holy presence is sensed in a special way as a prophecy speaks explicitly to the gathering. One may hear people crying or echoing words of agreement during the speaking of a prophecy and then worship, applause, speaking in tongues, or expressions of thanksgiving may be heard after it has ended.[9] But prophesying is not without listening as Poloma describes how individuals "who prophesy learn the art of listening and responding over time, often under the tutelage of more established prophets."[10] Both

---

6. Luhrmann, *When God Talks Back*, 46.
7. Harris, "Where Pentecostalism and Evangelicalism Part Ways," 31–40.
8. Harris, *God Conversations*.
9. Poloma, *Main Street Mystics*, 116.
10. Poloma, *Main Street Mystics*, 121.

prophecy and supplication involve a connection to communication since prior to speaking, there is listening.[11]

Pentecostals also commonly mention seeking God's direction or listening to God through their reading of Scripture. Scott Ellington speaks of the pentecostal approach to the biblical text in that they seek a fresh encounter with God and hear the Spirit in the text.[12] Keith Warrington echoes this in his writing on a pentecostal theology of the Bible by stating that pentecostals hold that believers are "to be aware that the Spirit is not as silent as many may assume but that he [the Spirit] desires to enlighten and encounter them as they listen to him [the Spirit] speaking to them through the text."[13] Luhrmann observes that pentecostal teaching (i.e., the sermon) has the Bible as its focal point. She remarks that it is called "teaching" because the one who teaches is "less important than [the] subject" being taught (i.e., God) for "God is speaking; the teaching begins to teach you how to listen."[14]

Yet, listening for pentecostals is not merely accomplished through a single bodily organ, the ear. Instead, pentecostals counter this popular cultural perception of listening by frequently engaging in listening through one's whole body. Michael Wilkinson and Peter Althouse discuss the Charismatic renewal of the Toronto Blessing in which they examine a form of bodily listening called "soaking prayer." As these authors explain, soaking prayer is a variation of an earlier pentecostal experience called "slain in the Spirit" in which "Pentecostals believed that the experience of God's presence was so real that they fell as if dead."[15] The phenomenon has also been given other names such as "resting in the Spirit" by some Charismatics of the 1960s.[16] *Soaking prayer*, as defined by Wilkinson, is "the deliberate practice of placing the body in a position of rest in order

---

11. Poloma, *Main Street Mystics*, 118.

12. Ellington, "Locating Pentecostals at the Hermeneutical Round Table," 217–18. Similarly, when Fee underscores the spirituality of the biblical text, he argues that when people are convinced that the Bible is God's Word, it is in and through the text "that here God speaks and we listen." Fee, *Listening to the Spirit in the Text*, 14.

13. Warrington, *Pentecostal Theology*, 200–201. Pentecostals also acknowledge that such messages from God via the text may not be identical for each person. As Warrington writes, pentecostals believe that the Spirit may tailor "different messages of hope, guidance, revelation and tuition depending on the cultural or spiritual context in which the believer is located." Warrington, *Pentecostal Theology*, 201.

14. Luhrmann, *When God Talks Back*, 12.

15. Wilkinson and Althouse, *Catch the Fire*, 5.

16. Wilkinson, "Pentecostalism, the Body, and Embodiment," 22.

to receive God's love."[17] It is described as being "nonverbal" as "[p]articipants do not pray to bring their cares and concerns in petition to God or intercede for one's needs or the needs of others. It is meditative prayer, where charismatics focus on being still or quiet in a posture of listening and receiving."[18] In addition to his research on soaking prayer at the Toronto Blessing, Althouse conducted interviews with three attendees of the Christian Healing Ministries in Jacksonville, Florida. One attendee, Louise, spoke how "soaking prayer was very important and changed her approach to prayer from talking out loud to God to listening without saying anything. It was a shift from being loud to learning to be still."[19]

Besides soaking prayer, other indications are evident that listening is carried out with the whole body among pentecostals. Travis Warren Cooper observes in his ethnographic study among Assemblies of God and Vineyard congregations how "Pentecostals conceive of their bodies as having the capacity to 'tune in' to divine 'wavelengths.'"[20] Cooper observed in an Assemblies of God congregation how periodically congregants bent their arms "at the elbows" and placed their palms "upward in postures of reception."[21] In this way, the congregants of Spirit-filled communities signaled through their bodies that they were attuned or listening to or for God. To summarize, both soaking prayer and bodily worship are pentecostal theological praxes that signify how pentecostals practice embodied listening. The subsequent section builds on this understanding by putting forth Lipari's interdisciplinary approach to bodily listening.

LISTENING AS AN EMBODIED, ETHICAL RESPONSE

When I consider the subject of listening, my mind cannot resist recalling the popular advertisement slogan, "Do you hear me now?" Yet, hearing and listening are not synonymous. According to Lipari, *hearing* involves perceiving and receiving so that it is focused more on the "self's experience," whereas *listening* concentrates more on "attention and obedience,"

---

17. Wilkinson, "Pentecostalism, the Body, and Embodiment," 23.

18. Wilkinson and Althouse, *Catch the Fire*, 5.

19. Althouse, "Emotional Regimes in the Embodiment of Charismatic Prayer," 44. Although many interviewees speak similarly about *soaking prayer*, Wilkinson and Althouse caution that it is a "multivariant term" in that it has "multiple meanings." See Wilkinson and Althouse, *Catch the Fire*, 5.

20. Cooper, "Worship Rituals, Discipline," 77.

21. Cooper, "Worship Rituals, Discipline," 81.

centering more "on the other."[22] Theologian Jennifer Baldwin, who highlights Lipari's work, describes *hearing* as providing "a more open, patient presence" when being with the other while *listening* is more "active," involving a "leaning in/forward."[23] In this light, perhaps the phrase that better serves my purposes is: "Are you listening now?" This section seeks to broaden the Western understanding of listening by challenging modernity's atomistic perception of listening. Drawing from Lipari, I aim to show how listening is a multi-dimensional, multi-layered, ethical activity, involving one's whole being, by addressing three common misconceptions of listening: (1) listening and speaking are two separate elements of communication, occurring in a linear fashion; (2) listening is only the translation of sounds through the organ called the ear; and (3) misunderstanding is to be overcome and avoided as it is an obstruction to quality listening.

Three Misconceptions of Listening

The first misconception is that speaking and listening occur in a linear fashion during the process of communication. This notion is evident if I identify listening as simply a matter of *catching* the other's words and offering a response in return, or as merely waiting for the other person to finish talking so that I may have my chance to speak. As one person told me, this is like, "listening to add my words, not listening to consume yours." Speaking and listening in this way are perceived as two separate acts that transpire in a linear fashion between Persons A and B, similar to using a tin-can phone. When two cans are linked via a string, Person A holds Can One close to the mouth while Person B has Can Two next to Person B's ear. Being careful to keep the string taut, Person A speaks into Can One while Person B listens through Can Two. This depicts communication as being a straightforward, uncomplicated, atomistic process in which speaking and listening are separate but equal. According to Lipari, this is called "the transmission model" in which ideas are moved "from one brain to another."[24]

---

22. Lipari, *Listening, Thinking, Being*, 75.

23. Baldwin, "Akroatic, Embodied Hearing and Presence as Spiritual Practice," loc. 1835–37.

24. Lipari, *Listening, Thinking, Being*, 23. This is not the only view of communication that Lipari describes as she includes descriptions of semiotic, ritual, and constitutive; however, each one in her view is "partial and incomplete." See Lipari, *Listening, Thinking, Being*, 26.

Contra to this misconception, Lipari writes that "speaking and listening are inseparable processes." Listening and speaking are not like persons on opposite teams. Instead, Lipari describes them as "counterpoints," such as when another melody is being played above or below a melody line or when a person offers a contrasting argument to the other's main viewpoint. They are interdependent. It is similar to touching. It is impossible for me to reach out and touch someone (to borrow from a vintage advertisement) without also "being touched."[25] This suggests that even when one converses with oneself, speaking and listening are transpiring concurrently. If I audibly tell myself, "Pam, how could you be so stupid," my self-talk may reveal how I have been listening to external voices, such as an experience that communicated that I was stupid or a family system in which a father repeatedly described himself as dumb. This conveys that I am not just listening and speaking to myself. As Lipari explains, inner voices are molded by public voices, and public voices are shaped by inner voices. It is "a blending of inner and outer."[26] Such a view rejects a rigid dualistic model that solely differentiates between inner/outer speech or speaking/listening and exchanges it for a more holistic model in which these distinct boundaries are blurred.

To support the so-called blurring of the boundaries of speaking, listening, and thinking, Lipari puts forth the term "interlistening." Lipari explains that *interlistening* is a description of "the ways communicative interactions transcend boundaries around time, place, and person."[27] I want to be clear that interlistening is not Lipari's effort to put forth some perfect model or lofty goal to which we are to aspire, but rather she is offering a description of listening. She describes listening, speaking, and thinking not as three distinct operations but an integration, or in her words "an integrated plural."[28] Namely, listening, thinking, and speaking are occurring all at once. They are not freestanding activities. Interlistening for Lipari "is itself a form of speaking" because speaking and listening echo everything in our past, present, and future. Whatever we have been told, pondered, spoken, scanned, or studied in our lives yesterday, today, or tomorrow are part of interlistening.[29] Such echoes impact our dialogue with the other and with ourselves. Every experience, be it sorrowful,

25. Lipari, *Listening, Thinking, Being*, 22.
26. Lipari, *Listening, Thinking, Being*, 171.
27. Lipari, *Listening, Thinking, Being*, 220.
28. Lipari, *Listening, Thinking, Being*, 220.
29. Lipari, *Listening, Thinking, Being*, 221.

joyous, traumatic, or victorious, and every relationship, be it good, bad, healthy, or unhealthy, join humans as they listen and speak. This is why it may be said that humans do not listen alone when they listen to the other or to themselves. If one person is talking before a group of hundreds who are said to be listening, simultaneously hundreds are talking and hundreds are listening. If only one is talking in a forest so that no one else is present to listen, there is still one who is listening.[30] Therefore, listening involves one's whole being—physical, mental, emotional, spiritual, and relational—and contains all voices, internal and external. Lipari calls this a person's *listening habitus*, which is the development of one's way of listening that is molded by "a combination of cultural, social, and personal experiences."[31]

No one listens with a clean slate or within a vacuum. Instead, I am naturally selective in my listening. Similar to walking through a food buffet, I automatically pick and choose what I hear and how it is heard, based on who I am in body, mind, and soul and how culture has shaped me. Such selective listening is exemplified while I am attending a concert of my favorite band. A drummer in the audience may pay particular attention to the band's rhythm section while I, who play guitar, center upon the sounds of the band's acoustic guitar. While a drummer appreciates the skills and sounds of the rhythm section, I may hear it as noise and occasionally overpowering to the point of irritating. Likewise, when I listen to the other, I am more attentive to certain phrases and concepts while closing myself off to other ideas, as discussed below.

The second misconception holds that listening is mostly the translation of sounds by using the organ called the ear. In contrast, Baldwin sees listening as engaging the other with one's whole body while attending "to the multidimensionality of communication."[32] Listening is more than merely deciphering sounds with one's ears such as *a, e, i, o, u*. As Evelyn Glennie, a deaf composer and percussionist, argues, humans "physically feel sound."[33] Physically feeling sound occurs more often than when one's chest is pounding due to the deafening sounds created by a church worship band. Instead, it transpires each time sound takes place. Glennie learned that sound did not merely come through the ears when her ability to hear began to deteriorate, leading to a reliance "on hearing aids" by

30. Lipari, *Listening, Thinking, Being*, 222.
31. Lipari, *Listening, Thinking, Being*, 77.
32. Baldwin, *Trauma Sensitive Theology*, loc. 2849–50.
33. Glennie, "Feeling Sound with Evelyn Glennie."

age twelve. At that time, she became curious about playing percussion instruments. Upon approaching a percussion instructor, he asked her if she could "hear more" by removing her hearing aids. After she removed them, the instructor inquired, "Where can you feel the sound?" As he hit a percussion instrument, her entire body had to become "patient" to genuinely listen to the sound so that it "seeped through [her] body." Glennie explains that initially the sound enters by way of the ear, "but the resonance" is "felt through the body" for all of us.[34] Today as a professional percussionist, she desires not only to generate a sound but also a type of feeling in her body, and she wants the audience to pay attention, open up their bodies, and feel it in their bodies, too.[35]

Yet the feeling in the body, or listening, also acknowledges uniqueness. For Glennie, listening is compared to playing a percussion instrument. When she strictly reads a musical composition by following "the instructions, the tempo markings, the dynamics," she is playing precisely as the sheet music dictates. In other words, she "translates" the music. However, when she interprets the music, the translation moves from being "shallow" to depth as it reveals her "sound color." In the same way that she must learn about an instrument and a musical composition to be able to interpret the music, so humans must also learn about the other to honestly listen, not just translate what they initially see and hear. She explains, "We all have our own little sound colors, as it were, that make up these extraordinary personalities and characters and interests and things." She indicates that technically listening to the letters and words is not enough; instead, genuine listening begins by listening to oneself,[36] and genuine listening to the other involves looking at the individual, not one's phone.[37] In both cases, listening occurs by attending to and opening up the body, which is lived out among pentecostals as they listen to the divine.

Listening with one's body appears in research that Lipari cites in which a listener's body matches the speech of the speaker as if the speaker and listener are dancing in rhythm to music. The listener's body synchronizes to the "pitch, intonation, volume, and tempo" of the speaking patterns of the other.[38] Lipari continues by noting other research involving

34. Glennie, "Listening Is about Looking at a Person."
35. Glennie, "Feeling Sound with Evelyn Glennie."
36. Glennie, "How to Truly Listen."
37. Glennie, "Listening Is about Looking at a Person."
38. Lipari, *Listening, Thinking, Being*, 226.

patients and doctors. Evidence shows the presence of an increased "sense of connection and therapeutic quality" when "doctors and patients" increasingly, but unintentionally, "coordinated" their body movements, such as their posture.[39] Additional research, which she refers to, demonstrates that speakers are dependent on the listener's body movements when they relate a story. The more attentive that I am as a listener with my body, the more the speakers remember the details of their stories and the better they relay them. Furthermore, research indicates that the listener and the speaker tell a story together. This means that a good listener becomes a partner in the telling of the speaker's story.[40] In short, physical attentiveness matters. Unfortunately, it is becoming increasingly rare amidst today's techno-focused world. As one grandmother tellingly remarked to another of her generation about their upcoming visit: "It will be nice to talk to someone who is not looking at their phone all the time."

The third misconception of listening states that misunderstanding is to be overcome and avoided because it is an obstruction to quality listening. When it is recognized that persons listen with their whole beings and partake of selective listening, it is possible to acknowledge that misunderstanding is part and parcel to listening. That is, it is constitutive of listening. Lipari explains that when I misunderstand you, I am being reminded that you are genuinely 'other' than I. Misunderstanding informs me that I am preoccupied with me and my own world. It tells me that I have a different history, customs, experience, and perception from you, signifying that my own self is not the totality of the world. Misunderstanding also reminds me that "perfection is impossible," and even though we may speak the same language, some human experiences are truly beyond words and comprehension.[41]

To put it plainly, misunderstanding cannot be circumvented because "I am not you, and you are not I." Rather, I am presented with an opportunity to see the other as a mystery, beyond my comprehension. Misunderstanding implies that the other is pushing back against me, suggesting that I cannot consume the other.[42] This indicates transcendence,

---

39. Lipari, *Listening, Thinking, Being*, 227.
40. Lipari, *Listening, Thinking, Being*, 229.
41. Lipari, *Listening, Thinking, Being*, 20.
42. As Anthony F. Beavers explains in discussing the philosophy of Emmanuel Levinas, "That which the self wants to enjoy but cannot is the other person. The reason that it cannot enjoy the other person is not rooted in some deficiency of sensibility, but in the other person who pushes back, as it were, who does not allow him/herself to be consumed in the egoism of my enjoyment. The other resists consumption. The presence

and as Anthony Beavers notes, the transcendence of the other "comes from beyond categories of my thought, from beyond the world."[43] Such otherworldliness beckons me to resist telling and instead to welcome the uniqueness of the other and my own one-of-kind self into the same space, thereby allowing the other to teach me. Within this same space with the other, as Lipari contends, listening becomes ethical, a responsibility for the other. This responsibility is illustrated by Emmanuel Levinas when I have an ordinary interaction with a man I do not know and I inquire, "How are you?" By simply asking this question, according to Levinas, I am "supporting and accepting" the fact that there is a "weakness" in him, "and so I bear it." By recognizing this weakness in the other, I then have a responsibility for the other.[44] As Bettina Bergo states in her description of Levinas's ethics: "[T]his other speaks to me, implores or commands me. In responding, I discover my responsibility to them" (italics in original).[45]

Of course, it is tempting amidst misunderstanding to avoid responsibility to the other by stomping away from or stopping the conversation. Such a temptation is evidence as to how much humans are drawn to sameness. We are attracted to sameness like a moth to a flame. We take great pleasure in sameness when we discover similarities with a stranger, but we may become exasperated and curt when differences dominate the encounter. Alternatively, if we adopt Lipari's view of misunderstanding (and difference), it becomes an opportunity "to move with more humility,

---

of the other, on this level, is not, properly speaking, known. The other person is encountered as a felt weight against me." Beavers, "Introducing Levinas to Undergraduate Philosophers," 5.

43. Beavers, "Introducing Levinas to Undergraduate Philosophers," 5.

44. Levinas, "Strong and the Weak (English subtitles)." For those who may be unfamiliar with Levinas, it may be helpful to provide some background. Levinas was born in 1906 to Jewish parents in Lithuania. During World War II, Levinas, who became a military officer, was captured and placed in a prisoners' camp in which he did forced labor. While his wife and daughter were hidden in France and survived the war, his parents and brothers were killed. See Peperzak, *To the Other*, 2–4. When I reflect on Levinas's life experience and recognize it was out of this that he argued for being responsible for the other, I perceive he is pushing back against the apathy towards the existence of the other, which in his case is being a Jew. As humans, we have a history of failing others amidst genocide. People fail to be responsible for the other (be it during the Holocaust or the conflict between the Hutus/Tutsis, etc.). They fail to guard the life of the other; to see the other; to value the life of the other; and to protect and keep the other safe. To be responsible for the other is to embrace the other's uniqueness while also upholding our common vulnerability/humanity. The uniqueness reminds us to cherish each life (or to use the words from a credit card's advertisement: "It's priceless").

45. Bergo, "Emmanuel Levinas," "2.3 The 'Treatise on Hospitality.'"

patience, and generosity than we might have otherwise."[46] In this way, it calls to us to invite the other into our life by moving towards, not away from, the other.

This became apparent to me when I conducted interviews with the survivor-participants. At times, as I listened to stories, I had an urge to place my fingers in my ears and rapidly chant, "la la la la." This impulse emerged periodically due to my own triggers as a survivor, but on other occasions, I was so repelled by the violence and suffering that I sought to shield my own being. However, as Lipari recognizes, if I would have turned "a deaf ear in order to protect the self-existing-I,"[47] I would have become complicit in their pain. The survivors, too, had yearned to safeguard themselves from a perpetrator, but they had been helpless to do so. By disciplining myself to listen, I joined the participants in their loss and grief, testifying to their pain, their healing process, and how they were changed, thereby changing me. Their being and their experiences of suffering challenged my present identity. As Lipari writes, to listen is to bear witness to the pain of the other, thereby becoming responsible.[48] This type of a listening ethic is what Lipari terms as "listening otherwise."

The Ethic of Listening Otherwise

Listening otherwise dispels a common mistaken belief that compassion for others flows from understanding others—that is, sameness. It assumes familiarity breeds understanding, which produces compassion. For example, it holds that unless I have experienced the death of a child, I cannot be compassionate and empathic towards parents who have experienced the death of a child, or unless I am a survivor of sexual violence, I cannot have compassion for survivors of sexual violence. In contrast, a foundational element of Lipari's *listening otherwise* is that humans can never have complete understanding. Lipari argues, "An ethics that depends on shared understanding will be a selective ethics—if it can even be called ethics at all. It will exclude from our moral consideration those who we cannot understand or who violate our understandings."[49] This

---

46. Lipari, *Listening, Thinking, Being*, 20.

47. Lipari, *Listening, Thinking, Being*, 248. Lipari is referring to her difficulty in reading Ralph Ellison's *Invisible Man* as she had to stop reading, but she challenged herself to continue.

48. Lipari, *Listening, Thinking, Being*, 248.

49. Lipari, *Listening, Thinking, Being*, 255.

type of ethics is choosy, listening only to those who are similar to us. Conversely, Lipari's *listening otherwise* hinges on the belief in the universality and uniqueness of suffering. Every person suffers while each experience of suffering is singular. Thus, suffering is a reminder that otherness, alterity, is "particular and ordinary." It is unique while being commonplace[50] (as in the survivors' unique healing journeys discussed in chapter 4). Thus, to say in response to the other's suffering, "Everyone goes through that" or "I know exactly how you feel" is to embrace suffering's universality while diminishing its singularity and the uniqueness of the other. However, when I recognize that suffering is universal, which connects me to the other, while also acknowledging that suffering is unique, then the other and the other's suffering is not absorbed.[51] Instead, it is welcomed "as an *other*, as a guest, as a not-me" inside of me (italics in original).[52] That is, as the listener, I do not lose the other's suffering "in its ubiquity nor in its singularity."[53]

Lipari's *listening otherwise* "challenges the ego and the illusion of control."[54] It surrenders our perceptions of the world on the altars of ambiguity and uncertainty so that we may, in Lipari's words "fully re-cognize the other," thereby becoming a type of a "host" to the other's suffering.[55] As such, it involves a self-emptying. Lipari summarizes *listening otherwise* as listening:

> from a space of unknowing, loss of control, loss of ideas and concepts; an opening to what is, not shrinking away, *being* there. And it is from this place that the ethical response emerges. Bearing witness gives rise to a listening without resorting to what is easy, what I already know, or what we have in common. It means that I listen for and make space for the difficult, the different, and the radically strange . . . listening otherwise also calls one to give attention to oneself, to heed the tumult of contradictory

---

50. Lipari, *Listening, Thinking, Being*, 252.

51. Lipari writes, "Listening otherwise is attuned to the suffering of others in a way that derives from regarding the other's suffering as a concern of mine not because I make some kind of cognitive leap or because of some strategic need I have of you, but because I feel *with* you, ineffably and irrevocably connected but not subsumed" (italics in original). Lipari, *Listening, Thinking, Being*, 256.

52. Lipari, *Listening, Thinking, Being*, 259. Lipari continues, "It doesn't insist on understanding or familiarity, or shared feelings." Lipari, *Listening, Thinking, Being*, 259.

53. Lipari, *Listening, Thinking, Being*, 260.

54. Lipari, *Listening, Thinking, Being*, 257.

55. Lipari, *Listening, Thinking, Being*, 258–59.

voices demanding to be heard, aware that our listening is itself a kind of speaking ... To *listen otherwise* with presence is to listen with all the presence of our being (italics in original).[56]

In sum, *listening otherwise* incorporates an emptying of the self, an ethical response towards the other. In the next section I turn towards Scripture and the ethics of the apostle Paul in which he, too, advocates for believers to be responsible for other believers, a self-emptying that parallels Lipari's *listening otherwise*.

PAUL'S ETHICAL CALL TO THE CORINTHIANS

This chapter began by drawing attention to the pentecostal characteristic of listening to God with one's whole body. It then supported this embodied action by asserting that listening involves a person's whole being, which Lipari turns towards being responsible for the other, *listening otherwise*. In this third section and in pentecostal fashion, I draw from Scripture a theological ethical praxis, similar to *listening otherwise*, that is put forth by Paul, as conveyed by Gorman. Prior to describing another divisive issue in the Corinthian church and Paul's ethical model, I offer a brief overview of the city of Corinth and of Paul's first epistle to them.

The Corinthian Overview

Scholars believe that the Corinthian Christian community mirrored the surrounding culture demographically, which also informed the patterns in how believers related to each other. Gorman highlights that a minority of the people in the Corinthian church were probably of the elite class since Julius Caesar populated Corinth with slaves, who had gained their freedom, and others, who were poor; thus, the majority of Corinth's population were "hardworking" individuals from the lower class who were using Corinth's location of more than one port to their benefit. Such a location granted Corinth the ability to dominate "the Asia Minor-Italy trade traffic," which generated opportunities for business, including the tentmaking activities of the apostle Paul.[57] Gorman describes those of the nonelite class as being "'upwardly mobile,'" who were striving to improve themselves by climbing up the "socioeconomic ladder." This drive

56. Lipari, *Listening, Thinking, Being*, 260–61.
57. Gorman, *Apostle of the Crucified Lord*, 274–78.

was accentuated since the Roman Empire fostered a "highly competitive social environment," and this was further stimulated by Corinth's being a rebuild and its ongoing reconstruction.[58]

Taking the church's milieu into account, the church not only reflected the population of Corinth with a larger number of the attendees belonging to the nonelite class (1:26), but it also simulated the culture's competitive nature, particularly in the members' relationships to each other, which Paul confronted in this first epistle. As Lipari asserts, people assimilate values from their culture concerning those who speak and those who do not and those who are heard and how they are heard.[59] Accordingly, the Corinthian church was naturally shaped by its surrounding, competitive culture as to how the believers related to each other so that they interacted with a propensity to jockey for position. Therefore, Paul's priority, as asserted by Gorman, was "to convince the Corinthians to embody the cross in daily life in light of the past resurrection and soon return of their crucified Lord." For Gorman, this is linked to the subject of spirituality, with the prevailing question being: "What does the life of a Spirit-filled community look like?"[60]

Yearning for them to portray the life of a Spirit-filled community, Paul confronts the Corinthians' competitive nature in this letter. First Corinthians 1 is a precursor to the entire epistle, with verse 10 summarizing the apostle's exhortation to the church: "I urge you, brothers and sisters, by the name of our Lord Jesus Christ, to agree together, to end your divisions, and to be united by the same mind and purpose." In the words of *The Message*: "You *must* get along" (italics in the original). This engenders Paul to address several competitive, divisive matters within the Corinthian church, two of which I have discussed in other chapters: The lack of respect for the non-elite members of Christ's body while partaking of the Lord's Supper (1 Cor 11) and the Corinthians not honoring each other and each member's gifts in the body of Christ (1 Cor 12, 14). The Corinthians' actions in these instances are indicative of how the community is not being responsible for the other through their failure to practice *kenosis*, or self-emptying. I now explore in this section

---

58. Gorman, *Apostle of the Crucified Lord*, 275.

59. Lipari refers to such selective listening as the "politics of listening." She explains, "[I]t relates to who speaks and who doesn't, what is and is not said, how what is said is said, as well as, of course, to whom it is said and what is and is not heard, and *how* what is heard is heard" (italics in original). Lipari, *Listening, Thinking, Being*, 78.

60. Gorman, *Apostle of the Crucified Lord*, 273.

an additional divisive matter found in 1 Corinthians 8 and follow that up with a discussion of the ethical example of Paul from 1 Corinthians 9.

The Eaters vs. the Abstainers

Amidst these divisive, competitive issues, Paul further speaks to the matter of eating meat offered to idols (1 Cor 8) and juxtaposes it with his own ethical pattern (1 Cor 9), which he instructs the Corinthians to copy. In considering this issue contextually, Jews religiously abstained from eating meat offered to idols as it was considered an idolatrous practice. As such, abstinence was included as one of the prohibitions instituted by the Jewish Christian apostles and elders in Jerusalem in regard to the Gentile believers (Acts 15:20, 28–29). Despite this directive, the church in Corinth was divided between those who ate meat offered to idols (the eaters) and those who did not (the abstainers). Some scholars speculate that Gentiles, possibly of the elite, were accustomed to socializing with friends during the festivals or at "private celebrations"; thus, they ate meat offered to idols at these events, which was the social element, while abstaining from worshipping other gods, the religious element.[61] Keener furthermore notes that leftover meat may be sold "in nearby restaurants and in the meat market," and it may not be labeled as being from the temple (10:25);[62] therefore, if Christians bought meat from non-Kosher places near the pagan temple, they may unknowingly be eating meat that had been offered to idols. In light of this context, the eaters argued that they had knowledge (*gnosis*) that gave them the freedom or right (*exousia*) to knowingly or unknowingly eat meat that had been offered to idols (8:1, 4–6).[63] Opposingly, the abstainers refused to eat meat that may have been purchased at non-Kosher places and thereby possibly offered to idols because they viewed it as idolatry.

When tackling this issue, the apostle partially agrees with the eaters while providing them with additional theological and ethical corrections. The eaters assert that they possess knowledge that idols are "nothing" since "there is no God but one" (8:4), to which Paul agrees. The pagan

---

61. Fee, *First Epistle to the Corinthians*, 362; Keener, *1–2 Corinthians*, 74.

62. Keener, *1–2 Corinthians*, 75.

63. Fee explains that the Corinthians hold that "Christian conduct is predicated on *gnōsis* (knowledge) and that knowledge gives them *exousia* (rights/freedom) to act as they will in this matter." Fee, *First Epistle to the Corinthians*, 363.

gods do not exist.[64] However, Paul disagrees that the eaters may do as they please and reproaches them: "Knowledge puffs up, but love builds up" (8:1).[65] Gorman explains, "An ethic grounded in 'knowledge' focuses on individual *freedom* and the exercise of one's *right* . . . An ethic of cruciform love, on the other hand, seeks to edify the other, taking account of the impact of one's behavior on one's siblings in Christ (8:11–12) and being willing to forgo the exercise of a right for the welfare of the other (8:13)" (italics in original).[66] In the words of Levinas: "Responsibility precedes freedom. It is more important than freedom."[67] Lipari explains, "To Levinas, ethics begins by renouncing the self's right to be, in favor, always, of the other. The self is called to responsibility for the other before it is free."[68] This indicates that the Corinthians are first and foremost responsible for each other prior to being free to act as they choose. Correspondingly, Paul cautions that the eaters' liberty may cause the abstainers (who Paul refers to as "the weak") to sin, meaning the eaters are also sinning against Christ (8:12).[69]

Paul's Embodied Ethical Model

Having now chided the Corinthians, Paul presents his own embodied ethical model for them to follow. Paul is communicating that they are not only to do as he says but also to do as he does. He will refuse to eat meat ever again if it causes the other to stumble (8:13), and he will become all

---

64. Gorman points out that Paul additionally affirms that since "all meat" is part of God's creation, it is "good" (10:26) so that whether believers eat or abstain from meat offered to idols, their relationship with God is not affected (8:8). Gorman, *Apostle of the Crucified Lord*, 307.

65. Paul states something similar later in this epistle in 13:2, 4.

66. Gorman, *Apostle of the Crucified Lord*, 307. Fee summarizes, "Christian ethics . . . springs not from knowledge but from love." See Fee, *First Epistle to the Corinthians*, 363.

67. Levinas, "Strong and the Weak (English subtitles)."

68. Lipari, *Listening, Thinking, Being*, 267.

69. Still, Paul disapproves of the eaters' behavior of knowingly eating meat that was offered to idols. For Paul, pagans are sacrificing to demons, not God; thus, Paul strongly forbids them to participate in eating from the table of demons (10:20–21). Keener clarifies, "Both priests (10:18) and Christians (10:16–17) partake of a sacrifice to God; by analogy, then, those eating idol food partake of a sacrifice to the demons the idols represent (10:20)." See Keener, *1–2 Corinthians*, 88. Nonetheless, the apostle makes allowances when eating meat purchased from a market or when dining at a non-believer's home if it is unknown if the meat was offered to idols. If a person states, however, that the meat was offered to idols, they are not to eat it (10:25–29).

things to all people so that he may save some (9:22). The autobiographical example of 1 Corinthians 9 establishes for Gorman a practical, distinct, ethical model that is patterned after Christ, which the Corinthians are called to emulate (11:1). For Gorman, Paul's ethical model is a specified pattern of: "although [because] *x*, not *y* but *z*." Gorman asserts that this pattern repeats throughout Paul's epistles as a description of himself but, more importantly, as a pattern of Christ. Gorman defines this distinct pattern as "*x* represents a status possessed, *y* a selfish action not taken, and *z* an alternative, selfless action."[70] This signifies that *x* is a right I have; *y* is not exercising that right; and *z* is responding through a counter-cultural act of self-denial. According to Gorman, the pattern is conveyed in Philippians 2 in reference to Christ and is imitated by Paul in 1 Corinthians 9. Gorman describes the *x, y, z* pattern in the *kenosis* passage (Phil 2:6–11) as:

- *x*: though he [Christ Jesus] existed in the form of God (v. 6a)
- *y*: [he] did not regard equality with God as something to be grasped, (v. 6b)
- *z*: but emptied himself by taking on the form of a slave, by looking like other men, and by sharing in human nature. He humbled himself, by becoming obedient to the point of death—even death on a cross (vv. 7–8).[71]

As shown, *x* is the right or status that Christ had as divine; *y* is the refusal to cling to that right or status that being divine afforded him; and *z* is the renunciation of self by his becoming human and his dying. Gorman continues by outlining 1 Corinthians 9 as Paul's imitation of Christ's ethical, kenotic pattern:

- *x*: For since I am free from all (v.19a; see also v. 20b)
- *y*: But we have not made use of this right (12b; see also vv. 15a, 18c)
- *z*: I can make myself a slave to all, in order to gain even more people (19b–c; see also vv. 12c, 20–22).[72]

70. Gorman, *Apostle of the Crucified Lord*, 508. The word "because" may possibly be preferred to the word "although," which, as Gorman states, conveys that Christ's action was not a "surprising *contradiction* of his divinity but a shocking *manifestation* of his divinity" (italics in original). Gorman, *Apostle of the Crucified Lord*, 508.

71. The *kenosis* text from Philippians 2 appears in a chart in Gorman, *Apostle of the Crucified Lord*, 310.

72. Paul's ethical pattern from 1 Corinthians 9 appears in a chart in Gorman, *Apostle of the Crucified Lord*, 310.

With Paul's supplying himself as an example, the Corinthians are to follow him by emptying themselves. They are to realize their rights so that they may refuse their rights and renunciate the self through a real action. More clearly, they are to resist clinging to the knowledge that other gods do not exist (x), by choosing not to use it as a defense for their freedom (y). Instead, they are to refuse to eat meat offered to idols so that others do not sin (z). In short, they are to live a life of cruciformity, not competitiveness.

Yet, Paul's model of self-emptying is not merely limited to eating meat offered to idols. If the Corinthians are to live as genuine Spirit-filled believers, it must be followed in every aspect of their lives. For instance, concerning the issue in 1 Corinthians 11 that even though some may have elite status, granting them the right to arrive early at the home church gathering to feast with their peers (x), nevertheless they are not to hold tightly to their elite status, taking advantage of this luxury (y); they are instead to share food with the non-elite who arrive late (z). Relating to the problems addressed in 1 Corinthians 12 and 14 that although they speak in tongues and although some members exercise gifts that cause them to be more visible than the other (x), nevertheless they are not to assert their liberty by extensively using their gifts, thereby barring the other from using a gift (y). In contrast, they are to encourage the other to use one's gift, which honors the other's voice as a valued member of Christ's body (z).[73] In view of the above issues, then, the Corinthian church is to embody what it is to be a Spirit-filled community by employing Paul's ethical, kenotic model. This ethical model of self-emptying is conveyed in Jesus's words to love my neighbor as I love myself. It appears in Levinas's ethics of "forbid[ing] the murderousness of my natural will to put my own existence first."[74] However, if Paul's ethical model is to be

---

73. Paul also addresses the matter of how the Corinthian believers align themselves with certain human leaders, thereby creating division in the church (1 Cor 1–4). Here I apply Gorman's pattern of *x, not y, but z* to this issue as well: "Even though some may be followers of Apollos and have benefited considerably from his teaching (x), nevertheless, they are not to exclusively endorse Apollos as the preeminent leader (y), but they are to recognize that God has gifted others in the church to be apostles, prophets, and teachers (12:28) and celebrate them, too (z)." Likewise, I apply Paul's ethical model to the matter of the Corinthians' taking each other to court (1 Cor 6): "Although the city of Corinth has granted people the right to take the other to court (x), they are to refuse to cling to this liberty (y) and choose to converse with the other in order to authentically connect with the other as another human being so that their differences may be resolved (z)."

74. Levinas, "Responsibility in the Face of the Other."

implemented, I argue below that Lipari's *listening otherwise* must already be in operation.

LISTENING AS A SPIRIT-FILLED KENOTIC PRAXIS

Having an aim to strengthen a pentecostal theological praxis of healing, I have described how pentecostals are characterized by a practice of embodied listening to God. I expanded on this by drawing from Lipari in which embodied listening includes being responsible for the other. I went on to explain how Paul exhorts the Corinthians to be responsible for each other over and above the advocation of their freedom when he urges them to imitate Christ's, and now his ethical, kenotic model. This self-emptying exemplifies what it is to be a Spirit-filled community. In this chapter's final section, I combine these three aspects (the pentecostal embodied listening to the divine; Lipari's view of listening to the other; and Paul's ethical model) to assert that prior to living out the kenotic model, embodied listening implicitly occurs. In fact, listening is required to live out a kenotic, Spirit-filled praxis, particularly in response to the other's suffering, thereby producing movement towards healing.

The significance of listening may be difficult for many Westerners to grasp. Counselor-participant Kiley seems to reflect this sentiment when she comments that we have a tendency as a pentecostal group "to go in and fix" it. This is also indicated when counselor-participant Shauna speaks of the unhelpful practice of pentecostals' both using "Christian clichés and throwing [S]criptures at people in ways that gloss over the atrocities and injustices." She continues, "I passionately love [S]criptures, but I have worked with many people who have been profoundly hurt by nouthetic counselors who dole out Bible verses in a way that feels 'cheap' and like a 'quick fix' that does not resonate with the humanity of the person in pain." Similar to these types of pentecostal responses and the emphasis on rhetoric in ancient Rome, Lipari asserts that "the Western conception of the *logos* [the Greek word for *word* or *speech*] emphasizes speaking at the expense of listening." This not only "ignores the importance of listening, but also . . . it obscures how listening makes the ethical response possible."[75] I cannot act ethically without first listening. Lipari contends that even in the category of ethics that centers on communication and rhetoric (dialogic ethics), listening is kept hidden and

---

75. Lipari, *Listening, Thinking, Being*, 263.

"rendered invisible." She argues that "the ethical response," put forth by such individuals as Levinas, "presupposes a hidden *listening*. For in order to respond, I must first listen—that is attend, observe, attune—and in doing so receive the otherness of the other. Without listening . . . there can be no genuinely engaged response" (italics in original).[76] Thus, if I am to live out the *x, y, z* pattern, I must begin by *listening otherwise*. Without this listening, a self-emptying (*kenosis*) fails to occur.

Listening otherwise is, in and of itself, kenotic. As suggested earlier, *listening otherwise* relinquishes (I empty myself of) my own preconceptions. I surrender my loyalty to what is known to me and what I perceive as certain and the way I see life so that I may completely see the other. To employ Lipari's words, I give up my insistence to understand the other and the other's suffering in accordance with "my terms" and with "my cognitive preconceptions and categories, simply assimilating what I already know, or think I know, about the other or his or her point of view."[77] I am emptying myself of my own notions of how the world operates and presumptions about what the other is experiencing, and I am permitting the other to teach me. I surrender. I forfeit. I empty myself in order to receive and learn.

Such an emptying is indicated as transpiring both with pentecostals and the Corinthians. Pentecostals set aside their own agendas, understandings, and the right to speak in order to listen to and receive from God, who is Holy Other, when they practice soaking prayer or tune into God during a worship service. These pentecostals no longer speak by making requests to God, but they surrender themselves as they listen with their whole being. When pentecostals embody listening to the divine, they are allowing themselves to be healed by emptying themselves. Survivor-participant Jade illustrated how she emptied herself through "carpet time," in which she was "on the floor to receive from God." She had a memory of being horrifically abused at eighteen months old, but she was at a loss regarding how to attend to it. During her healing journey, this abuse was addressed when Jade was experiencing "carpet time" during a church service in which she sat on the floor, "rocking back and forth, wailing uncontrollably." For her, the rocking and the wailing signified her meeting with God as an eighteen-month-old, and God was

---

76. Lipari, *Listening, Thinking, Being*, 249.

77. Lipari, *Listening, Thinking, Being*, 257.

"allowing her to release that pain," or I would say, empty herself. Jade was letting herself be healed through this self-emptying.

This was not the only occasion Jade listened in order to receive from God. She recalled another experience that transpired during regular pentecostal evening church services. She noted that an evening service allowed for a lengthened worship time in contrast to a morning service, giving her the opportunity to stand and become lost in her connection with God. As such, over a period of several months, she repeatedly had this image of Jesus and her being alone in a ballroom. She was dressed in a long evening gown when Jesus approached her in a tuxedo with tails and invited her to dance. After several months of envisioning Jesus and her dancing during Sunday night worship, she said, "I really like dancing with you, but I am puzzled as to why this keeps happening." Jesus responded by saying, "I am restoring your dignity." As she stood in worship, Jade was *attending, observing,* and *attuning* to God, allowing herself to be healed.

Similarly, *listening otherwise* is implied in each of the issues that Paul addresses in Corinth. It is only after the members of the body *listen otherwise*, or *attend, observe,* and *attune,* to each other that they may enact Paul's ethical model. For instance, during a church gathering, the elite need to *listen otherwise* to the nonelite who arrive late prior to abstaining from their gorging on the available food. It is necessary for members of the body to stop speaking in tongues and *attend, observe,* and *attune* to other members of the body in order to embody Paul's ethical model. The eaters are to *listen otherwise* to the abstainers before surrendering their right to eat meat. With each issue, then, *listening otherwise* implicitly precedes, or is an unseen integral component of, Paul's aforementioned ethic. Such listening involves *listening the other to speech*, a practice in which I reverse the "normative social arrangement" of my culture. This means I no longer muzzle the non-elite, but I *attend, observe,* and *attune* to the misfit or outcast, thereby enabling the other to move toward wholeness.[78] Feminist theologian Nelle Morton states, "We empower one another by hearing the other to speech. We empower the disinherited, the outsider, as we are able to hear them name in their own way their own oppression and suffering."[79] Such hearing, Morton says, is with "the whole body . . . evok[ing] speech—a new speech—a new creation."[80]

78. I am drawing from Lipari, *Listening, Thinking, Being,* 280.
79. Morton, *Journey Is Home,* 128.
80. Morton, *Journey Is Home,* 128.

In considering how pentecostals *attend, observe,* and *attune* to God and how the Corinthians need to listen to the other, I propose that the call to empty ourselves to *listen otherwise* is foundational to living a Spirit-filled life. It resists the desire to consume or compete with the other as if I own the other, but instead it becomes responsible for the other upon seeing the other's face. This priority on listening specifically came to the fore in Jade's story above in which the pentecostal pastor refused to *listen otherwise* but sought to control and convince Jade through telling. Jade may have responded more positively if the pastor had chosen survivor-participant Frances's preferred response. When I asked Frances what she wanted to say to other pentecostal survivors, she told me how she first would "really want to listen to them more than" she "would want to tell them anything" in order to "hear where they are at." Frances based this response on her own journey of healing from sexual violence. She recognized that she had experienced various stages during her healing journey, including her becoming angry if someone attempted to tell her anything in connection "to pentecostalism and healing from sexual violence." Therefore, Frances has placed a priority on listening before speaking. In other words, she seeks to *attend, observe,* and *attune* to other survivors.

Counselor-participant Shauna indicated the importance of *listening otherwise* when I asked her what she desired to communicate to other pentecostals. Shauna said, "One of the greatest ministries we can offer to a precious individual who has survived sexual violence is to offer presence in a way that feels honoring of the survivor's need for boundaries and their ability to inform their community of what feels supportive and encouraging to them individually." For Shauna, this is different from "imposing what we 'think' they need which can inadvertently induce more secondary trauma as we speak for them or try to make decisions for them, etc." In other words, we may do harm by not *attending, observing,* and *attuning*.

When I asked the participants what they wanted to say to pentecostal leaders and congregants about healing from sexual violence, more than one survivor stated, "Listen." Sutton mentioned that one way some pentecostals were unhelpful for him was when they "sought to deliver [him] from demons of molestation or fear when what was needed was a listening ear and carrying the burdens of suffering and shame." Jade, too, wanted pentecostals to "listen to . . . survivors and believe them when they talk about how long that journey has been, how difficult it's been, and how painful it's been." She said of church leaders, "They need to actually listen to the person who comes to them, not try and give answers." Counselor-participant Shauna understood the significance of listening over telling when she commented, "Be careful not to be like Job's friends who talk instead of listening. Rather than your clever words of encouragement, it is your unconditionally accepting presence in this person's life that provides medicine to the soul of the survivor."

This type of listening, then, calls for an emptying of myself and *listening otherwise* so that the speech of the other is birthed, and healing emerges. It is when I practice self-emptying that others can discover their own voices. This means I must set aside my certainty and preconceptions in order to fully welcome others and their suffering into the same space where I am. I am putting aside my competitiveness for cruciformity. It is only then that I am in a place to act both ethically toward and responsibly for others via listening. Through *listening otherwise*, I am acting ethically, responsibly for them, caring for them, which in turn empowers them. Therefore, rather than placing my hands over my ears and closing my eyes, I am truly seeing the face of the other and listening. Bearing this in mind, a Spirit-filled believer, who employs Lipari's *listening otherwise* with Paul's ethical pattern of *although x, not y but z*, may have the following internal response to the other who is suffering: Although I have obtained wisdom from my past suffering, nevertheless, I will not insist on sharing my story and the wisdom I have previously gained, but I will empty myself by suffering with those who suffer by *listening otherwise*— that is, *attending, observing,* and *attuning*. This will allow the other to learn amidst his/her pain while I resist the belief that I understand. In short, I will *listen the other to speech.*

CONCLUSION

This chapter sought to augment the element of embodied listening within pentecostalism by emphasizing how a Spirit-filled community is to be characterized by kenotic listening. They are not only to listen kenotically to the Holy Other but also to the human other, thereby strengthening a pentecostal theological praxis of healing. I assert that a sign of a Spirit-filled community is less about speaking in tongues, giving an interpretation of tongues, or prophesying (which have their place) and more about self-emptying by *listening otherwise*. It is less about being empowered to proclaim the gospel and more about a kenotic response of listening that is followed by the ethical action of *although x, not y but z* that demonstrates those who are the people of the Spirit. The next chapter continues this theme by centering on another praxis grounded in pentecostalism and linked to listening, which is embodied waiting.

7

Wait with Me in My Story

I felt they [pentecostals] just didn't really understand the length of the journey. And so, I believe that God wants to come and partner with us and walk with us, but he understands how fragile and how much any type of abuse . . . causes such a fracturing at a very core level of the person's identity, and that needs to be very gently and carefully put back together again.

—Jade, survivor-participant

We cannot prescribe a timeline or a kind of a linear path. It's not subsequential. There's nothing linear about healing from trauma at all. There's nothing linear about it.

—Megan, a counselor-participant

It's not a simple process of healing. People need more than just to hear you're going to pray for them and to get over it . . . They [survivors] actually need your presence and you [to] walk alongside [them]. Don't expect them to be farther than where they are [but] accept and encourage them where they are.

—Dayton, a counselor-participant

THE BIGGEST LESSON THAT Elizabeth learned on her healing journey from sexual violence was, "just how few people can do messy."[1] After

1. Portions of this chapter were presented as papers at SPS. Engelbert, "Wounds that

being sexually assaulted as an adult by a person of the same gender, she sought support for healing from those in the church. What she soon learned was that the church still has taboos, rules about which topics are and are not available for discussion.[2] Ultimately, she became "separated . . . from many" in the church when they learned about the sexual assault. This, in turn, drove Elizabeth to ask God for prayer warriors who refused to "shy away" from such personal information and be willing to battle with her "for the long haul." The ability to go the distance was crucial as her experience with the church, by and large, "was an expectation that healing would be immediate," providing she had faith, believed, and gave it all up, whatever that meant. Elizabeth did not doubt that instantaneous divine healing was possible. During the interview, she stated that she was "willing to try anything to not be completely broken forever." Thus, at one point she attempted *Sozo*, which she described like a prayer journey that was more formulaic and centered on instantaneity. However, she came to realize during her healing journey that instantaneous healing was just "not the journey that God had for" her. In the beginning, she genuinely believed for a healing that could be characterized as more linear and immediate. Now, Elizabeth implies that she is waiting for her complete healing: "I had to learn from the beginning that it will leave a scar, but that scars heal, and the only scars in heaven are not ours. I don't know if that's true, but that's what I believe . . . scars . . . [are] with us here, but up there, I just believe we're going to be healed from that." In the meantime, she is learning to trust God for healing by way of a journey that is long and messy. In her words, "[T]here is nothing nice about this process."

According to Elizabeth's story, many pentecostals, when faced with suffering, initially seek instantaneous healing, whether they be survivors like Elizabeth or potential companions to the hurting. This is to be expected given that praying for immediate healing is part and parcel of pentecostalism since pentecostals believe in intense, supernatural experiences

---

Instantaneity Forgot" and Engelbert, "Tell Me the Story of Trauma."

2. The subject of taboos concerning which topics may or may not be discussed in the church surfaced in the research of Yuvarajan and. Stanford, in which clergy were asked about their perceptions of sexual violence. A theme that arose was the belief among clergy that one of the reasons survivors avoided talking about sexual violence with clergy was because it was a taboo subject in the church. Yuvarajan and Stanford, "Clergy Perceptions of Sexual Assault Victimization," 598.

of the Spirit in the here and now. Therefore, such a prayer for instant healing is not to be confused as the main problem. Instead, the issue is a triumphalist attitude that may accompany it by dogmatically asserting the necessity for instantaneous healing and victorious Christian living.

This chapter seeks to counteract the aforementioned pentecostal pattern of congregational care by offering another attribute that has historically been a part of pentecostalism, which is *waiting*.[3] Thus, I am asserting here that instantaneity is not the only acceptable pentecostal path toward healing, but that pentecostals are inherently in a unique place to provide long-term congregational care by drawing from the concept of *waiting*. Building on this pentecostal trait, I seek to contribute to pentecostal congregational care for survivors of sexual violence by offering a praxis of embodied waiting. This will occur in four movements: (1) by addressing the matter of time in relation to healing from sexual violence; (2) by asserting that eschatological embodied waiting is a characteristic of believers as seen in 1 Corinthians; (3) by describing a historical and contemporary pentecostal practice of waiting; and (4) by presenting a praxis of active, embodied waiting by drawing from concepts of time and story.

WAITING AS A MATTER OF TIME

The very nature of healing from sexual violence, as it was described by the research participants, warrants the need for a different pentecostal theological praxis other than an assumption of instantaneous healing when offering care to survivors.[4] This section juxtaposes the experiences of healing described by the participants with the general narrative of Western time. I propose that the healing praxis of waiting is essential since each survivor-participant experienced an extended healing journey that has continued for years.

More than one counselor-participant affirmed that the healing journey from sexual trauma endures for a long period of time. When I asked counselors what they perceived as the biggest challenge or surprise for pentecostal survivors, both Megan and Dayton mentioned the length of the healing journey. Megan reasons that pentecostals are "waiting for that

---

3. Frank Macchia also highlights the tension between *waiting* and *hurrying* when he discusses the father and son duo, Johann and Christoph Blumhardt. Macchia, "Waiting and Hurrying."

4. Haley French addresses this issue of time in "Marginalization at the Altar."

divine healing" to "just take it away." The fear of pentecostal survivors in Megan's experience is if they are not healed in "a few months," they perceive themselves as "indulging" because they are "not trusting God enough," "praying enough," or "doing enough." This notion is in contrast to the reality of trauma, which Megan depicts as involving a lengthy process as a survivor first wrestles with the shock of having experienced the unexpected. The person spends weeks and months attempting to acknowledge the reality of what occurred apart from attending to other aspects of sexual trauma. Dayton agrees, "This process is slow. It's not a quick prayer" and neither does the survivor simply "pray for ten weeks" and then is "over it."

When asked how pentecostals and/or pentecostal beliefs were unhelpful, Megan used the metaphor of Friday, Saturday, and Sunday in which pentecostals are awaiting the resurrection on Sunday. She said, "As pentecostals, we run for Sunday." Thus, she saw survivors believing that they need "to leave their Fridays and . . . their Saturdays sooner than what is actually helpful." She explained how survivors are not permitted to "be in death" even though "a horrible kind of violation" has transpired. They have experienced "the most intimate connection" that humans were meant to have with another person, but now this intimate connection has occurred by way of violation, a way in which "God never intended." In our responses to survivors, we as pentecostals tend to "push people to Sunday." Dayton similarly described how pentecostals seem to lack "the capacity for long-term." For Dayton, this emerges from the belief that says, "You just need to pray more and just get over it and let God heal you," which is to say, it is up to the survivor. This points toward the cultural influence of the can-do attitude that is part of the United States and Canada. This attitude seemingly establishes no limits in the formation of the rule: "I can do anything if I just work hard enough." An issue for survivors and companions to survivors is that healing from sexual violence does not play by this rule. No amount of increased effort, prayer, or faith will guarantee a speedy healing.

Several of the survivor-participants also desire to educate other pentecostals about the long duration of their journeys. Dominique underscores that pentecostals are to be compassionate because healing from sexual violence is not "an overnight thing." Jade wants survivors to know that "the journey is long" and "difficult" but not to let that deter them from taking the journey. She also highlights her own journey when she says, "I went on this journey to come to the very depths of my being, and when I got there, I discovered God was there waiting for me." She offers hope through her firm belief that if survivors choose to walk the path of healing, they will find God and God's love. For Jade, it is God's love that brings "healing to them."

Destiny and Jackson both attest that healing is not a quick fix, like "a one and done" type of experience. Destiny sees it as "a lifelong journey," and Jackson characterizes healing as "a thousand-mile journey" as "the pain and memories" remain part of who the survivor is while becoming "less intense." Counselor-participant Megan concurs when she notes that pentecostal survivors are often seeking the "invisible finish line" when they ask, "When do I get to run through the tape?" They are surprised when Megan responds, "Heaven." Megan will clarify this to them: "Your trauma will be with you the rest of your life, but you won't think about it every day, and it won't be the only thing true about you." She will underscore that for a time the trauma will be "center stage," which calls for the survivor "to be a good host to it." Eventually, the trauma will become part of the survivor's "backdrop, but it will show back up" when the body perceives a threat, engendering the survivor to engage it again. Survivor-participant Sutton affirms this when he speaks of his surprise of "how long memories remain and the randomness of smells and sounds to stir up memories." This perception is supported by Herman when she writes, "Resolution of the trauma is never final; recovery is never complete. The impact of a traumatic event continues to reverberate throughout the survivor's lifecycle. Issues that were sufficiently resolved at one stage of recovery may be reawakened as the survivor reaches new milestones in her development. Marriage or divorce, a birth or death in the family, illness or retirement, are frequent occasions for a resurgence of traumatic memories."[5]

The Narrative of Western Time

The above descriptions of prolonged healing from sexual violence are in opposition to the story of time in Western cultures. The narrative of time within the United States and Canada is often perceived as linear with an emphasis on instantaneity. Linearity denotes events directly following

---

5. Herman, *Trauma and Recovery*, 303. While Herman uses the word "recovery," as mentioned previously (chapter 1), I choose the word "healing" (or "reconciliation") in relation to healing from trauma and grief because a person is never the same and cannot return to who they once were, which *recovery* suggests.

one after the other. The problem with linearity as it relates to sexual violence is the effects from sexual trauma do not conduct themselves along a direct path but rather are chaotic, in which the past erupts and disrupts the present at any moment. The danger of focusing on instantaneity, in conjunction with a survivor's healing, is the centering on time, not healing. Instantaneity, which (for this study) is located inside a culture that worships at the feet of accelerated time, seeks efficiency in time. An accelerated-time-centered culture tends to measure progress by means of competition so that the prize is awarded to the most efficient and competent. Efficient time is implied in the similar responses that survivors Dominique and Jade heard, such as, "You're not going through that right now . . . So why is it still bothering you?" This suggests, as with efficient time, a survivor's healing is orderly and streamlined.

Efficient time follows the rhythm of the ticking of the clock as today is viewed as sliding into tomorrow. Japanese theologian Kosuke Koyama agrees, "[T]ime slips away without the aid of anyone or anything."[6] This is a reminder how humans are powerless to stop the unceasing movement of time. Time marches on, unabated. *Tick. Tick. Tick.* To circumvent time's independent power, residents in the United States and Canada strive to control it by abiding by strict schedules according to the clock. Practical theologian John Swinton explains, "[The clock gives] the impression that we can *control* time. When we look at a clock, we imagine that we can see time. When we see something, we are able to name it. When we can name something, we feel that we can control it" (italics in original).[7] But such control is an illusion. We cannot stop or slow time down and neither can we propel it[8] or tame it to do our bidding. Yet, we continue to avoid peering behind the Wizard's curtain through busyness. Our busyness intensifies the illusion of our ability to preside over time. The busier we are, the more productive we perceive ourselves and the more successful we appear to others. James K. A. Smith writes about the absence of hope in busyness, which is grounded in a belief that it is all up to me: "Our frenetic busyness is so often a practical outworking of an unconscious despair, for it is a refusal of hope. It is a refusal of hope because it is,

---

6. Koyama, *Three Mile an Hour God*, 16.

7. Swinton, *Becoming Friends of Time*, loc. 538–39.

8. Koyama writes, "[T]ime flows away without my pushing it." This is in contrast to other objects, such as a coffee cup, which I can push. Koyama, *Three Mile an Hour God*, 16.

functionally, a refusal of trust and dependence."⁹ In the end, we have only deceived ourselves. Power over the clock is not power over time. These attempts to have power over time and escape the God-given constraints are a refusal to embrace our finitude and thereby strive to be like God.

As such, there is no time or place for brokenness within the narrative of Western time, only efficiency and productivity. Efficient time denies space for unique journeys of healing, or even yielding time for a journey. Journeying on a path toward healing is simply not a wise, economical use of time. African theologian David Ngong points out that a "view of time" which holds "to increasing human progress or improved material or spiritual well-being is a mirage often rooted in the dominating politics of Western modernity." Rather than being linear, Ngong asserts, "[T]ime . . . moves forward and backward, folding and unfolding, intertwining and intermingling, sometimes holding several times together at the same moment."¹⁰ This description of time is more congruent with healing from sexual violence, which is disorderly. It does not flow in a manner that is the shortest distance between two points, which, according to Koyama, "is artificial," not natural.¹¹ Instead, as Elizabeth stated above, it is messy. Other participants, whether counselors or survivors, seem to agree as they paint images of wrestling matches. Narratives of healing from sexual violence tell of stories of the past's bleeding into the present and the present's entering the past as survivors grapple with stories of healing alongside stories that consist of damage from the violence. At times, the stories predominately paint the harm that results from sexual violence, e.g., shame, anger, dissociation, etc., and at other times, they depict the grace, courage, and strength in the spaces where healing has emerged. These stories indicate that healing is juxtaposed with suffering. That is, healing is made visible against the backdrop of the trauma from sexual violence. Since linearity and instantaneity are not the most suitable descriptors concerning healing from sexual violence, I offer below a scriptural foundation of an embodied active waiting.

---

9. Smith is asserting that "eschatological people" are to have an element of unhurriedness about them, to be people of rest. Smith, *How to Inhabit Time*, 168.

10. Ngong, "No Condition Is Permanent," 22. Ngong is asserting that African Christian theology has been expressed through a lens that is modern and linear and argues that it is better conveyed through palimpsestic time.

11. Koyama, *Three Mile an Hour God*, 40. Koyama rightly points out that it is technology that has produced straight lines, which are "symbol[s] of streamlined efficiency," not nature; one simply needs to consider the bodies of humans and creatures to notice nature emphasizes curves. See Koyama, *Three Mile an Hour God*, 40.

WAITING AS A BELIEVER IN CORINTH

The foundation for forming a pentecostal healing praxis of waiting is the recognition that the whole of the Christian life is one of waiting. The believer's very existence revolves around expectant waiting for the Lord Jesus Christ's Second Coming, the time when all of creation will be renewed and, to paraphrase the apostle Paul, "Death, where is your everlasting triumph as you will definitely die" (1 Cor 15:55). This is the Christian hope, and it is to govern how believers are to live in the present—it is to be embodied. It is this type of eschatological embodied waiting that I maintain is a theme in Paul's first letter to the Corinthians. After briefly explaining my connotations of *waiting* and *eschatology*, I underscore in this section the direct and indirect references to eschatological waiting in 1 Corinthians. I emphasize how a believer's eschatological waiting is embodied, duly influencing how the believer inhabits this life. I conclude this section by discussing three issues in the church that Paul connects to eschatology, or an embodied eschatological waiting.

Connotations of Waiting and Eschatology

Prior to exploring the references to eschatological waiting, it is important to provide a few comments about the words "waiting" and "eschatology." The image of waiting in the United States and Canada is often illustrated as biding my time, such as waiting impatiently at a red light, drumming my fingers on the steering wheel. It is frequently pictured as sitting in a doctor's office, watching the minutes slowly tick by. Both portrayals depict *passive waiting*, in which I do very little as I wait for something, or someone, who holds the power over my time. What I see in 1 Corinthians, however, is an *active waiting*, in which the past and future connect in the present, transforming the actions of my being. Thus, as I await the full revelation of Christ (1:7), my future impacts how I live now. Jesus Christ's crucifixion in the past and his Second Advent in the future are present in my actions today as I live out a life of cruciformity. It is this type of waiting that I perceive in Paul's admonitions to the Corinthians.

Concomitantly, active waiting is to be seen as a form of participation in Christ's ministry, not an orchestration of the Second Advent. Some pentecostals have employed Matthew 24:14 to promote the church's power to accelerate Christ's return by preaching the gospel to every tribe and tongue. This understanding believes that the church has been given a responsibility to usher in Christ's Second Coming. It essentially advocates for human agency over divine agency by implying that Jesus is waiting for the church, not the church is waiting for its Coming King; thus, it shifts the power to the church. In contrast, I am stressing an active waiting that perceives believers as participants in Christ's ministry through the power of the Spirit. They are not the orchestrators nor the custodians of the timing of Christ's Second Coming. To borrow from Smith, Christians are not undertaking "some Pelagian 'planning'" since we are not the engineers of the future.[12] Active waiting refers to the church's responsibility to trust in God's grace that the Spirit is already ministering in the world and then to join with the Spirit in that ministry. In accordance with Smith, waiting is not "passive quietism" nor "Pelagian activism" but involves "hopeful trust."[13]

Concerning the word "eschatology," which is the study of last things, the popular perception in the United States and Canada evokes pictures of highly detailed charts, describing the end times. As a youth, I recall attending multiple end-times seminars that delineated the future events of the Rapture, Tribulation, Antichrist, the Mark of the Beast, the Millennium, and the Apocalypse (these are capitalized to indicate their marked singularity as they each highlight one significant event or person). If I was not fully convinced through a presenter's teaching about a specific timeline, I was swayed by vivid images in the 1972 movie *The Thief in the Night*; the movie thoroughly captivated my childhood imaginations by generating nightmares about the possible terror of being left behind. Unfortunately, a focus on the events of the Last Days routinely fails to produce personal transformation in the current day. There is instead a preoccupation on situating today's events on the charts of tomorrow, not on seeking to align my current way of being with the coming reign of God. An overt attentiveness to timelines may contribute to a triumphalist attitude that is far removed from the humility of living the cruciform life through relationships. Smith describes this kind of eschatology as being "*above* history," in which "[h]istory is the regrettable grind of waiting, the churn of degeneration, the countdown of demise" (italics in original).[14] In other words, waiting becomes an endurance of all that transpires until the end finally comes. In contrast, the eschatological waiting that I see

12. Smith, *How to Inhabit Time*, 150. Pelagius was a theologian during the 300s who emphasized human choice and human effort for salvation.

13. Smith, *How to Inhabit Time*, 164.

14. Smith, *How to Inhabit Time*, 6.

in 1 Corinthians is embodied in that believers are to actively, relationally live out cruciformity. That is to say, how Christians wait for Christ's return is associated with how they relate to each other today, or to use a phrase from Smith, "living futurally" presently governs the Christian's relationships.[15] Smith explains, "I *am* what I am called to be" (italics in original).[16] Therefore, as Smith writes, eschatology's concentration is not merely emphasizing expectations of the future "but also a recalibration of our present."[17]

An additional and essential piece that informs my embodied view of eschatology in 1 Corinthians is the apostle's usage of the Greek words for *wait* that are also linked to an eschatological theme. The first epistle to the Corinthians contains two words that may be translated *wait*. The first is *apekdechomai*, which carries the meaning to "expect," "wait," or "look for," as in 1:7: "so that you do not lack any spiritual gift as you *wait* for the revelation of our Lord Jesus Christ" (italics added). Paul utilizes this verb only in relation to eschatology as in anticipating the end (i.e., Rom 8:19, 23, 25; 1 Cor 1:7; Gal 5:5; Phil 3:20).[18] The second is *ekdechomai*, and it denotes to "receive from another," "expect," "look for," "wait for," or "wait." Paul uses *ekdechomai* in 11:33 in reference to partaking of the Lord's Supper: "So then, my brothers and sisters, when you come together to eat, *wait* for one another" (italics added). *Ekdechomai* is also translated *expect* when speaking of Timothy in 16:11: "So then, let no one treat him with contempt. But send him on his way in peace so that he may come to me. For I am *expecting* him with the brothers" (italics added).[19] I will later discuss in more detail how *ekdechomai* is used in 11:33, linking it to embodied eschatological waiting.

The Corinthian Thread of Waiting and Eschatology

Having clarified the words "waiting" and "eschatology," I now move to examining these themes in 1 Corinthians. Overall, this first letter to the Corinthians contains bookends of direct and indirect references to eschatological waiting. Paul begins his letter by explicitly speaking of the

---

15. Smith, *How to Inhabit Time*, 152.
16. Smith, *How to Inhabit Time*, 152.
17. Smith, *How to Inhabit Time*, 149.
18. This is confirmed by Fee, *First Epistle to the Corinthians*, 42n36. Also of note, Heb 9:28 uses *apekdechomai* in an eschatological context.
19. See other uses of *ekdechomai* in Acts 17:16; Heb 11:10; 10:13; Jas 5:7.

Corinthians awaiting the Lord's return in 1:7, and towards the end of his letter (chapter 15) he discusses the resurrection extensively and then closes with a straightforward eschatological reference: "Let anyone who has no love for the Lord be accursed. Our Lord, come!" (16:22). While a word for "wait" is not in 1 Corinthians 15 nor 16:22, an expectation or a hope is clearly found; this glimpse of the believer's future calls for waiting for the time when the Lord will come (16:22) and God will be all in all (15:28). As Smith writes, Christians live eschatologically since we "are a futural people. Every day we pray for God's kingdom *to come*. But as long as we are praying it, it hasn't yet arrived, which means we are also a *waiting* people" (italics in original).[20]

Between the eschatological bookends of 1:7 and 16:22 is an eschatological thread that is visible throughout this first correspondence to the believers at Corinth. The eschatological thread is identified by David Garland when he notes, "Paul plays the eschatological card in every issue he addresses in the letter except the one concerning headdress in 11:2–16."[21] Richard Hays also endorses this view as he perceives that "virtually every page of Paul's letter seeks to reframe the Corinthians' vision of existence within this 'already/not yet' eschatological dialectic."[22] An eschatological theme suggests waiting. The linking of eschatology to the problems in the Corinthian church indirectly communicates their behavior is to imitate their eschatology—it is to be an embodied eschatological waiting, which is an active waiting.

Ciampa and Rosner contribute to the above understanding by associating eschatology with the cross. For them, Paul's message of Christ's "death and resurrection" is an appeal for the Corinthians "to enter the new eschatological age established in and by" Christ. This means that the Corinthians, and thereby all believers, are to live out a life of the cross. This life is "other-person-centered," namely a life of cruciformity.[23] A life of cruciformity is an embodied eschatological waiting as indicated when Paul addresses the current problems of the Corinthian church by speaking of the past (the cross) and the future (the eschaton). By connecting the Corinthians' present problems with eschatology, Paul is calling for

---

20. Smith, *How to Inhabit Time*, 148.

21. Garland, *1 Corinthians*, 17. Keener agrees but adds that even the issue of headdress includes an eschatological reference in 11:10. See Keener, "Overrealized Eschatology or Lack of Eschatology in Corinth?," 43.

22. Hays, *First Corinthians*, 19.

23. Ciampa and Rosner, *First Letter to the Corinthians*, 26.

the Corinthians to live out their future—the coming revelation of Jesus Christ—in the present. By linking the church's issues to the cross of Christ, the apostle is beckoning the Corinthians to mirror in the present a past event—the death of Christ—in and through their relationships. Therefore, the embodiment of their eschatology (the future revelation of Christ) and the embodiment of cruciformity (the past death of Christ) are two congruent avenues to describe how believers are to actively wait in their present community. That is to say, the believers will be living a life of cruciformity like Jesus Christ in the eschaton. Garland provides a list of the issues that are linked to the eschatological theme: "factions (2:6–8; 3:10–15, 16–17), incest (5:5), lawsuits (6:2–3, 9–10), sexual immorality (6:14), marriage (7:29–31), idol food (9:25; 10:11–13), the Lord's Supper (11:26, 32), and spiritual gifts (13:8, 12)." He goes on to note that the list's climax is "the long discussion of the resurrection" (1 Cor 15), ending with Paul's exclamation of 16:22.[24] I highlight below three of the connections between the church's problems and eschatology: factions, sexual immorality, and the Lord's Supper while showing how the influence of culture played a role in these issues.

Factions, Immorality, and the Eucharist, O My!

I begin by calling attention to the possible reason for Paul's emphasis on eschatology prior to highlighting the three issues. Many New Testament scholars maintain that Paul's focus on eschatology was probably evidence of the Corinthians' deficient eschatology as demonstrated in how they excessively mirrored the pagan, non-eschatological culture.[25] Keener supports this view by writing that the Corinthians "interpreted Paul's teachings in light of their own cultural assumptions and more so after his

---

24. Garland, *1 Corinthians*, 17.

25. See Hays, *First Corinthians*, 70; Garland, *1 Corinthians*, 14; Wright, *Resurrection of the Son of God*, 279–80. Other scholars have put forth an alternate theory as to the reason for Paul's eschatological theme. Commentators (such as Thiselton, "Realized Eschatology at Corinth," 510–26; Thiselton, *First Epistle to the Corinthians*, 40; and Fee, *First Epistle to the Corinthians*, 46) have argued that Paul is addressing the Corinthians' *overrealized eschatology*, in which they were living as if Lord Jesus Christ has already come so that Christ's kingdom was already present. Hays offers a definition of *overrealized eschatology* as "a belief that the kingdom of God had already arrived in all its fullness and that they were living already in a state of eschatological blessedness, like angels in heaven." See Hays, *First Corinthians*, 70.

physical departure from them."[26] As Keener explains, the Corinthians' lack of eschatology pointed toward the influence of Greek and Roman philosophy and even some cultural aspects of the Diaspora of the Jews.[27]

Issue 1: Factions

The influence of philosophy particularly appears in the issue of factions. As I mentioned previously, the Corinthians had a modified, ancient rendition of children arguing, "My dad is better than your dad," as they were divided over which teacher was the best (1 Cor 1–4). Oropeza explains that the Corinthians were "scrutinizing preachers," and it is possible that "the faction loyal to Apollos" was more vocal in its criticism (see 1:12).[28] In essence, these personality cults were comparing, contrasting, and competing with each other. Oropeza underscores that criticism was also an issue in the second letter as "certain Corinthians" were displaying "contempt for the apostle's speeches and physical presence (2 Cor 10:10)." Oropeza mentions that such criticism reflected the cultural priority placed on "oratory performances" due to the influence of the "sophists and philosophers who preached publicly" in Corinth.[29]

Not only did the style of speaking influence the Corinthians but so did the teaching of the philosophers. Ciampa and Rosner comment that the philosophers of Stoicism and Cynicism exhorted followers to imagine "oneself to be filled, rich, and reigning," and evidently, the Corinthians had "adopted the inflated self-understanding of pagan philosophy."[30] This causes Paul to write, "Already you are rich! You have become kings without us!" (4:8). Ciampa and Rosner summarize that the Corinthians were boasting about the "wisdom and power" of their favorite teachers and "Paul's deficiencies in these areas."[31] Paul stresses eschatological judgment (3:10–17; 4:4–5) in opposition to the Corinthians' self-aggrandizing. N. T. Wright explains that in light of the eschatological judgment, the Corinthians are to "realize that their posturing, their puffing-up of themselves, are simply a way of reinforcing their standing within the

---

26. Keener, "Overrealized Eschatology or Lack of Eschatology in Corinth?", 43.
27. Keener, "Overrealized Eschatology or Lack of Eschatology in Corinth?", 43–45.
28. Oropeza, *1 Corinthians*, 33.
29. Oropeza, *1 Corinthians*, 33. See also 31.
30. Ciampa and Rosner, *First Letter to the Corinthians*, 179–80.
31. Ciampa and Rosner, *First Letter to the Corinthians*, 70.

present age, while Paul's apostolic labors and the hardships he endures are a sign that he is living at the point where the two ages, the present and the future, overlap and grind together like millstones."[32] The Corinthians' attempts to possess this present age's power and wisdom for the purpose of a higher status or position are not representative of actively awaiting the Coming King. Instead, Wright points out, "they need to be energized by the divine Spirit so that they live in the present age in the light, and by the standards, of the age to come."[33]

Issue 2: Sexual Immorality

Embodied eschatological waiting appears in the issue of sexual immorality in which some believers were having sexual relations with prostitutes (6:12–20). Concerning this matter, Hays perceives the influence of Stoic philosopher Epictetus in the Corinthians' assertion, "I am free to do anything" (v. 12). Such a belief system gave priority to the freedom of the philosopher, and Hays posits that the Corinthians incorporated this belief into the teachings that they received from Paul.[34] In response, Wright views that Paul contends (vv. 13–14) that "what is done with the present body matters precisely because it is to be raised" by God's power. Wright explains that Paul is describing a "continuity between the present body and the future resurrection body," which indicates that what we do with our bodies in the present matters in the future.[35] Once again, this demonstrates an embodied eschatological waiting as believers are to presently live out in their bodies their future life of the resurrected body as they actively wait for the advent of the fullness of God's kingdom.

Issue 3: The Eucharist

The final example of embodied eschatological waiting that I highlight occurs in Paul's teaching on the Lord's Supper (11:17–34). I substantially argued earlier (chapters 2, 3) that the church's partaking of the Eucharist is the embodied telling of the story of Christ's trauma (crucifixion). However, the Corinthian church was not relationally embodying the story they were telling at the Lord's Supper, but rather they failed to embody an

---

32. Wright, *Resurrection of the Son of God*, 286.
33. Wright, *Resurrection of the Son of God*, 286.
34. Hays, *First Corinthians*, 101.
35. Wright, *Resurrection of the Son of God*, 289.

eschatological waiting (this comes clearer in vv. 27–32). I briefly described how the Corinthian culture understood power and how the Corinthians were embodying this understanding as they partook of the Lord's Supper: the rich were shaming the poor at the Lord's Table. Paul was providing the words of institution of the Eucharist to serve as a reminder of the way in which the Lord Jesus had entered into humanity's death experience as an act of ministry. Since God was ministering to the Corinthians in this manner, they were to respond similarly by ministering to others by entering into their death experiences. Despite God's ministry to them, the elite Corinthians' behavior was contrary to Christ's as they exhibited a *power over* rather than a *power with* or *for* the poor. Gorman describes this latter power: "Cruciform love and power are ways of being for others, expressions of commitment to the weak, to a larger body, and to enemies."[36] The rich were to enter into the poor's death experience of lower status without shaming them but rather caring for them. By entering into the other's death experience, believers were participating in God's story through acts of ministry. Now, as Paul concludes his discussion on the Lord's Supper, he points out that to fail to do so has dire consequences.

The apostle begins this section (vv. 27–32) by admonishing that whoever partakes of the Lord's Supper "in an unworthy manner" is liable for Christ's death. Fee notes that Paul is focused on how the meal is being taken, not on the lack of worthiness of the person.[37] Fee believes that Paul's "concern is not simply personal or introspective," which suggests the main issue is overlooked if the Table is viewed "only in terms of our needs and not also in terms of those of others."[38] The apostle then exhorts the Corinthians to examine themselves (v. 28). Fee remarks how such a self-examination, which is to occur each time they take the Lord's Supper,[39] will determine if their behavior toward and treatment of others at the Table testifies to Christ's gospel that "they claim to embrace" (v. 26).[40] If so, they are participating in God's story (not their own) via an act of ministry (an event) by entering into the poor's death experience.

---

36. Gorman, *Cruciformity*, loc. 4141–42.

37. Fee, *First Epistle to the Corinthians*, 560. I am mostly following Fee throughout this section. See Fee, *First Epistle to the Corinthians*, 558–69.

38. Fee, *First Epistle to the Corinthians*, 558.

39. According to Daniel Wallace, the verb for the word "examine" functions as an iterative present imperative, which is a "repeated action"; thus, whenever the Lord's Supper is observed, this examination is to occur. See Wallace, *Greek Grammar*, 722.

40. Fee, *First Epistle to the Corinthians*, 562.

Paul continues by describing their stance and conduct towards others as not discerning the body, resulting in judgment (vv. 29–30). In light of the context, partaking of the Lord's Supper "without careful regard for the body" speaks of the Corinthians' lack of discernment for the corporate body.[41] By not discerning the corporate body, the Eucharist is no longer a meal of mutuality and solidarity but of disparity and divergence. It is no longer a meal with a sense of belonging and inclusivity but of alienation and isolation. Due to a lack of regard for the body of Christ, the Corinthian church is experiencing judgment in their midst: some of the Corinthians have become sick, and some have even died. Such discipline (v. 32) by the Lord appears to be judgment for their refusal to minister to the other by entering into the other's death experience. The wealthy are not treating the poor with respect and honor by recognizing the poor's situation and being present to them in their death experience, the lack of societal honor due to their lower status. Instead, the wealthy are bringing the poor's lack of honor to the fore by treating those of identical status with dignity while shaming those of the lower class. Such behaviors and attitudes—that is, the absence of acts of ministry—are sin (see also Matt 25:41–46).[42] To use Gorman's word, they are being judged for their failure to live a life of "cruciformity."[43]

---

41. I agree with those scholars who perceive that within the context the phrase "discerning the body" indicates the discerning of the corporate body. See Blomberg, *NIV Application Commentary: 1 Corinthians*, 231; Fee, *First Epistle to the Corinthians*, 562–63; Keener, *1-2 Corinthians*, 99.

42. Root writes, "To refuse the acts of ministry—no longer seeking justice and loving mercy (Mic. 6:8)—is to refuse the being of God." Root, *Pastor in a Secular Age*, 253. Root continues by drawing from Ezekiel and the valley of dry bones. He asserts, "Ezekiel knows that these bones of which God speaks are dry because they are not only surely and completely dead but also disobedient. These elect ministers are dry bones because they have sinned. Can dry bones live if they are dead because they are unfaithful? They were not unfaithful at the periphery but at the center, opposing God's ministering nature by being like all the other nations. What if they have denied their ontological state as ministers, by taking on actions in opposition to ministry? Can God resurrect, reversing death and bringing new life to those who have sinned against ministry and turned their back on the God who arrives to save?"; see Root, *Pastor in a Secular Age*, 253. He also states, "Though we die, we are promised new life, not because our own life is so grand, for we all have sinned and denied ministry, refusing and opposing God's being by treating our neighbor as nothing but dry bones. We have denied God, opposing his very being by disobeying his commands and refusing to be our brother's keeper, leaving him for a bone pile where all ministry is lost." Root, *Pastor in a Secular Age*, 256.

43. Gorman says, "In response to the problem at Corinth, the link Paul makes between communion with the Lord and loving communion with others is as creative as it is profound. The Lord's supper is a proclamation of the Lord's death (11:23–26). As such

The significance of embodied waiting becomes particularly apparent in verse 33: "So then, my brothers and sisters, when you come together to eat, *wait for* [or *receive*] one another" (italics added). As mentioned above, verse 33 uses *ekdechomai* rather than *apekdechomai*. Scholars are divided as to the best translation for *ekdechomai*, whether it be *wait* or *receive*.[44] For my purposes, Paul is calling for a living out of both Christ's crucifixion (the past) and Christ's coming (the future) in the present, no matter if the translation be *wait* or *receive*. The past and future tenses are to meet in the present tense through embodiment. Receiving the other includes waiting for the other, and waiting for the other includes receiving. Both are acts of *cruciformity* and *living futurally*, and like the partaking of the bread and the cup, they are to continue as believers actively wait for the Lord's return. A life of cruciformity and living futurally is portrayed as believers "receive," "wait," "accept," or "welcome" (*ekdechesthe*) others (v. 33).[45] That is, the proclamation of the Lord's death and his coming kingdom is not only with the words of institution; it is not only by eating the bread and sipping the cup, but it is also through embodiment—living out the crucified Christ and the future returning Christ by welcoming the other today.

WAITING AS A PENTECOSTAL

I have just described how being a follower of Christ involves the characteristic of waiting as portrayed in Paul's first epistle to the Corinthians. Pentecostals, too, have stressed waiting. As Vondey comments: "The entire tone of Pentecostal worship has been described at times as 'one of waiting.'"[46] My foundation for establishing embodied waiting as a form of healing praxis within pentecostalism is to briefly describe how both historical and contemporary pentecostals accentuate waiting. I begin laying

---

it must reflect the cruciform love of the Lord; otherwise it is a mockery of his death." Gorman, *Cruciformity*, loc. 2736–38.

44. See Oropeza, *1 Corinthians*, 152–57; Winter, *After Paul Left Corinth*, 143–52. A scholar's preference is linked to whether or not *prolambanō* in verse 21 is "to take before another" or simply "to take." In other words, the question remains whether *prolambanō* includes a temporal aspect or not. If it does not include temporality, then *ekdechomai* is translated "to receive." See Talbert, *Reading Corinthians*, 94–100; Thiselton, *First Epistle to the Corinthians*, 898–99; Blomberg, *NIV Application Commentary: 1 Corinthians*, 228–32; Fee, *First Epistle to the Corinthians*, 567–69.

45. Fee, *First Epistle to the Corinthians*, 567–68.

46. Vondey, *Pentecostal Theology*, 62.

this foundation by highlighting how waiting is expressed in the stories of survivors-participants.

Waiting as a Survivor-Participant

Coinciding with Elizabeth's above discussion on instantaneity, survivors spoke about waiting. Frances recounted her waiting to speak in tongues when she was a child, even though she did not receive tongues at that time. Destiny, as a result of being sexual violated, suffers from ongoing PTSD, for which she is "waiting on the Holy Spirit" for direction and healing. Dominique described her prayer life during her healing journey as having occasions when she would "earnestly pray and pray." These instances involved an element of waiting, as she was determined not to stop praying until she sensed God. Dominique said, "It might take awhile, but then when God comes in, when the Holy Spirit moves in, you know he'd done moved in, and you were a lot more lighthearted. You had a clear mind. [It was] not always completely clear, but it was clearer." Dominique's latter comments illustrate a pentecostal practice that has been assigned a variety of labels, including "praying through," "waiting on the Lord," or "tarrying." Dominique's description is explained by Vondey as a "practice" in which there is "an emphasis on sustained prayer until the results of that prayer are manifest[ed]."47 I view this concept of waiting among pentecostals as a foundation for building a helpful healing praxis.

Waiting as an Early Pentecostal

Older pentecostals may recall the frequent usage of the word "tarrying," particularly in relation to lingering at the altar after a Sunday evening service or after a sermon during revival or camp meetings. *Tarrying* is the KJV translation of *kathizō* in Luke 24:49 in which the disciples are instructed to "tarry" (*wait, remain,* or *stay*) in Jerusalem until they "have been clothed with power from on high." David Daniels comments how African American pentecostals assigned "theological significance" to the KJV use of the word "tarrying" by equating it to mean "prayer as waiting on God."48 It is not surprising, then, that Cecil Robeck describes the "tar-

---

47. Vondey, *Pentecostal Theology*, 86.

48. Daniels, "'Until the Power of the Lord Comes Down,'" 178. Similarly, Daniel Isgrigg's study on the reception history of Luke 24:49 underscores that the phrases

rying meetings" to receive the Spirit baptism in the "upper room" of the Azusa Street Mission as lasting "anywhere from several hours to several days" as they waited for God.[49] Important for this study is Castelo's perception that "[t]arrying is an *embodiment* and demonstration of human desire in search of being ordered by God's very presence" (italics added).[50]

In light of the above discussion, it may be said that early pentecostals viewed the call to tarry as a priority to encounter God. Daniels especially affirms this by describing the practice of tarrying as "the core of African American Pentecostal spirituality"[51] that provides a firm basis for the experiences of salvation, sanctification, and Spirit baptism—encounters with God.[52] There are several characteristics of African American tarrying services that are significant for this discussion. Typically, African American tarrying services continue for extended periods of time with an exhortation to continue seeking the Spirit baptism if a person did not experience it. These tarrying services additionally incorporate an embodied, active waiting that includes one's whole being, involving bodily movements such as swaying, kneeling, handclapping, etc. Moreover, African American practices of tarrying are not done in isolation but rather are a communal affair, unlike Dominique's above story of waiting on the Lord.[53] Hence, the community is partaking in God's ministry to the whole being of the seeker. The local church body is participating

---

"tarrying for the baptism" and "waiting on God" were used synonymously. Isgrigg examines eighty instances of Spirit baptism as reported in the *Apostolic Faith* newspaper. See Isgrigg, "How Long Shall We Tarry?," 178–81.

49. Robeck, *Azusa Street Mission and Revival*, 140.

50. Castelo, "Tarrying on the Lord," 50. Isgrigg found in his reception history of Luke 24:49 that the text does not simply engender tarrying to be an aspect "of Pentecostal spirituality" but "an apostolic standard" established by the Lord Jesus Christ. See Isgrigg, "How Long Shall We Tarry?", 180. Yet, similar to the aforementioned research participants, waiting was juxtaposed to instantaneity in early pentecostalism. For example, early pentecostals did not necessarily always wait for the baptism of the Spirit. Isgrigg comments that for William Seymour "receiving the baptism in the Spirit" was not "inherently" an extended process but rather a "properly prepared seeker should have 'no trouble in receiving the Pentecostal baptism.'" Corresponding with Seymour's beliefs, Isgrigg perceives that of the testimonies studied, 45 (56 percent) experienced Spirit baptism "immediately or within the same day." See Isgrigg, "How Long Shall We Tarry?", 184.

51. Daniels, "'Until the Power of the Lord Comes Down,'" 175.

52. Daniels, "'Until the Power of the Lord Comes Down,'" 176.

53. Daniels emphasizes that "tarrying is not a private experience" but "a communal event" that is accompanied by the encouragement and prayers of the congregants. See Daniels, "'Until the Power of the Lord Comes Down,'" 178.

through the power of the Spirit in the ministerial dance of the divine to the seeker's whole person. It is Christ's community who enables the seekers to tarry for extended periods, providing support for seekers to persevere.[54]

According to Daniels, tarrying among African American pentecostals also places prominence on God while the person is actively waiting. This surprised me as I previously understood the focus of waiting to be more anthropocentric, in which the person was responsible to receive from God by preparing the self; hence, lack of receiving meant lack of preparation. While Daniels underscores both human and divine agencies at work, he prioritizes God's initiative.[55] Daniels writes, "Through tarrying, God makes people ready to be encountered by God. The stress falls on God making ready the praying person's whole being, not the person or God making the praying person worthy."[56] That is, the emphasis is on God is God. God is doing the work.[57]

---

54. Isgrigg's study underscores this aspect when he perceives that "the power of tarrying meetings" was not the length of time individuals waited to receive the baptism in the Spirit, but "it was the hunger engendered within a supportive communal environment." This prompts Isgrigg to conclude from his study that since so few receive the Spirit baptism alone, it is important "for 'non-glossolalics' to become initiated into the Spirit-filled life" through "atmospheres in which there is a communal practice of glossolalia and encouragement for believers to seek the baptism." Isgrigg, "How Long Shall We Tarry?", 192.

55. Daniels, "'Until the Power of the Lord Comes Down,'" 179. See also Isgrigg, "How Long Shall We Tarry?", 181.

56. Daniels, "'Until the Power of the Lord Comes Down,'" 180. To gain a fuller picture of the characteristics of tarrying meetings among African American pentecostals, I offer the following extensive quotation from Teresa Reed's portrayal of a typical tarrying service at her church: "[C]andidates who were ready to be filled with the Holy Ghost . . . would gather at the Saturday-night prayer meeting designated specifically for this purpose. Typically, the tarrying service would begin when a song leader initiated a repetitive, call-and-response, congregational song, usually to the accompaniment of hand-claps, foot-stomps, tambourines, drums, and keyboard instruments. To the sound of this music, the 'seekers' would be encircled and encouraged by helpers who assisted with prayer and praise until the achievement of infilling became evident. Often, the text of the opening song would give way to the rhythmic, continual repetition of the phrase 'Thank you Jesus.' After continuous repetition of the phrase, the evidence of the candidate's infilling . . . by the Holy Ghost was in whether or not he or she spoke in tongues. At the conclusion of tarrying service (which usually lasted for hours), candidates were asked to give their testimonies, and the leader judged at that point which cases of infilling were genuine and which were not. Those who had failed to become filled with the Spirit were admonished to return for the next week's tarrying service." See Reed, "Shared Possessions," 15.

57. I am drawing from Root's portrayal of the ministry of Johann and Christoph Blumhardt who taught Karl Barth to embrace "God is God." Root, *Churches and the Crisis of Decline*, particularly chapters 2, 3, 4.

Waiting as a Contemporary Pentecostal

The concept of waiting continues to be a major factor in the lives of pentecostals. Although waiting today may not always be equated with extended times of prayer during services, waiting still happens among pentecostal communities.[58] Luhrmann in her study of Vineyard churches recounts a period of waiting during church services: "On Sunday mornings the band would pause after a few songs and the leader would pray softly into the silence. 'God, we love you so much. Help us to hear you clearly today. Come into our midst . . . Come, Holy Spirit, come . . . Come . . .' And people waited (even the coffee drinkers) to let God come."[59]

Sometimes waiting entails the ability of a person to hold ideas in tension. This tension appeared among pentecostals in Catherine Bowler's research on healing. Bowler's study concentrates on the Victorious Faith Center in Durham, North Carolina, an African American church that adhered to the prosperity gospel. Bowler describes how dedicated congregants prepared themselves for Sunday morning worship by praying and sometimes fasting during the week. She then speaks of how a level of intensity of expectation appeared on Sunday morning, especially for individuals who were "waiting to hear answers to their prayers." Bowler notes that congregants repeatedly heard that God's provisions were directly available to them, yet Bowler perceives that "some language suggested a circuitous route between the waiting believer and his or her personal miracle."[60]

Harris in *God Conversations* includes waiting as a major part of her life as a pentecostal and describes numerous occasions where she has prayed and waited. She incorporates these contemporary experiences of waiting with biblical examples, such as Mary's waiting for three months in her cousin's Elizabeth's home; Hosea's waiting for his wife to return to him; and the Lord's telling Habakkuk to wait (2:2–3). For Harris, waiting is crucial both in listening to God as well as in God's fulfillment of the

---

58. Many pentecostal churches, particularly those of a White, bourgeois ethos, no longer practice an extended time of waiting on the Lord in a communal setting. Poloma and John Green note that many contemporary Assemblies of God churches in the United States have exchanged "extended revival meetings" and "times for 'tarrying' prayer" for abbreviated "services to accommodate time-conscious Americans" despite some congregants' recollection and yearning for a time of "waiting for the Holy Spirit to move in the gathering." See Poloma and Green, *Assemblies of God*, 218, 109.

59. Luhrmann, *When God Talks Back*, 5.

60. Bowler, "Blessed Bodies," 90–91.

promises spoken to her; this kind of waiting resulted in her waiting for weeks, months, or years.[61]

Similarly, a promise was made to survivor-participant Jade at a critical turning point in her healing journey when God spoke to her about waiting. At the time, Jade was lying in a fetal position, experiencing such waves of pain that she believed she was about to die. Amidst this harrowing experience within death's shadow, the Holy Spirit promised her: "If you will wait, you'll see the goodness of God in the land of the living." Jade was unacquainted at that point with Psalm 27:13 from which these words originated. She was also unaware that she could wait or that waiting even existed. But these words of promise cultivated a tiny seed of hope, as Jade thought, "I've not seen any goodness yet, but maybe there is such a thing as goodness." Hope was birthed amid her discovery of waiting when she realized, "Oh, there is something better than just all this pain." Like some of Harris's experiences, Jade's waiting for the fulfillment of a promise has been lengthy. Although it has been a long, hard journey, Jade said, "I now can say that I have seen the goodness of God."

As illustrated by Jade, Harris, and others, waiting remains an integral part of pentecostalism even though it may have shifted in focus among some pentecostal groups through the years. This type of pentecostal waiting, which accompanies hope after having received a promise, may be comparable to the aforementioned embodied eschatological waiting, in which Christians wait for the Blessed Hope. As Smith points out, this hope is "unhurried" and makes space for rest because of a trust that God is moving and acting "even in spite our own labor."[62] In the next section I connect the healing praxis of waiting to storytelling.

WAITING IN STORIES

I turn my attention in this section to a more detailed image of pentecostals actively waiting alongside survivors. By considering the previous explorations, I seek to answer the question, "What does a healing theological praxis of embodied eschatological waiting alongside survivors of sexual violence look like?" Thus, a healing praxis of active waiting, or embodied eschatological waiting, takes into account the matter of time, eschatology/cruciformity, and the championing of God is God. It resists

---

61. See Harris, *God Conversations*.
62. Smith, *How to Inhabit Time*, 169.

Western perceptions of time, namely instantaneity and linearity by accepting how efficiency fails to control time. As such, it upholds hope as it trusts that God is already at work, thereby stressing divine agency over human agency. It seeks to live out in the present both the past event of the cross of Christ and the future event of the return of Christ through relationships, and in so doing so, it enters into the chaos of time and space of survivors in which the past and present are muddled. This calls for emptying self of preconceived timetables, the drive for efficient time. It receives the other by patiently waiting and waits for the other by patiently receiving, which models mutuality, a *power with* the other rather than a *power over*. It attempts to live futurally by entering into the other's losses or death rather than pushing them out of the chaos. Like pentecostals who tarry, it acknowledges God prepares the other, and God is the healer who is already at work both in the other and in me. That is, God is God. It is communal as it waits together for God's intervention. With the above elements in mind, an active waiting that includes these traits is listening. While previously I detailed a praxis of healing alongside the other as embodied listening, I continue here with this theme by emphasizing *to what* pentecostals are to listen, which is stories, and *how long* they are to listen, which entails being in step with the non-linear healing process.

It goes without saying that stories and storytelling are central to pentecostal theology, whether it be personal testimonies or biblical stories, such as accounts from the book of Acts. Therefore, it seems appropriate to employ stories as a means for healing from sexual violence. Stories often push against linearity and instantaneity in the Western concept of time, thereby reflecting an alternate conception of time. Unlike linear time, stories may be characterized as matching the chaotic rhythm of healing from sexual violence. As Ngong remarks, "[S]tories, like life, are often nonlinear."[63] Ngong references African theologian Musa Dube when he notes how "many of the stories that seem to be linear are the stories of the privileged, who often avoid setbacks in life."[64] Likewise, the traditional narrative of the United States and Canada tends to paint life as being formulaic, a self-determined trajectory of success devoid of trauma, and if pain happens to enter one's life, a formulaic resolution may be implemented. This corresponds with a formulaic response some survivor-participants heard, "Since you have prayed, you are healed."

63. Ngong, "No Condition Is Permanent," 34.
64. Ngong, "No Condition Is Permanent," 34.

Survivor-participant Mackenzie described her pastor's wife, who also served as co-pastor, as praying for Mackenzie's healing from sexual violence and then indicating that Mackenzie was now completely healed, much to Mackenzie's annoyance. Survivor-participant Jade talked about having this type of expectation during her healing journey: "When I first began, I thought it would be instantaneous. I thought, 'If I do the things [that] they tell me to do, . . . I'll get better quickly.' Many times, when people prayed with me, I thought, 'Oh, good. This is done. Now I'm healed. Now I can get on with life.'" Unfortunately, healing was not transpiring in the instantaneous manner that Jade and others had believed it would. As a result, pentecostals appeared to become upset with her when they said, "Oh, you're not doing it right. You're not trusting God enough. You're letting your emotions control you." This illustrates how conservative, White evangelicals and pentecostals perceive the individual as powerful, with the ability to make choices that garner favorable outcomes in a linear fashion.[65] In contrast to such formulas, stories mirror healing from sexual violence in that they may place events non-sequentially, shifting details around in an infinite number of ways. Ngong validates this view: "Stories can be both past and contemporary at the same time."[66]

The telling of a story is also tailored by the storyteller and/or the audience by eliminating some details in one telling but expanding said details in another. Thus, the details of a story are not always constant but pliable. Such subtractions and additions correspond with the effects of sexual trauma and healing from it since the effects are unpredictable by nature. Ngong supports this characteristic of stories: "Story is therefore a malleable form that may be used to form people who are also seen to be malleable."[67] This also points toward the impact of the audience, be it one person or a group of persons, in how the story is told. Annie Brewster, the founder and executive director of Healthy Story Collaborative, underscores this point: "A sense of shared humanity prevails. Audience members are not simply passive recipients; rather, they enter into the stories as new characters and change the shape of each story going forward, actively engaged in the healing process."[68] Because of the audience,

---

65. I am drawing from Maros, *Calling in Context*, 162. She is pointing out the differences between liberal and conservative Christian views of power; the former underlines social systems and the latter stresses personal power.

66. Ngong, "No Condition Is Permanent," 34.

67. Ngong, "No Condition Is Permanent," 34.

68. Brewster, *Healing Power of Storytelling*, 120.

a story may not only change but also have an everlasting characteristic. Dube explains, "A story may also be told to a group of listeners who add their comments and questions. This makes storytelling itself (and the story itself) a moment of community writing or interpretation of life rather than activity of the teller or author. The teller or writer thus does not own the story or have the last word, but rather the story is never finished: it is a page of the community's fresh and continuous reflection."[69] This, then, is similar to healing from sexual violence, which lasts a lifetime. Like healing journeys, stories are without ending; they may be told and then repeatedly retold in diverse ways, even long after the person's life is over.

Yet, it is not only the story that changes. Both the storyteller and the audience may also undergo transformation. Wendy Ryden witnessed healing transformation when she taught a writing workshop that assisted attendees in writing about their experiences of cancer. She saw how the "audience plays an important role in healing function of illness narratives." She noted that several attendees saw the healing value of the workshop.[70] Arthur Frank argues in his work that a community is created from the telling of stories in relation to illness:

> The claim to speak in one's own voice and tell one's own story is *not*, however, a claim that this story is exclusively one's own. On the contrary, what is claimed is membership in a community of those who share one's story ... Stories are told as claims to membership in communities, but the community is not already there, waiting for the story. Communities are formed out of stories; the story is the reflexive affirmation that a gathering of people *is* a community, or even that two people can become a community. The communal act of telling, hearing, and recognizing a story is how a group becomes a community ... Stories tell individual people's experiences, but in storytelling, individuality folds into community (italics in original).[71]

Therefore, listening to stories is not a form of passive waiting, but active waiting. Active waiting, or an embodied eschatological waiting, calls for listening with one's whole being, discerning what is transpiring in the storyteller, the storylistener, and in the space between them. Active waiting strives to maintain a stance of humility as the audience embodies the posture of learning. This type of waiting seeks to be taught

---

69. Dube, "Introduction," 3.
70. Ryden, "Stories of Illness and Bereavement," 72.
71. Frank, "Enacting Illness Stories," 36–37.

by survivors (as will be discussed in the next chapter) as they tell the stories of their journeys towards healing. This willingness to learn is an approach to active waiting that communicates patience and stands in contrast to tapping one's fingers and looking at the clock, which are common mannerisms of passive waiting that communicate impatience. The listener takes on a kenotic attitude, emptying self of any time-focused agenda, in order to unite with and learn from the survivor. Like a child, who desires to hear the same story repeatedly, listeners clothe themselves in this childlike frame of mind and actively wait by patiently listening as stories from the healing narrative are told and retold. As stories are repeated, both the storyteller and storylistener learn and thereby are transformed. Active waiting, then, is neither Pelagian acts of dispensing advice nor the making of plans but embodied patience that is welcoming, a good host to the stories.

CONCLUSION

In this chapter, I have taken the experiences of pentecostal survivors and counselors and combined them with culture, Scripture, theology, and psychology to form an embodied healing praxis of waiting. It could be said that a depiction of active waiting, or embodied eschatological waiting, within a community is seen in the apostle's description of love (1 Cor 13). Love is characterized as patient and kind as they wait together rather than bragging or being puffed up, which mirrors the philosophies of Stoicism, Cynicism, or American-can-doism. It is not self-serving like those who participate in inappropriate sexual relations or sexual violence, and neither is it rude by not waiting nor receiving each other during the partaking of the Eucharist. Instead, they wait for the Spirit's baptism or supportively wait with a survivor for healing. Love is displayed in an attitude of mutuality within the community by suffering and rejoicing with one another, no matter if one is rich/poor, baptized/not baptized, or healed/hurting. Drawing from Smith, embodied eschatological waiting is the practice of "a theology of public life, the life we share in common in the meantime."[72]

---

72. Smith, *How to Inhabit Time*, 155.

8

Learn from My Story

I think educating is super important.

—Kiley, a counselor-participant

If they don't already know this, how prevalent [sexual violence] is [and] to get trained on trauma informed care.

—Dayton, a counselor-participant

We need to do just a better job of being able to even understand the complexities of trauma. Go read about it. Go learn about it. Ask questions. Because the more you educate yourself, when you encounter it, the more you . . . [will] be able to offer.

—Megan, a counselor-participant

Survivor-participant Frances taught me about being more circumspect in how I present God, holiness, sexuality, and the cross to others if I am to help form a safe place for survivors. Frances was introduced to pentecostalism at approximately seven years of age when her family began attending a pentecostal church. Although her family had stopped attending by the time she was twelve years of age, she continued going, particularly to youth group. When she described attending the church, she recalled having experiences with God, such as going to the altar and being slain in the Spirit. But church was not the only place she experienced God. She talked about always feeling a connection to God. For instance, she was quite young when she sensed a big warm hand of God holding her while she was praying beside her bed. Thus, Frances said that experiencing God was something "I always felt connected to, but my church just made it so scary." Frances heard a "really strong fear message" at the pentecostal church so that when she prayed at the altar to receive tongues but did not, she concluded that there was "something really wrong with" her. By age fourteen, she stopped attending.

As a survivor, she told me how the holiness message was problematic. She received the unintentional message from the church that a person must be holy to receive the Spirit baptism with evidence of speaking in tongues. As mentioned previously (chapter 5), she surmised that she was impure because she did not speak in tongues. She believed, "I was tainted, dirty." In Frances's experience, the pentecostal church carries the idea that holiness is "purity, and if something happens that makes you impure, you can't have a relationship with God." This coincided with the pentecostal message on sexuality. Frances remembered hearing that if she slept with someone prior to marriage, she was similar to "a piece of chewing gum that had been chewed up" before being with her husband. In another analogy, sexual purity was compared to a piece of tape. When tape is first adhered to a surface and then peeled off, it is still real sticky; however, if the tape is used too many times, it loses its stickiness—that is, purity. Unfortunately, these teachings about being sexually pure avoided offering a caveat for those cases where consent was not given; therefore, as a young survivor of sexual violence, Frances inferred she was sullied.

Frances underscored holiness, sexuality, and the cross when I asked her what she desired to say to pentecostal leaders. Concerning holiness, Frances affirmed that holiness is important while also longing for leaders to be very careful as they discussed holiness in combination with sexuality. She cautioned about communicating to youth that if they failed to say 'no' firmly enough, they have disappointed God and damaged their holiness before God forever. She invited leaders to consider the love of God in relation to sexuality rather than conveying fear for being a sexual being. Frances warned leaders about declaring who is considered to be holy and who is not considered to be holy in connection to sexual holiness.

Frances also desires leaders to be careful about how they speak about the cross. She had heard how God poured "out God's wrath on Jesus," which Jesus "took for all of us." This seemed to reinforce her sense of unworthiness, which did not ease her fear of God. Today, Frances's view of the cross indicates God's love for her and her healing. When she was experiencing immense pain, the cross was more than God's knowing about the pain and identifying with the pain, but it was God's taking that pain from her. For Frances, Jesus is the one who takes the pain and makes us new. Jesus restores us through Jesus's own life and death. Frances believes that this is now "the promise of what the Christian community can be," which is healing. And so, she asks: Are we agents of healing? Are we living into this message of healing for people who hurt? Concerning sexuality, how are we talking about it? Are we shaming women, such as the way in which they dress? Or are we being Christ's agents of healing?

⁂

Frances's story invites reflection and transformation, both in the individual and in the church, in order to create a safe place for survivors. The preceding two chapters discussed the pentecostal healing praxes of listening and waiting. These praxes are not an end in and of themselves, but embodied listening and embodied waiting may lead to embodied learning. When speaking of learning, I am not referring to a style of learning that occurs as if I am depositing propositional knowledge from my brain into yours. Neither am I discussing survivors' conducting a lecture on healing and sexual violence. Instead, I am referring to a multi-faceted style of learning that impacts all of me. This style of learning involves embracing the praxes of listening and waiting. As I actively engage in the praxes of listening and waiting, I may simultaneously deepen my ability to listen and wait as I increasingly fine tune (learn) how to listen and wait through my practice of it. At the same time, through my listening and waiting, I am learning about (or being trained in) sexual violence and how survivors heal. Thus, as we listen to and wait with survivors in an embodied way, we open ourselves to embody learning. We may learn about God and how God heals others and who God is. We may learn how to respond to survivors of sexual violence. We may learn about ourselves and experience healing in ourselves, involving our own transformation. It may even be said that this entire book is an opportunity for embodied learning, which is transformative. While each chapter pursues transformation among pentecostals and in the church in how we respond to survivors and sexual violence, this chapter is more direct in its focus in this regard with an emphasis on praxis. After highlighting the perspectives of the participants, I set forth a pentecostal praxis of embodied learning by: (1) employing elements from Jack Mezirow's transformative learning theory; (2) demonstrating how transformative learning is a characteristic in pentecostalism; and (3) outlining how transformative learning calls for humility in ministry as stressed in 1 Corinthians.

THE NECESSITY FOR LEARNING

My purpose here is to underscore the need for training on trauma and how to care for people with trauma. Stated simply: learn about it. Learning about sexual trauma contributes to our willingness to discuss it in our churches, and this may have a positive impact on a survivor's healing journey. More than one counselor-participant urged pentecostals, especially leaders, to receive training about trauma and how to care for those who have experienced sexual violence. Dayton commented that one of the challenging aspects of his work is "a lack of training and understanding about . . . the impact of . . . [sexual] trauma and what it takes to heal." Without training, potential companions may re-traumatize the survivor by insisting on instantaneous healing (previous chapter). Dayton illustrated how re-traumatization may appear in a survivor: "Well, we said that prayer, and I'm still having these symptoms. I didn't get healed, so God must not love me or is [not] interested in me or is distant from me." Both the pentecostal companion's response and the impact on the survivor depict how "churches just are ill-equipped to provide [the] kind of support that people need . . . People are not trained in just holding presence and listening and holding space, and that's what people need." And, unfortunately, Dayton is "only one of a handful of specialists" in his area. He receives calls every week from potential clients who he is forced to turn away because he does not have the space in his schedule. He pointedly said, "The need is so great, but the church, and even therapists, are ill-equipped to handle it."

Some survivor-participants echoed the counselors' sentiment. Mackenzie said, "If you really want to be Christ, then you need to realize that there are many people in your church who are struggling right now, and you need to be able to minister [to them]." She commented on those who cannot afford to see a counselor by encouraging pastors to consider helping congregant-survivors financially "or at least guide them." Jade appealed to church leaders and non-leaders "to become more educated about the effects of trauma." She mentioned that ministers in her pentecostal tradition who graduated with a Master of Divinity degree have "no idea what to do with trauma. They have no idea what to do with people who've been sexually abused, physically abused, [and] verbally abused. They have no clue what to do." She strongly believes that all pentecostal leaders "should get training in trauma."[1]

Counselor-participant Megan demonstrated the necessity for more training when she spoke about being surprised by "the amount of harm and . . . awful theology that people are offering" in relation to "healing from trauma." She noted how potential companions frequently utilize such clichés as, "God uses everything. Look for the lesson in this," or "God allowed this." Megan agreed that God will use everything, indicating that Romans 8:28 is true; however, if this verse is given "to someone who is in the throes of shock in the midst of trauma," pressure is added. Megan likened it to putting "a weighted blanket on someone," but the person is unable to support it because that person is "already holding so much." In the end, it crushes them. Megan continued, "We can do damage with verses that are true when we misapply them or bring them way too soon." Timing matters. As Megan clarified, "The Bible can be a weapon, or it can be an absolute salve to somebody's soul, depending on how you bring it and when you bring it." Counselor-participant Shauna also said in her advice to church leaders: "Please be mindful of the messages you may be inadvertently giving the survivor, i.e., you may be sharing a truth or a principle." She admits that what the church leader may be "saying is true." However, when "the person is in pain," the "words are often used by the enemy to make the survivor feel condemned/misunderstood/judged, etc." She admits that this may not be the leader's "intent," but "people are especially susceptible to misperceiving our words."

Counselor-participants also urged churches to learn to communicate about sexuality and sexual violence rather than follow the inclination to plug their ears and close their eyes. Kiley referenced this when she advised churches to teach about consent and healthy boundaries in the area of sexuality. She was raised in a pentecostal church culture that was sometimes quite "hierarchical" and "prim and proper" in the way things were done. Unfortunately, this translated into a lack of conversation

---

1. This was supported by Yuvarajan and Stanford who said that among the clergy interviewed, none of the ministers had received training in relation to helping survivors of sexual violence during their educational training to be ministers. Yuvarajan and Stanford, "Clergy Perceptions of Sexual Assault Victimization," 600.

surrounding consent and boundaries, which has an impact on survivors. For Kiley, it is important to train congregants that "if you want to say 'no' to that hug, you can say 'no' . . . Even if Pastor was just up there saying, 'Go give your neighbor a hug,' it's okay."

Megan iterated the call to communicate about sexuality when she highlighted areas where the church could improve: "We need to learn how to talk about sexual assault in more honest ways." The church also needs "to be able to talk about sexuality" in healthier ways that will "really help people." She demonstrated this need when she spoke about the church's tendency to "have a distortion of bodies." This distortion surfaces when women are told that their virginity is "a present to offer" so that if a woman removes the wrapping, she is giving her "husband an unwrapped gift." Megan echoed Frances when she said that one issue concerning these analogies is no one ever considers that the gift may be "unwrapped unwillingly." As a result, a female survivor is only left with the church's message that it is her fault that she is no longer pure.

Megan continued by asserting that if the church is to begin to have "honest conversations" about sexuality, they must "start long before" sexual violence ever happens. She perceives that "the church does a lot of damage [when] the church itself does such a poor job . . . talking about sex." In other words, before sexual violence appears on the church's doorstep, churches must "learn how to talk about it." The church must question, "What messages are we sending about our bodies?" Without healthy, honest, ongoing conversations about sexuality within the walls of the church, a survivor's healing journey may be compounded and lengthened. As a case in point, Megan contends that conversations about sexuality are to include the subject of "arousal structures." When some survivors experience an orgasm or arousal amidst the assault, they unfortunately may think, "Oh, I liked it. I participated. I did something." Megan counters this belief: "No, your body is literally responding the way God designed [it]. It's responding to sensual touch . . . That doesn't mean you're complicit. It means that your body responded in the way it was intended but in the wrong context. Our bodies can't read context . . . That's the brilliance and . . . the stupidity of our bodies. It just responds to stimuli. It can't differentiate where it's coming from. That's the work of the rest of our systems that's able to do that, but our limbic system simply responds to sensual touch. Period."[2]

2. Sarojini Nadar and Johnathan Jodamus put forth a way to discuss sexual ethics within pentecostalism, which tends to demonstrate a body-spirit dualism and

Training is also necessary for the church because believers can be vital in the survivor's healing journey. Megan puts it simply: "Learning how to sit better with people is essential." For Dayton, congregations can be "a critical part" of survivors' healing because congregations "can offer safe spaces and community," which the sexual violation damages within survivors. These safe spaces and community are ways for survivors "to learn how to be safe with another person" and "how to begin to build trust." This means that such a community can be like a "corrective emotional experience" through relationships "with people." Safe communities may help rebuild emotional experiences (e.g., trust) that have been taken from them, robbed, through the sexual violation. Similarly, counselor-participant Shauna describes the role of the companion as "essential." She challenges potential companions to "remove [their] agendas" (such as "immediately trying to cheer them [survivors] up") and become companions "who can sit with them in the pain in a way that offers warmth, connection, and reminds them of their inherent worth apart from their works/performance/right theology." Shauna argues that being present is a "profound change agent" that assists survivors in "restor[ing] their belief that God is good" and that God, too, "sit[s] with them in [their] dark places." She paints a picture of how essential companions are for survivors: "You hold hope for the suffering person, without being obnoxiously cheerful, but gracious, patient, warm and present in a way that instills confidence that they will get through this and [that] they are not alone because you and others ARE there with them in their dark night of the soul" (all caps in original). But this means training, which implies learning.

EMBODIED LEARNING AS TRANSFORMATIVE

Having underscored the participants' insights concerning the need for church communities to learn about sexual trauma and about appropriate responses to survivors, I assert that the idea of training is not foreign to pentecostalism, but that it has been historically, albeit often indirectly, a part of it. Training implies learning, and learning implies the possibility of transformation, a dynamic that is deeply embedded within

---

a puritanical sexual ethic. The authors assert that the pentecostal liturgical practices indicate that the sexual is plentiful, such as Jesus being portrayed as a lover in worship. This opens a door for pentecostals to move towards a more embodied theology and a way to sanctify sex. Nadar and Jodamus, "'Sanctifying Sex,'" 1–20.

pentecostalism's DNA. But in order to first connect learning to transformation, I stress in this section an overview of Jack Mezirow's transformative learning theory along with a description of some of the theory's characteristics and ingredients, which is followed by examples from the participants.

An Overview of Mezirow's Transformative Learning Theory

If one is to grasp the concept of *transformative learning*, one begins by distinguishing it from *learning*. According to educator Patricia Cranton, sociologist Jack Mezirow believed that learning can transpire when one acquires "new knowledge" or expands one's "existing knowledge without calling into question any previously held assumptions or beliefs."[3] Learning is when I take in recently discovered information and insert it into my prior understanding or expectations. I am merely adding to my habituated assumptions or perceptions. An analogy may be adding salt to an old family recipe for tomato pizza sauce, an ingredient which only enhances the flavor without changing the basic recipe. Or it may be like an artist who paints a traditional water-color picture of a family farm and later inserts a cloud in the painting, which does not radically transform the artist's rendition. Learning is my putting new information inside my already existing framework of how I believe the world operates. Consider a female survivor who tells her story of sexual trauma to pentecostal congregants. Church members may acknowledge a sexual incident occurred, but they may find fault with the survivor because of their assumption that such things do not happen to good pentecostal women; thus, she must have gone alone to a place at night, or she must have she dressed inappropriately or led him on.

Learning, as described above, differs from Mezirow's transformative learning, which is defined as "*learning that transforms problematic frames of reference to make them more inclusive, discriminating, reflective, open, and emotionally able to change*" (italics in original).[4] Elsewhere, he writes more succinctly that *transformative learning* is "the process of effecting

---

3. Cranton, *Understanding and Promoting Transformative Learning*, 13. Mezirow writes, that learning is "the process of using a prior interpretation to construe a new or revised interpretation of the meaning of one's experience to guide future action." See Mezirow, "Transformative Learning Theory," 22.

4. Mezirow, "Transformative Learning Theory," 22.

change in *a frame of reference*"⁵ (italics in original). This suggests that an individual undertakes a course of action to change one's persistent assumptions, expectations, and impressions about life and how they operate.⁶ In the case of sexual violence, pentecostal congregants may try to push past the ingrained assumptions of their church culture by seeing, listening to, and believing a survivor instead of blaming the female survivor for the sexual violence. As Cranton clarifies, "[T]ransformative learning involves a deep shift in perspective and . . . leads to a way of seeing the world that is more open."⁷ It entails questioning my deeply held beliefs about how the world works. When this shift occurs, I cannot return to my previous view of the world, be it in major or minor ways. My old glasses are no longer helpful to me, prompting me to replace them. Returning to the illustration of tomato pizza sauce, transformative learning could be like reassessing my ancient family's recipe for pizzas that involved the use of a sauce that had been spread on pizzas for generations. Going against tradition, I make a pizza with a creamy, garlic sauce after tasting a pizza without a tomato-base sauce or after experiencing a shortage of tomatoes. Or it could be like an artist being exposed to new information about the farm and other painting styles; therefore, the artist's perception of beauty is altered, causing the artist to paint an abstract picture of the farm.⁸

5. Mezirow, "Transformative Learning," 5.
6. Mezirow, "Learning to Think Like an Adult," 7–8.
7. Cranton, *Understanding and Promoting Transformative Learning*, 13.
8. Mezirow's transformative learning theory came about when Mezirow noticed an unparalleled influx of women, including his wife, pursuing higher education in the 1970s, resulting in his engaging in research to explain this phenomenon. See Mezirow, "Transformative Learning Theory," 19. See also Mezirow, "Conversation at Home with Jack Mezirow." It is also to be noted that since it is an educational theory, Mezirow's theory seeks to cultivate transformation by "teaching for change." See Taylor, "Fostering Transformative Learning," 3. Mezirow discovered a ten-phase process that the women experienced when their prior assumptions and expectations were transformed as a result of their learning. The ten phases are: (1) encountering a disorienting dilemma; (2) undergoing self-examination; (3) engaging in a critical assessment of one's assumptions; (4) recognizing a connection between one's discontent and the process of transformation; (5) exploring options for new roles, relationships, and actions; (6) planning a course of action; (7) acquiring knowledge and skills for implementing one's plan of action; (8) trying on various new roles and evaluating them; (9) building competence and self-confidence in new roles and relationships; and (10) reintegrating new perspectives into one's life. See Mezirow, "Transformative Learning Theory," 19; Cranton, *Understanding and Promoting Transformative Learning*, 16. Mezirow saw that change in the women's perceptions began due to a disorienting event or problem, which was followed by undergoing a self-examination and critically assessing their assumptions. This in turn led to their putting on new lenses with a different outlook and/or new actions.

It could be said about our frames of reference that we are our stories (histories). As an American, my life is shaped by stories from America's past, including the stories of independence and the right to pursue happiness. While these stories mold my understanding of how the world operates, my assumptions will vary from other Americans based on American stories of race, ethnicity, and gender. These latter stories will be influenced by regional stories that stem from being raised in the South or being brought up in the North, East, or West. All of these broader stories of the United States, race, ethnicity, gender, and region are further molded by my own familial stories of multiple generations. Each of these broader to narrower stories influence how I live, what I believe, and how I interpret what happens to me. Unknowingly, I make sense of life and life's experiences by drawing from these stories.

The drawing from our stories was illustrated by counselor-participant Megan in her account of how some pentecostal women interpreted sexual assault. Megan's description portrayed how pentecostal women employed their frames of reference, which particularly included church messages about sex. One message communicated to women was that losing their virginity was like a lollipop that they opened, and somebody else licked it, and they put the wrapper back on and handed it to their husbands. This message may influence unhelpful responses to female survivors, such as survivors needing to repent because they had an affair when they were sexually assaulted.[9] This in turn may lead some survivors, in drawing from their frames of reference, to believe, "If I had an affair, I was complicit," even though mutuality was absent from the sexual violation.[10] Thus, chaos is heaped upon chaos as survivors, who are "in the

---

While many of Mezirow's phases accentuate planning and executing a plan to adopt a new outlook, or action, Cranton comments that more attention is currently being placed on the first three phrases, which focus on a disorienting situation and reflection on one's expectations. See Cranton, *Understanding and Promoting Transformative Learning*, 16.

9. As a case in point, John Wigger reports this transpired with Jessica Hahn after Jim Bakker sexually assaulted her. Wigger, "Jessica Hahn and Pentecostal Silence on Sexual Abuse," 26–30.

10. McFarlane and van der Kolk state, "Traumas provoke emotional reactions in proportion to the degree of threat and horror accompanying them. One way of dealing with these intense emotions is to look for scapegoats who can be held responsible for the tragic event. Family members and other sources of social support can be so horrified at being reminded of the fact that they, too, can be struck by tragedies beyond their control that they start shunning the victims and blame them for what has happened—a phenomenon that has been called 'the second injury' (Symonds, 1982). Many personal testimonies of trauma survivors indicate that not being supported by the people they

throes of trauma," are faced with further pain from which they need to heal. In Megan's words: "It's not okay to put it all on the victim; you have to make room to engage the perpetrator."[11] If the church is to make such a shift, the church must become open to the changing of its expectations about life and how life operates. It is the changing of these foundational expectations that is the focus of transformative learning theory.

As seen above, the theory postulates that each of us has assumptions, expectations, and impressions on which we base our thinking, moods, needs, and automatic responses.[12] They are our filters through which we interpret life's experiences.[13] They are our lenses through which we attempt to navigate the problems that life presents to us. These assumptions, expectations, and impressions are the building blocks of our *frames of reference*, which Cranton calls "habitual expectations." She describes *habitual expectations* as "what we expect to happen based on what has happened in the past," indicating that they are rooted in our experiences from our upbringing, relationships, society, etc.[14] We remain unaware of our internalizing of our frames of reference (habitual expectations) from our family of origin, friends, church, community, and culture, yet, according to Mezirow, we are able to see their results.[15] The effects are seen at work when we are faced with a situation, and we automatically employ our frames of reference to determine our next steps, expecting it to be resolved as it was in the past. This appeared when counselor-participant Dayton spoke of pentecostals who have said to survivors: "We're just going to pray for healing. The Holy Spirit is going to come down and just

---

counted on, and being blamed for bringing horrendous experiences upon themselves, have left deeper scars than the traumatic event itself." McFarlane and van der Kolk, "Trauma and Its Challenge to Society," 27.

11. Studies show that blaming the victim is an ongoing and major part of survivors' experiencing stigma due to sexual violence. Murray et al., "How Can We End the Stigma," 285.

12. Mezirow, "Transformative Learning Theory," 22.

13. Mezirow writes, "Frames filter sense perceptions, selectively shaping and delimiting perceptions, cognition, and feelings by predisposing our intentions, purposes, and expectations." Mezirow, "Transformative Learning Theory," 22.

14. Cranton, *Understanding and Promoting Transformative Learning*, 7. Mezirow offers multiple examples of possible frames of reference: "rules, criteria, codes, language, schemata, cultural canon, ideology, standards . . . paradigms . . . [p]ersonality traits and dispositions, genealogy, power allocation, worldviews, religious doctrine, aesthetic values, social movements, psychological schema or scripts, learning styles, and preference." See Mezirow, "Transformative Learning Theory," 22.

15. Mezirow, "Transformative Learning Theory," 22.

take it away." Dayton continued, "But that's not how trauma works." This "lack of understanding about trauma . . . actually reinforces the trauma on the victim," meaning it "can re-traumatize." Their frames are informing these would-be companions how to "understand" and respond to needs for healing while assisting them in how to explain their world.[16]

Typically, we are inclined to hold to our frames of reference so strongly, that Mezirow says we unknowingly "reject ideas that fail to fit" our assumptions. He explains that we might label the ideas outside our frames as being "unworthy of consideration" as they may be seen as "aberrations, nonsense, irrelevant, weird," or just plain wrong.[17] Maybe the family rejects the using of another kind of pizza sauce, evaluating it as ungenuine, or the artist's family sees the abstract painting of the farm as not art when they say, "A child could do better than that!" Cranton rightly points out that continuing to uphold indefinitely our perspective of "distortions, prejudices, stereotypes, and simply unquestioned or unexamined beliefs . . . is safe,"[18] whereas it is a risk to transform our assumptions and expectations. It is a dive into the unknown.[19]

Incidents in the participants' stories in the preceding chapters illustrate how some potential pentecostal companions maintained their habitual expectations when faced with a problem. I formerly mentioned one of Jade's pastors, who she had approached for prayer in relation to her depression (chapter 6). The pastor responded by unknowingly employing his habitual expectations by saying he had been depressed once and resolved it by choosing not to be depressed, and so should she. He drew from the belief in American-can-doism, which was supported by his own experience. Habitual expectations of how God operates also appeared in some of the survivors' descriptions of how pentecostals responded to their need for healing: "Since we have prayed, you are now

---

16. Mezirow, "Transformative Learning," 5.
17. Mezirow, "Transformative Learning," 5.
18. Cranton, *Understanding and Promoting Transformative Learning*, 18.

19. Consider an example of persons who have not experienced a death of someone close to them. These individuals may hold that mourners quickly return to life as normal, believing that mourners who fail to do so are emotionally unstable or not trying hard enough. While facilitating grief support groups, I have heard mourners say more than once, "I have apologized to my friends for my previous responses when their person died." The participants' disorienting experience of a death of a loved one modified their understanding of grief, causing them to become more open and empathic towards others, showing transformative learning at work.

healed" (chapter 7). Their frames of reference remained unshaken as they grasped dogmatically to the belief: God heals when we pray.

Characteristics and Ingredients of Transformative Learning Theory

If our habitual expectations, like those above, are to change, transformative learning theory contends that several ingredients need to be present. Before mentioning these factors, I draw our attention to some characteristics of transformative learning. Cranton speaks of transformative learning as involving "a process of critically questioning ourselves and the social systems within which we live."[20] It must entail a shift in our habitual expectations if it is to be classified as transformative learning. The circumstances, however, in which this type of knowledge or learning transpires, is an unknown, suggesting that one cannot create a formula as to the kind of learning that will produce transformation.[21] (This coincides with mysticism which believes that we cannot predict or force a divine encounter for God is God.) According to Cranton, Mezirow believed that transformation of our assumptions, expectations, and impressions may happen gradually or developmentally (*incremental*). They may also take place due to a dramatic singular event (*epochal*) or occur from a combination of the two, in which the pronounced event begins the gradual transformational process.[22] Transformation that emerged incrementally, epochally, or in combination was portrayed in the lives of the survivor-participants' shifts in their God images (chapter 5), which I reference here for illustrative purposes only (as this chapter centers on the transformative learning of companions, not survivors). Some survivors, like Jackson, spoke of a developmental transformation in their experiential-relational understanding of God as they shifted from a harsh judge to

---

20. Cranton, *Understanding and Promoting Transformative Learning*, 11.

21. Cranton writes, "As useful as it would appear on the surface to be able to say that 'this is going to be transformative learning' and 'this cannot be transformative,' I think we would do ourselves a disservice to try to define types of learning out of context. We know that transformative learning involves a deep shift in perspective and that it leads to a way of seeing the world that is more open. But we cannot say what kind of a learning experience will promote this shift in perspective in any person or any context." See Cranton, *Understanding and Promoting Transformative Learning*, 13.

22. Cranton, *Understanding and Promoting Transformative Learning*, 56. Cranton writes, "Even if the precipitating event is abrupt, it seems to be followed by a process of unfolding, including critical reflection, discourse, and a conscious revision of assumptions." Cranton, *Understanding and Promoting Transformative Learning*, 56.

a loving God. Others, such as Mackenzie and Dominique, underscored a combination of incremental and epochal learning in which they had mystical experiences while they also studied the Scriptures.

Yet, despite the occurrence of an unexpected event, Cranton notes that an ingredient necessary for transformative learning to occur is *volunteering* to revise one's habitual expectations. That is, transformative learning is not automatic. A disorienting, and perhaps even earth-shattering, event does not always translate into changing one's embedded assumptions. Instead, the element of choice is a determining factor.[23] This means that just because individuals undergo training on sexual trauma, which may disrupt their assumptions about the world or the providence of God, one should not conclude that these individuals will inevitably experience a transformation of their frames of reference. It is much easier to add information to our understanding since transforming it often requires unlearning what we already believe—a far more arduous task. Cranton goes on to point out that while our experiences may provide opportunities to transform our frames of reference (e.g., receiving training on trauma; hearing a survivor's story; a mystical encounter with God, etc.), our experiences must also be accompanied by the ingredient of critical *reflection* for transformative learning to occur.[24]

I believe Megan illustrated the power of volunteering and reflecting when she recommended that potential companions are to "learn how to help people stay in their story." In other words, companions are to learn how to sit with others rather than hurriedly attempt to propel survivors out of their pain. Unfortunately, many would-be companions employ their habituated assumptions by focusing on the survivor's possible long-term gains with clichés like, "Your mess became your message"; "It's now

---

23. Cranton, *Understanding and Promoting Transformative Learning*, 6.

24. Cranton, *Understanding and Promoting Transformative Learning*, 7 and also 25–26. Cranton specifies three kinds of reflection: (1) *content reflection* describes the problem by answering, "What is happening here? What is the problem?"; (2) *process reflection* describes the problem-solving strategies being used by asking, "How did this come to be?"; and (3) *premise reflection* inquires, "Why is this important to me?" See Cranton, *Understanding and Promoting Transformative Learning*, 26–27. This carries some resemblance to Richard Osmer's assertion that practical theology has four tasks: (1) *descriptive* seeks to deeply describe the experience by inquiring, "What is going on?"; (2) *interpretative* reflects on the experience with the aid of science and culture by asking, "Why is this going on?"; (3) *normative* continues to reflect on the experience by drawing from theology and Scripture with the question, "What should be going on?"; and (4) *pragmatic* provides a new action in light of the reflection that wonders, "How might we respond?"; see Osmer, *Practical Theology*.

your testimony"; or "Look for the lesson." In drawing from Ezekiel's valley of dry bones, Megan explained that prior to life's coming into the dry bones, "there is a long season that those bones are still on the ground." In like manner, it is a "healthier process" to allow survivors to "stay on the ground a lot longer" than what either the survivors or potential companions think is "comfortable." *Staying on the ground longer* means that survivors are able "to walk into the stories and look at each individual piece." Survivors need "time to sit with it so that when it does reform, there's actually strength to it." Sitting with it, however, begins with would-be companions who are willing to be transformed in how they accompany survivors and who are willing to reflect on both their previous and new understandings. This in turn allows them stay *on the ground* with survivors. As such, they may no longer push survivors toward a future, but they may respond more like Megan. When Megan sits with survivors, she tells them that they never have to say, "I'm so glad this happened to me, or God ordained this to happen so [that] I would get this revelation or this gift." For her, a survivor is not required to find the lesson in the trauma. She informs survivors, "You never ever have to bless your trauma. Ever. But you can keep any gift that comes out of it." The ability of companions to sit with survivors' trauma, then, is correspondingly teaching survivors to sit and reflect on their trauma. Shauna puts it this way: "As you can sit with him/her, you are helping the individual feel that they can sit with their own trauma."

Moreover, in conjunction with self-reflection, Mezirow saw *dialogue* (discourse that involves "the assessment of beliefs, feelings, and values") as a crucial ingredient if transformative learning was to take place.[25] Conversations in a safe, open, nonthreatening, empathic, and comfortable environment nurture transformation.[26] For me, this is particularly the case when considering the relationality of storytelling and storylistening. Dialogue bolsters the prospect of transforming the church in relation to sexual violence, an aspect of social justice. Dialogue that involves embodied listening to and embodied waiting alongside survivors' stories, which is followed by critical reflection, reinforces the potentiality to challenge and change ingrained assumptions and expectations within pentecostalism in relation to sexual violence, God, and healing. If we as a church are to learn and change, it is imperative that we embody listening to the

25. Cranton, *Understanding and Promoting Transformative Learning*, 19.
26. Cranton believes that dialogue is not a necessary component to the theory. Cranton, *Understanding and Promoting Transformative Learning*, 7.

stories of survivors and embody waiting with survivors while becoming circumspect, both individually and communally. As survivors tell their stories, pentecostal embodied listeners and waiters may learn how their former assumptions about sexuality no longer work in regard to sexual violence and healing from it, and this may transform their habituated pentecostal expectations of healing and caregiving.

I turn again toward the stories of the survivor-participants to be a representation of how transformative learning may emerge in a person's life while reminding the reader that this chapter's focus is on companions. I learned from Elizabeth about one of her earlier expectations: if a person is churched, pure, and a passionate Christ follower, that person is exempt from sexual violence. She now realizes sexual violence can happen to anyone, even those who are passionate for Jesus. She asserted, "Just because we're churched doesn't mean we're exempt."

I learned from Jade about the importance of listening to each other's stories and teaching on sexual violence in the church. As a youth, Jade thought sexual abuse was customary in families until a friend's home environment demonstrated otherwise. Jade said, "I truly believed that what was going on in our home, . . . the sexual abuse between everybody, . . . was just normal. This is what families did. I had no frame of reference to know [differently] . . . until I went to my friend's house." Her friend was an only girl with five older brothers. While staying overnight with her friend, Jade assumed that the friend was being sexually abused by her brothers; however, the friend insisted that those things never happened in her home. Jade thought to herself, "Oh, my God, what goes on in our home is not what happens in everyone else's home." This conveys how dialogue played an important part in Jade's transformative learning. Her story also raises the matter of teaching and discourse on sexual violence within the context of pentecostal churches. Yet, it is important that such dialogue involves the entire body of Christ, males and females. Pentecostal Tanya Riches points out that when issues of gender, intimate partner violence, etc. were openly explored in women's groups in the church while being omitted among congregations as a whole, these issues were amplified as being that of women (they were "'femininized'"), which "reinforc[ed] gender dominance."[27] If issues of sexuality, consent, boundaries, and sexual violence are not presented to the entire church, some congregants may remain unaware of wholesome relationships

---

27. Riches, "Nevertheless, She Persisted," 57.

because they are only acquainted with sexual violence and dominance. It is their frame of reference.

PENTECOSTALISM'S EMBODIED LEARNING

As shown above via transformative learning theory, learning may be connected to transformation, which I believe connects learning to pentecostalism. I refer to this type of learning as embodied learning. By embodied learning, I am emphasizing a learning that changes our being and/or the actions of our community. It is a learning that goes beyond merely cognitive learning. Many of us may remember studying dates, facts, figures, and theories in school in order to inhale them for the purpose of exhaling them on a test, never being forced to recall them again. We may remember information in order to use it in a presentation, soon forgetting it after completing the task. These are examples of cognitive learning, which is disconnected from reflection and action, and therefore not embodied. The type of learning to which I refer impacts the whole being and/or the community as it becomes a part of our actions. It changes us cognitively, psychologically, spiritually, and relationally. Concerning my purposes, transformative learning means we are transformed in how we interact relationally with survivors; how we think about sexual violence and healing from it; how we respond emotionally to sexual violence and healing from it; and how we understand and interact with God. Embodied learning is transformative, which connects it to pentecostalism.

It is not a stretch to say that inherent within pentecostalism is the pursuit of transformation, both personally and socially. Transformation is linked to sanctification, which contains the two elements of being positionally sanctified and progressively sanctified. Warrington describes the latter as "a life of ongoing discipleship, demonstrated by commitment to a transformed lifestyle."[28] Sanctification is a major component of pentecostalism as it appears in the pentecostal five-fold gospel of Jesus as Savior, Sanctifier, Baptizer, Healer, and Coming King. Transformation is important in relation to divine encounters—it is a necessary element in determining whether or not an encounter with God is genuine; without it, pentecostals tend to doubt that the experience with God is real. To this point, a person may hear a pentecostal preacher on any given Sunday call for transformation of the congregants, exhorting them to put off

---

28. Warrington, *Pentecostal Theology*, 206.

the deeds of the flesh. In more recent years, pentecostals are increasingly pursing transformation in society. Donald Miller and Tetsunao Yamamori research the social ministries of pentecostals around the world.[29] Collected essays in *A Liberating Spirit: Pentecostals and Social Action in North America* seek to answer the question of whether or not pentecostals in North America are involved in social issues such as race, ecology, poverty, and justice.[30] Thus, pentecostals are embodying learning through their emphasis on transformation, both individually and culturally.

Furthermore, I stressed in the forgoing two chapters how characteristically pentecostals listen to and wait for God as they long to connect with God. Through their embodied listening and embodied waiting pentecostals desire a connection with the divine. A connection is a sense of aliveness, or an energy, in which one knows that one has been seen, heard, and valued in that moment. When pentecostals embody listening to and waiting for God, who is Holy Other, and they connect with God, they are setting into motion the possibility for embodied learning and thereby transformation. As pentecostals open themselves to listen to God and wait for God, yearning for a connection, they are opening themselves up to learn and be changed. They are humbling themselves by way of embodied listening and embodied waiting while hoping for a connection with their Creator. Through embodied listening and embodied waiting, they are nurturing a welcoming stance. As such, they are inviting God to transform their assumptions and see life and themselves through God's eyes. In short, they are teachable.

The above listening and waiting for a divine encounter has implications for potential companions to survivors. First, teachability, which flows out of embodied listening and embodied waiting, is also essential as a potential companion to survivors. It mirrors professionals in the fields of medicine, psychology, and research who have learned about humanity while learning about the impact of trauma from survivors of sexual violence. Through survivors' telling of their experiences (stories), they have taught professionals about flashbacks, dissociation, anxiety, fear, etc. that result from sexual violence. In response to hearing about these experiences, professionals have developed theories and practices that assist in understanding and moving survivors toward healing, such as EMDR, Internal Family Systems, and various neurological theories (some of

---

29. Miller and Yamamori, *Global Pentecostalism*.
30. Wilkinson and Studebaker, *Liberating Spirit*.

which were discussed in the previous chapters). In this light, pentecostal companions are in one sense returning to school—they are becoming students of the survivors and their humanness.

Second, when potential companions embody listening and waiting, they are nurturing an opportunity for connection with the survivor. As embodied waiting needs embodied listening, so transformative learning requires both embodied listening and embodied waiting. As we listen to and wait with survivors, we are hoping for a connection to transpire in which there is a dynamic that says, "I have just now been seen, heard, and valued!" A connection may lead toward a learning that transforms previously held habitual expectations about the world, ways of understanding, doing, and being. But such transformative learning—embodied learning—requires humility.

LEARNING THROUGH HUMILITY

Thus far, I have outlined how learning may become transformative, a major building block of pentecostalism. I drew from Mezirow's transformative learning theory to stress traits that generate a type of learning that changes us both personally and socially, which I refer to as embodied learning. One caveat is necessary in light of the above discussion. While the praxes of embodied listening and embodied waiting are definitive acts of ministry, the praxis of embodied learning differs in that the praxis is more of a posture of learning—a teachability. This is due to the presence of mystery and unpredictability, the attendants of transformation. As in mysticism, I cannot force transformation to occur. Similar to encounters with God, I cannot determine what will definitely bring about transformation. I can, however, be open. I can cultivate teachableness while choosing to volunteer, reflect, and dialogue to potentially be transformed through learning. This transformative learning, or embodied learning, will challenge our habitual expectations and assumptions, which are unknowingly and unquestioningly accepted. Events, which may or may not be earth-shattering while containing aspects outside our realm of expectations, can be the catalyst to change our frames of reference in relation to God, suffering, healing, humanity, sexuality, violence, etc. By choosing to reflect on our assumptions, expectations, and impressions of others or events of which we have become aware, we may move toward a more open, empathic, and teachable stance. Teachability suggests clothing ourselves in humility, placing ourselves in a position to experience transformative learning. Humility accepts our finitude over and above the can-do-Pelagian attitude that dominates Western culture and influences pentecostalism. To underscore the importance of humility when ministering to the other, I turn towards the first epistle to the church at Corinth.

It is tempting for those of us who are not facing difficulties to display a subtle (and perhaps nonconscious) arrogance of having the answers as we minister to the hurting. Perhaps it emerges because of our belief that we somehow have superhuman powers and can take charge of a situation. If we are the holders of the so-called answer to the problem, we may be convinced that we possess the unknown key to unlock an intervention to save persons from their pain. As such, we may subtly believe we are the bearer of precious knowledge that others are incapable of receiving for themselves. In this case, we view ourselves, instead of the sufferer, as the expert of the sufferer's pain. In our desire to be their savior, we end up wielding power over those who are suffering by quickly supplying advice rather than approaching others with humility that is accompanied by a desire to learn. Some of us may perceive that this is what it means to minister to others: Being ready to dispense our wisdom to solve others' problems. However, I suggest that this may be an *anthropocentric* (a human-centered) approach to ministry rather than *theocentric* (God-centered) perspective, an issue that was surfacing among the Corinthians. Let me be clear: a human-centered approach to ministry is not the same as affirming our humanity. When we genuinely welcome our humanity as pentecostals, we recognize our limitations in that we are created creatures, and this, in turn, moves us toward God, our Creator, in the face of our impossibilities. When our ministry is human-centered, however, we rely on a can-do, we-know-best attitude, acting as if we are the center in our acts of ministry, not God. We might seek to put forth our brand or believe that it is up to us to generate growth and change, either in the individual or the church (I allude to this in the foregoing chapter in relation to eschatology). This advocates self-agency, not divine agency.

The term "anthropocentric" is the word Gorman uses to describe the Corinthians' "understanding of ministry and community," which Paul is seeking to correct in 1 Corinthians 4.[31] Members of the Corinthian church, who are simultaneously immersed in a status hungry, competitive

---

31. Gorman, *Apostle of the Crucified Lord*, 290.

society, are arrogant. As I have discussed earlier, they are boasting about their wisdom, their leaders, their permissive sexual morals, their freedom to eat meat offered to idols, their elite status, their spiritual gifts, and their speaking in tongues. Concerning this lack of humility, two words emerge more than once in this first correspondence to the Corinthians that indicate their vanity. The word translated *proud*, *arrogant*, or *puffed up* (*physioō*) is seen on multiple occasions in this first epistle. Paul uses this word to depict the members of the church at Corinth (see 4:6, 18, 19; 5:2) and to describe the end result of knowledge (see 8:1). He also uses it to show that it is not a characteristic of love (see 13:4). An additional word that speaks of their arrogance is translated *boasting* or *boast*, and it underscores their pride in their flesh (3:21a), in their gifts (4:7), and in their loose morals (5:6). Such boasting implies an unwillingness to learn or to be taught and to assert their own power over others. Paul seems to be calling for humility throughout this letter as displayed through a life of cruciformity, but this call particularly appears as an overarching theme in his discussion on ministry in 3:1—4:21, of which I will briefly highlight some themes contained in these verses.

The background of the issue that is represented in 3:1—4:21 is found at the start of the epistle. The evidence that the Corinthians' view of ministry was anthropocentric is seen in their argument concerning which human leader was better than the other. This is an ongoing issue in the church as contemporary pentecostals have also experienced similar attitudes by following specific charismatic leaders based on which one is deemed more spiritual or more anointed. As previously discussed (chapters 5, 7), divisions emerged as some championed Paul, some Apollos, and some Cephas (1:12, 13). Gorman notes that such "allegiance . . . was typical among disciples of competing teachers in antiquity but which contradicts the gospel."[32] As Gorman mentions, the apostle proffers an alternate perspective to the Corinthians' competitive perception of "human leaders" by presenting a "theocentric tone" in 1 Corinthians 3.[33] Paul continues to address the divisions in 1 Corinthians 3 and 4, in which he writes of jealousy arising in the community. Oropeza notes that the word for jealousy (*zēlos*) carries the meaning of being harmful, not helpful, to others, in that it is "concerned primarily about one's own advancement." It can also imply "competition" that assists "one's group while leading to

---

32. Gorman, *Apostle of the Crucified Lord*, 286.
33. Gorman, *Apostle of the Crucified Lord*, 290.

dishonor others."³⁴ It seeks to get ahead, stepping over and on others in the process, if need be. It is anthropocentric—human-centered and arrogant by refusing to learn from others who are deemed less worthy.

After discussing the proper role and attitude for servant-leaders in the church by using both himself and Apollos as examples (3:5—4:5), which is in contrast to the Corinthians' arrogance, Paul more broadly addresses influencers in the Corinthian body. While Paul started with talking about his own life in these verses, Oropeza asserts that the apostle shifts to all "laborers" in the Corinthian body with the usage of the phrase "each one" (3:10). This indicates that whether they be teachers, leaders, or any influencer of others in the church, each laborer in the Corinthian body is to be attentive "to the way they build up the community in Christ" (3:10). For Oropeza, this also takes into account those who "exercise spiritual gifts that are supposed to edify members."³⁵ Therefore, each one who has any sway over any other is to be humble, recognizing that each one is a participant in God's ministry, building on the foundation of Jesus Christ (3:11). On Judgment Day, it is God who will test the work of each one, not humans, and then it will be clearly revealed to all which works survive (3:12–15).

Paul eventually moves to a call for the Corinthians to be willing to be teachable or learners, not arrogant. The apostle writes, "I have applied these things to myself and Apollos because of you, brothers and sisters, so that through us you may learn 'not to go beyond what is written,' so that none of you will be puffed up in favor of the one against the other" (4:6). Here are two words that are in direct contrast to each other: *to learn* (*manthanō*) and *to be puffed up* (*physioō*). Scholars have wondered and debated about the meaning of the phrase "not to go beyond what is written."³⁶ Whatever the meaning, the Corinthians are to be learners who apply what they have been taught through the example of Apollos and Paul (who are not status-hungry, competitive ministers) rather than being arrogant through their favoring "the one against the other."³⁷

---

34. Oropeza, *1 Corinthians*, 43.

35. Oropeza, *1 Corinthians*, 45–46.

36. Two of the five possibilities introduced by Oropeza are: a saying known by the Corinthians or an earlier citation of Scripture by Paul. Oropeza, *1 Corinthians*, 55. Oropeza believes it is a combination of these two. Keener proposes it possibly carries the idea of, "Do not boast beyond the appropriate station God has given each one." Keener, *1–2 Corinthians*, 45.

37. Oropeza, *1 Corinthians*, 54.

The Corinthians' learning calls for a turning away from their ingrained cultural upbringing of seeking status and power and be transformed by demonstrating a change in their actions. This type of learning seems to be a priority as Oropeza notices that this section contains several "pedagogical words, including the necessity to learn (4:6), tutors (4:15), parental guidance (4:15), imitation (4:16), remembrance (4:17), and teaching (4:17)."[38] By using these pedagogical words, Paul is repeatedly calling for a posture of humility and transformative learning. These are to be portrayed by living out the apostle's example (4:16) rather than living out society's example of boasting. Oropeza outlines the "three rhetorical questions" that Paul asks in 4:7, providing the grounds for their humility:

- "Who regards you to be superior (to others)?" of which the answer is "no one."
- "And what do you have which you did not receive?" of which the answer is "nothing."
- "And, why do you boast as though not the receiver?" of which the answer is, "I should not be boasting; all that I am and everything I receive is a gift from God."

Therefore, they are to shun their being puffed up with pride in relation to others. Instead, they are to humbly realize that everything that they have—their salvation, their knowledge, the manifestations of the Spirit, the church's apostles, pastors, and teachers—are granted by God as gifts, not earned by their own accomplishments.[39] This is a theocentric perspective of ministry.

Theocentric ministry in regard to sexual violence and healing from it contains several qualities, as discussed in the previous chapters. It humbly trusts that God is ministering to survivors as they tell their stories. It validates and normalizes the unique journey of each survivor. It is not fearful when the survivor's God images begin to change. Theocentric ministry seeks to empty the self—it is kenotic. It embraces cruciformity, recognizing this is part of the path toward transformative learning. It admits its own limitations in having the ability to fully understand. It holds that although I have wisdom from my own healing journey, I resist the urge to advise. Instead, I listen and wait while being open to learn—that is, it practices *although x, not y but z*. Theocentric ministry maintains a

38. Oropeza, *1 Corinthians*, 56.
39. Oropeza, *1 Corinthians*, 58–59. The quotation of 4:7 is Oropeza's own translation.

trust that God is God while waiting for healing for the other. It recognizes that I am a participant of Christ's ministry as Christ is the healer, not I. I am not the authority on healing. Healing is God's department. It humbly embraces my own limitations in order to prepare me to learn and thereby becoming open to transformation.

CONCLUSION

Drawing from the participants' perceptions, I have combined the theory of transformative learning, pentecostalism's emphasis on transformation, and Paul's instruction on humility in 1 Corinthians to propose a pentecostal praxis of embodied learning. I opened with the story of Frances, who offered a lens through a survivor's eyes of how it is to hear certain pentecostal messages about God, holiness, sexuality, and the cross. She desired the pentecostal church to learn from her experience and be transformed in order to provide a safer environment for survivors. But such changes imply learning in a way in which transformation is generated. By using transformative learning, this chapter invited pentecostals to consider opening themselves up to changing their own ingrained, nonconscious expectations and assumptions by listening to the stories of survivors. Embodied listening along with embodied waiting may cultivate a soil that creates the possibility for listeners to be transformed in their thinking and responses. I refer to this learning that is embodied as a pentecostal praxis because it is transformative. It presupposes a teachability that clothes itself in humility. As seen in 1 Corinthians, humility is necessary if we are to participate in God's ministry. Paul's theocentric view of ministry is in contrast to the Corinthians' anthropocentric one. An anthropocentric view clings to human status and power. It is revealed when I center on building my own brand or believe that it is up to me to provide a solution to a person's pain. Its focus in ministry is on me and what I must do. It differs from Paul's theocentric view, which has a posture of humility. In such a view, God is the center of ministry, and we are participants in God's ministry. We are participating in God's ministry of seeing, hearing, and believing survivors because, as Elizabeth noted, God sees, hears, and believes them. This implies learning: learning what God is doing in the other, in me, and in the space between us.

9

The Theory of Relational Trauma Training: The Conclusion

You can get to the point where you can say, "It is well with my soul." You can get to that point in your life because it is. It is well. It is well.
—Dominique, survivor-participant

I'm just so different... I feel like I'm more present to my body. I feel that I'm not afraid. I'm open. I talk openly about the fact that I was sexually abused, and so I'm not ashamed of that anymore... I feel that I'm much stronger. I feel that I'm able to solve problems now that before I just believed that all problems were just too big for me.
—Jade, a survivor-participant

The distance in time and coming to grips with the realities of my abuse have helped to mitigate pains even as it has not removed painful memories or fears altogether. Particularly fears for my own children. I find much more freedom now to talk about the abuse without the same levels of shame and guilt.
—Sutton, a survivor-participant

My personal experience is so much more robust because I've had to trust at such a high level. And so emerging from this has been incredible. The truth is that sometimes I have good days, and sometimes I have not so good days ... [but] this is the biggest part that I want to share is there is redemption.
—Elizabeth, a survivor-participant

THE PREVIOUS PAGES HAVE been a journey that we have taken together while correspondingly inviting us to reflect on our future steps as well as to evaluate where we are in the present. The preceding chapters have put forth a pentecostal theological praxis of healing that may be summarized as a theory called *Relational Trauma Training*. It implies that the entirety of this book is a training manual. Thus, when a companion journeys alongside a survivor, the companion is involved in relational trauma training. This theory, which is based on this qualitative study, consists of the act(s) of sexual violence followed by seven healing elements:

- see, hear, and believe;
- survivors tell the story;
- the unique story of healing;
- the story of healing God images;
- healing through embodied listening;
- healing through embodied waiting; and
- story as a way to embody learning.

The theory may be illustrated by using the following diagram:

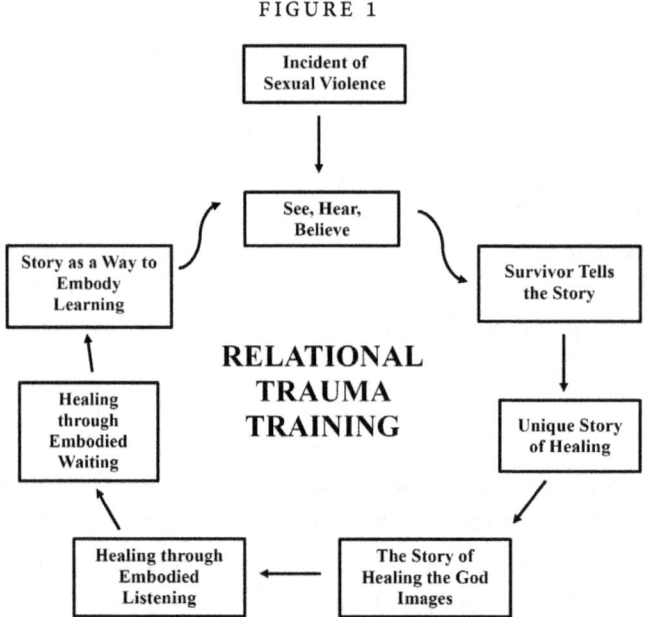

Figure 1. Eight elements of the theory of Relational Trauma Training

The first element is the precipitating act of sexual violence. The next four elements contain characteristics of the survivors' healing journeys, and the last three elements are specific healing praxes in response to the survivors. The theory also includes throughout repeated sub-themes such as relationships, body, and story, indicating a multi-dimensional theory rather than individual elements. Unfortunately, the above diagram is restrictive in its portrayal in that it is slightly misleading in its sequential pattern. While the first aspect, the incident(s) of sexual violence, does not repeat within the theory, the remaining seven healing aspects recur again and again and sometimes simultaneously. The survivor is seen, heard, and believed as the stories are repeatedly told, including the telling of the person's unique journey and of the healing of the relational false images of God. As the companion fully listens to and waits amidst the telling of the stories, the companion to the survivor is potentially taught about sexual violence and healing from it. That is, some companions are embodying learning as they embody listening and waiting. The result: when the survivor is being seen, heard, and believed, it prompts the survivor to retell the stories again, causing elements of the cycle to be repeated. As is the case, the seven healing elements of the theory may not emerge in a predictable sequence even though they are presented above in a circular, set pattern but arise concurrently in a fluid, organic manner.

The three praxes of embodied listening, waiting, and learning are constantly in play alongside the other elements of the journey. These three interlocking praxes are necessary for engendering healing for each part of the survivor's journey. The praxes are first put into action following the event of sexual violence, such as when survivors initially reveal the incident to others and then when they continue to tell the stories again and again. The praxes remain crucial as survivors talk about the unique characteristics of their healing journeys and experience healing of their false God images. The companion's use of the praxes, then, implies that companions are an essential part of the healing journey as the audience plays a needful role in the telling and hearing of the stories. Relationality becomes key in the survivors' healing. Without the companions' listening, waiting, and learning, healing movement does not transpire. One way to illustrate this fluid, recurring dynamic is through a never-ending spiral, which I have attempted to portray here:

218 PART TWO: PROVIDING A SAFE PLACE FOR SURVIVORS

FIGURE 2

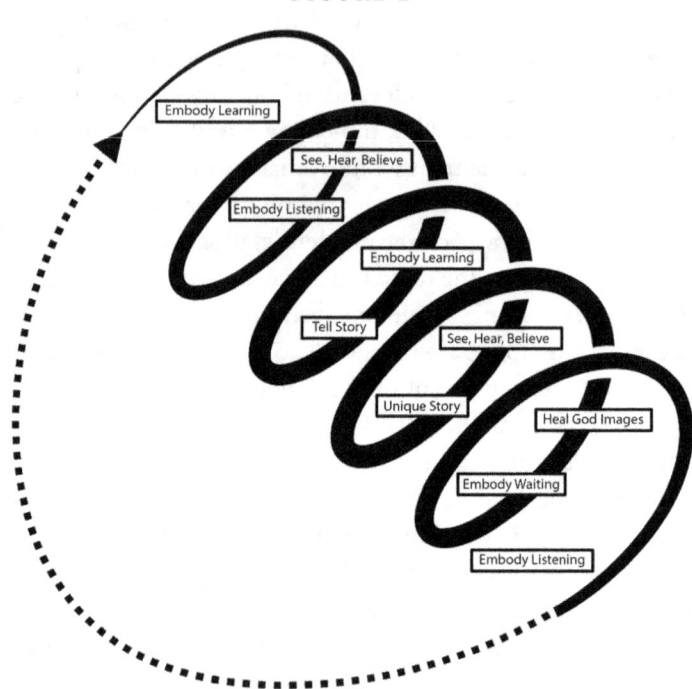

Figure 2. Interconnection of the elements

Within a spiral, the elements of the theory move in and around, folding and unfolding one upon the other. With that being said, in what follows, the theory will be reviewed one element at a time for the purpose of simplification, with the understanding that multiple aspects may be operating concurrently. I begin with the possible elements that are included in the survivor's healing journey, which will be followed by the three praxes of a companion.

WHERE HAVE WE BEEN

The precipitating element, which is the non-repeating element of the theory, is *the act of sexual violence*. This act of violence involves a relationship whether it is with a stranger or a friend or family member. The range of the type of relationship between the survivor and the perpetrator may vary such as: person-to-stranger, a perpetrator who is never seen before or after the sexual violation; person-to-acquaintance, in which only the

THE THEORY OF RELATIONAL TRAUMA TRAINING: THE CONCLUSION 219

perpetrator's name may be known; or person-to-familiar, where the survivor knows the perpetrator well. In the cases of this study's participants, the acts of sexual violence were committed by persons exceedingly familiar to the survivors—they were trusted attachment figures. No matter the type of relationship, however, power is exerted over individuals as they are dishonored by being sexually assaulted. These abusive relationships leave persons shattered to the core, impacting survivors physically, cognitively, emotionally, socially, and spiritually. Nothing of the survivor is left untouched.

If a wound occurs from violence within a relationship, then healing occurs through companioning relationships. The first element named in the diagram is the need to be *seen, heard, and believed*, which demonstrates the importance of relationships. A priority for survivors is to have their experiences of sexual violence acknowledged and their reactions to the sexual violence validated and normalized, not to have their theology corrected nor their response to the violation regulated. Being seen, heard, and believed is connected to recognizing that sexual violence is an issue in our world. Survivors long for their churches, communities, and culture to know about the prevalence of sexual violence. They want people to see, know, and believe the statistics. When survivors are not seen, heard, and believed, further violence is committed on top of the sexual violence. Unfortunately, according to the participants, ignorance about the prevalence of sexual violence is a common feature of the church. As one counselor mentioned, an incongruity exists between the great need and lack of resources in the church. Survivors are in our pews and pulpits. Are we aware of them? Are we creating safe spaces for them?

Since the survivor longs to be seen, heard, and believed, *the story is told*, which is the second element named in the diagram. The story is told both bodily and verbally. The body will tell the story of sexual violence even when the survivor fails to verbally use words. The body remembers. The story told by the body is more implicit, but it is a telling, nonetheless. It may be told through a variety of means, such as strong emotions, nightmares, sleep disturbance, flashbacks, or flight/fight/freeze reactions, which may seem to others as overreactions. To borrow from van der Kolk, *the body is keeping the score* as the story of sexual trauma will be told one way or another.

The longing to be seen, heard, and believed emerges as the survivor *verbally tells another person* about the sexual violation. As humans, we are storied-people. Both the nature of stories and the acts of storytelling and storylistening impart healing to us. Telling and retelling the story is how survivors move towards healing. In short, you must tell it to heal it. For the survivor, it is how the body learns that the person is no longer in danger. If the survivor is not seen, heard, and/or believed in the telling, more pain is inflicted on the wounds. Both implicit and explicit cues by the audience either help the survivor heal or generate more hurt. This telling and retelling of trauma is not foreign to pentecostals, nor to the early church. Believers through the ages have told and continue to tell the story of Christ's trauma on the cross by way of partaking of the Lord's Supper. This telling and retelling by participating in the eucharistic meal is an opportunity to move believers toward healing and wholeness and is to continue until we are completely whole in the eschaton.

Seeing, hearing, and believing involve survivors *telling their unique stories of healing*, the third element named in the diagram. In the same way a single human being is unique, so is each survivor's healing journey. As a unique story, it may contain elements that are similar and/or different from others. Uniqueness may include: the relationship with the perpetrator; the circumstances of the sexual violence; the survivor's unique personality; the survivor's family system; the survivor's gender and gender roles; the survivor's religious/spiritual background; the support system of the survivor; the use of various healing resources; and other miscellaneous factors. There is no basis for competition or one-cure-fits-all because each healing journey is unique. This is similar to the gifts in the body of Christ in which there is no foundation for competition as God has placed each member in the Christ's body as God has determined.

The fourth element named in the diagram that involves seeing, hearing, and believing is the *healing of the survivor's faux images of God*. False gods are those images that we create from our insecure relationships with attachment figures who care for us. We unknowingly place the qualities of those who are wiser and stronger in our lives onto our experiential-relational images of God, creating false images of God. These God images differ from our concepts of God, which are cognitive descriptions that are based on what we were taught about God, such as through doctrinal classes or in church. If any of us are asked to describe God, we draw from our God concepts. We may say, "God is loving, all powerful, and all knowing." However, when difficulties emerge, we often draw from our God images by possibly saying, "God has abandoned me! God is punishing me and hates me!" While God concepts and God images are not as separate and distinct as I have described here, such a separation assists in understanding their definitions. The changing of our unknown God images comes when God enters into our impossibility through a divine encounter and reveals who God truly is.

The next three elements of the relational training theory of trauma are interlocking praxes, which the church and companions to survivors may employ to engender a safe, healing space for survivors. The first praxis that is required for survivors to be seen, heard, and believed is *embodied listening*. The embodiment of listening is a pentecostal characteristic in which pentecostals are in the habit of listening to God who is Holy Other. This may occur individually as pentecostals read the Word or in a church body as congregants become still during worship to listen for God to speak. It transpires in services when pentecostals experience soaking prayer or are being slain in the Spirit. Drawing from this historical pentecostal characteristic, I assert that listening otherwise is a natural part of offering care to survivors for pentecostals. It involves a self-emptying that pentecostals implement in their services and in private prayer times as they listen to God. In a similar way that they attend, observe, and attune to God, this praxis attends, observes, and attunes to survivors. Both of these generate healing movement: first for the pentecostal listening to God and second for the survivor who is being seen, heard, and believed.

Embodied waiting is the second praxis that is needed for survivors to be seen, heard, and believed. Similar to embodied listening, embodied waiting is also a traditional pentecostal characteristic as seen in their waiting on the Lord at the altar and in their waiting for the Lord's Second Advent. As such, embodied waiting in relation to survivors recognizes that complete healing is not instantaneous but will transpire when God's kingdom has fully come. Embodied waiting resists the Western story of time, which includes linearity and instantaneity. Unlike the Western view of time, healing from sexual violence does not follow predictable, sequential paths and neither does it transpire in a flash. Instead, it embraces an active waiting, or an embodied eschatological waiting, that lives out a life of cruciformity. This type of waiting accepts that God is God; is communal in that it waits together for healing; and lives out both the cross (the past) and the eschaton (the future) in the present.

The third praxis that is necessary for survivors to be seen, heard, and believed is the *embodiment of learning*. Such learning means clothing ourselves in humility if we are to be open to transformation. Humility indicates that I am free to be a creature while God is the Creator. I resist attempts to be superhuman in order to be the survivor's savior. Instead, I accept my finitude with humility. If I am to embody learning, I must embody listening and waiting as these praxes are necessary ingredients to foster an opportunity to experience a connection with survivors, which may lead toward transformative learning. As a companion, if my focus remains on the self, my status, and a can-do attitude, I am living out an anthropocentric form of ministry. However, if I welcome my limitations with humility, I nurture a theocentric form of ministry that recognizes I am a participant in Christ's ministry to the survivor. I am humbly accepting my limitations, which include my lack of understanding, knowledge, and power. I then am emptying myself, becoming willing to connect and learn in a transformative way. This type of transformative learning has also been a traditional part of pentecostalism as pentecostals have historically prioritized sanctification—that is, transformation—in the life of the disciple.

A type of learning, which produced change, was suggested by several counselor-participants when I asked, "How has this work changed you?" Joel noted that a portion of this personal transformation was "getting past the mystique" of sexual violence. He told me about the calling of both he and his wife: "God has called us to run towards the people everybody else is running away from." Megan has discovered the privilege and "honor to store people's trauma" in her body, illustrating to me the impact that a survivor's story may have on a companion. In other words, she "make[s] room [within herself] for people who need a safe haven," which is not something she considered at the beginning of her counseling practice. She said, "I actually get to be a container, and I'm a vessel that gets used by God." Kiley implied that she learned more about accepting her humanity, particularly as a person who was driven and a perfectionist, as she has had to learn to practice self-care. It has been a process for her to find more balance in her life. Dayton admitted that not all of the changes in his life are positive. Negatively, he is becoming increasingly cynical of the church because he is "really being exposed to the underbelly of the church and all of its dysfunction and . . . abuses and how they perpetrate abuse generally but sexual abuse particularly." He sees "how people who come with their sexual wounds" have been "treated" in the church, which "reinforces [their] trauma." Positively, he believes that God has generated growth "in the capacity to sit with wherever people are in the midst of their pain and . . . suffering [while] holding space for their emotions and all . . . parts of self, and . . . allowing them a safe place to do that. In that way, I always say I have a front row seat in watching the Holy Spirit show up and do deep inner healing work."

WHERE WE ARE TO GO

After considering this research project, I now invite readers to reflect on, "Where do we go from here?" It is my sincere hope that once individuals have completed reading these pages, this work will continue through a variety of paths. I foresee that the preceding chapters call for a response in at least three ways. First, there is a call to learn about sexual violence and healing from it. While the #MeToo Movement has exposed the epidemic of sexual violence being committed specifically against women, sexual violence is occurring among all types of humans, no matter how they identify themselves. How will the church respond to this exposure of the dark places on which the Spirit is shedding light? It is my hope that we as the church, and pentecostals in particular, will not miss an opportunity to be prepared to point survivors to professional help while being able to offer safe spaces of healing.

In regard to professional help, more than one counselor raised concerns about pastors sending survivors only to counselors who are Christian without placing a priority on whether or not the counselor is trained in sexual trauma. Using parallel reasoning, I doubt few pentecostals have sought out a Christian general practitioner for brain surgery if the recommended brain surgeon was a non-Christian. While persons may be trained in counseling and licensed, individuals who are not equipped to assist with sexual trauma may do more harm. Like medical professionals, counselors have specialties; thus, caution is to be exerted when recommending professional help. Personally, the pace of my own healing journey increased exponentially when I saw a non-Christian counselor who was trained in EMDR while I was also seeing a pentecostal mental health practitioner.

The rationale for pentecostal governing bodies to provide and encourage training on sexual violence and healing from it for pastors, leaders, and congregants involves the practicality of being supportive. It is first a priority to understand the impact of sexual violence so that churches and congregants may be prepared to supply survivors with a list of *qualified* professionals. Understanding the effects of sexual trauma is additionally important because non-licensed professionals (e.g., church leaders or congregants) are highly needful during the healing journey. These persons may offer safe spaces for survivors as well as prayer. Survivors are in our churches. They may be sitting in the pew or standing on the platform. What is being done to support them?

Second, this research project is a call to learn how to listen. When I have taught an online class on pastoral counseling, I have invited students in their video introductions to state what they hope to gain from the class. Inevitably, some students expect to learn the type of advice to express in a pastoral counseling session, such as how to employ Scripture in response to a congregant's problem. This expectation is understandable when it is recognized that culture and the educational system stress speaking, not listening. And if listening is discussed, it is believed to be a gap in the conversation in which I am preparing to give my answer or response. The higher educational system, too, is not immune to a depreciated view of listening. As Lipari suggests, except for specialized fields, such as psychology, a course on listening is usually not required in undergraduate or graduate education.[1] This is evident in the curriculum for degrees in Christian ministry or theology in which course requirements frequently include homiletics, apologetics, and/or evangelism. A student who primarily seeks to become proficient in speaking to congregants during pastoral counseling sessions is more than likely endeavoring to resolve congregants' problems by giving them advice—that is, convince and control them—and therein signaling a need to learn how to listen. Such a student may be surprised, or disappointed, in my course since I have underscored listening, not speaking. Listening involves multiple aspects that include listening to the other and being self-aware of what is happening inside of us. As pentecostals, I have taught that listening includes three aspects: listening to what the Spirit is doing in me; listening to what the Spirit is doing in the other; and listening to what the Spirit is doing in the dance between us.

Third, this book is a call for further research, both quantitative and qualitative. The forgoing chapters are only an introduction to learning about the impact of sexual violence and providing care to survivors. As a

---

1. Lipari writes, "The few domains with a more nuanced approach to listening—such as spiritual traditions and psychological practices—are so small and specialized that the majority of us encounter none of these insights in our everyday experience. Rather, the dominant emphasis in U.S. culture—in education, politics, law, or religion—is on speech and speaking rather than on listening. High schools have debate teams, colleges teach courses in 'Public Speaking,' 'Persuasion' and 'Argumentation.'" Lipari, *Listening, Thinking, Being*, 12.

limited qualitative study, it is inappropriate to generalize the experiences of these participants onto all others. For example, it is possible that not all survivors experience a healing of their God images. It is vital, therefore, to expand the research by testing the results of this limited study by interviewing: more survivors and counselors on the subject of the healing journeys from sexual violence; Christian leaders and congregants about their awareness of sexual violence and providing care for survivors; and organizations who supply healing ministries to survivors. A limitation of this study is it contains participants who are White, middle-class citizens from the United States and Canada. It is essential that further studies include participants of other races, ethnicities, cultures, and economic status.[2]

WHERE WE ARE NOW

Today, the pentecostal church, with its emphasis on healing, has a beautiful and sacred opportunity to participate in Christ's healing ministry in the world with regard to survivors of sexual violence. Let us humbly welcome our humanity and the humanity of others by embodying listening, waiting, and learning to become holy vessels of healing to the broken. As Don MacNeill, Douglas Morrison, and Henri Nouwen write, "Compassion asks us to go where it hurts, to enter into places of pain, to share in brokenness, fear, confusion, and anguish. Compassion challenges us

2. An example of a similar study is Elizabeth Odette Pierre's practical theological dissertation and her article based on her dissertation called "Sexual Violence: The Sacred Witness of the Church," in which she sought to learn "how Black Christian women recover from sexual violence" while she also discovered the church's response to these survivors. Pierre's qualitative study involved five women, a majority of whom were raised in Black pentecostal churches, but only two continued to attend church. Pierre explored how atonement theology operated in these women's lives by seeking to answer, "How does the knowledge of Jesus Christ's death and resurrection affect their healing journeys?" Pierre also uncovered that the women were reluctant to disclose to anyone in the church about their experiences of sexual violence in part because sexual violence was not discussed in their churches. If the participants did speak of it with a person in the church, with the exception of one woman's pastor, the women were not usually supported. Pierre concludes that sexual violence "marked" the participants, which is similar to how Jesus's wounds marked him in order to "demonstrate" to his disciples that "what happened to him was real"; however, as his crucifixion and resurrection were "not the only part of the story," sexual violence was "not the only part of" the participants' stories. "They have experienced healing, joy and deep love from God that resonates deeply within them." See Pierre, "Black Christian Women and Sexual Violence: Caring for the Souls of Survivors," 172. See also Pierre, "Sexual Violence," 362–71.

to cry out with those in misery, to mourn with those who are lonely, to weep with those in tears. Compassion requires us to be weak with the weak, vulnerable with the vulnerable, and powerless with the powerless. Compassion means full immersion in the condition of being human."[3] While this is a conclusion to this book, the reality is: no conclusion exists on this earth in the survivors' healing processes. However, there is hope of healing movement, as illustrated in this chapter's epigraphs, which are a few of the survivors' responses to the question, "How are you different today?" As the survivors continue to experience healing, so also may their companions continue to learn. Survivors and their companions have the opportunity to walk an ongoing path of healing and learning. Since neither of which will conclude until Jesus's reign is fully established in the eschaton, today is our opportunity to participate in this sacred honor of Christ's healing ministry in the world. Let us be a church who is humble, welcoming hosts to the condition of being fully human.

---

3. MacNeill et al., *Compassion*, 3–4.

APPENDIX A

The Process of Identifying, Collecting, and Coding Data

To find participants who were survivors, I relied heavily on postings on social media, websites, and the word of mouth of others. I purposely did not contact survivors but chose to create opportunities for potential survivor-participants to hear about the project and to contact me. To find counselors, I contacted friends, ministers, professors, and counseling centers to inform them about this project. This means that the participants for this qualitative study were not personal friends at the time of the interviews.

When a potential survivor-participant contacted me via email, I sent them a screening questionnaire to verify they met this study's criteria. Each survivor was to be at least thirty years of age; regularly attend a pentecostal meeting or church; have been on a healing journey for more than a year; and be able to identify someone to whom they could turn in case they were triggered. After receiving their screening questionnaire, I arranged for a shorter conversation via telephone or videoconferencing. This shorter conversation provided an opportunity for the researcher and potential participant to become acquainted prior to partaking in an extended interview.

When a potential counselor-participant contacted me via email, I inquired via email about their current practice, training/licensure, and identity as a pentecostal. Potential counselor-participants were to have obtained training to assist survivors of sexual violence; be licensed within their state/region; and consider themselves a pentecostal. When potential counselor-participants met the aforementioned criteria, I invited them to participate in an extended interview.

The interviews for both survivors and counselors were semi-structured with six and four main questions, respectively, and ended with the question: "Is there anything else you would like to tell me?" The participants received the main questions in advance along with some sub-questions to help minimize any uncertainty and to empower the participants. They were also required to sign an informed consent form prior to the interview. The recorded interviews were conducted via videoconferencing (e.g., Zoom) and averaged sixty to ninety minutes in length. One participant chose to answer the questions in writing rather than participate in a formal interview.

I also developed a written survey via Survey Monkey that was available online for approximately four weeks in an attempt to increase the number of survivor-participants. Pentecostal survivors of sexual violence were informed through various posts on social media and other websites of an opportunity to tell their stories via a survey. The survey began with several questions to determine if potential participants met the necessary criteria to participate. If so, individuals were invited to continue with the survey by answering open-ended questions about their healing journeys. If necessary, participants were able to pause the survey and return to it at a later time. The identities of the participants remained anonymous unless they chose to identify themselves. One person qualified and completed the survey as a result of this method.

After I personally recorded and transcribed the interviews, I entered into a detailed process called *coding*. This process involves reading the interviews multiple times to discover the various themes that were contained in the data, out of which categories were formed. These categories have provided the bare bones of the chapters of this book.

APPENDIX B

Interview Protocol for Survivors

1. What does it mean to you to be a pentecostal?
   a. How would you define a pentecostal?
   b. What do you think makes pentecostalism different from other Christian traditions?

2. Describe for me your faith journey.
   a. How was faith viewed and/or practiced in your family growing up?
   b. What is your salvation story?
   c. What have been some of the major turning points in your relationship with God?
   d. What is a story about your relationship/experience with God that stands out to you?
   e. What was/is your family's and/or church's understanding and/or belief about divine healing? About God interacting with the world?
   f. In what ways has your understanding of divine healing shifted during your faith journey?

3. This interview focuses on the journey of healing from sexual violence. However, to discuss a healing journey, there must be something from which to heal. You have already shared some details in the questionnaire. However, is there anything about the sexual violence that you experienced that you desire me to know in order to help me understand your healing journey?

Some of those things may be: your age or the number of years ago; single or multiple incidents; perpetrator being a believer or part of the church; and whether or not you were in pentecostalism at the time.

4. Tell me your story about your healing journey from sexual violence.
    a. How did your healing begin?
    b. What resources were used on your healing journey?
    c. What resources were the most helpful and/or unhelpful on your healing journey?
    d. What were some of the major turning points on your healing journey?
    e. If you were to use a word or phrase to describe your healing journey, what would it be? Why?
    f. What has been most surprising to you on your healing journey? Why?
    g. Describe what has been and/or is the most challenging for you on your healing journey.
    h. How has the pandemic influenced your healing journey?
    i. From the time you purposely began this healing journey, how are you different today?
    j. How would you describe where are you today on your healing journey?

5. Describe how your healing journey has had an impact on your walk with God.
    a. How have you experienced God on this healing journey?
    b. How has your relationship with and/or beliefs about God been influenced during your healing journey?
    c. In light of your healing journey, what is your favorite story in Scripture and why?
    d. How has your pentecostal faith, belief, and/or practices been a help and/or hindrance in your healing journey?
    e. How have other pentecostals been helpful and/or unhelpful on your healing journey?

6. What would you communicate to other pentecostals about sexual violence and healing from it?
    a. What would you say to other pentecostal survivors of sexual violence?
    b. What would you say to pentecostal pastors or leaders about sexual violence?
    c. As a survivor of sexual violence, how would you describe healing to other pentecostals?

7. Is there anything else you would like to tell me?

APPENDIX C

Interview Protocol for Counselors

1. What does it mean to you to be a pentecostal?
    a. How would you define a pentecostal?
    b. What do you think makes pentecostalism different from other Christian traditions?

2. Tell me your story how it is you became a licensed counselor who specializes or helps those who have experienced sexual violence/trauma.
    a. How are you different (personally and/or in your beliefs) since you started or because of this type of work?
    b. What is most surprising to you in this work?
    c. What is most challenging in this work?
    d. What is a key for you in maintaining self-care?

    Other:
    - What have been some of the major turning points in your practice?
    - How have you experienced God in your practice?
    - What is a story about an experience with God amidst your practice that stands out to you?

3. Describe in general the healing journey of pentecostals who have experienced sexual violence.

You may want to consider:
- How do they experience God in their healing journey?
- What is most surprising to them in their healing journey?
- What is most challenging to them in their healing journey?
- How have pentecostal beliefs and/or practices been helpful and/or unhelpful to them?
- How have other pentecostals been helpful and/or unhelpful to them?

Other:
In general, how does their relationship with and/or beliefs about God change during their healing journey?

4. What would you communicate to other pentecostals about sexual violence and healing from it?
   a. What would you say to other pentecostal survivors of sexual violence?
   b. What would you say to pentecostal pastors or leaders about sexual violence?
   c. How would you describe healing of sexual violence to other pentecostals who have not experienced it?

5. Is there anything else you would like to tell me?

Bibliography

Adams, Lucy. "Sex Attack Victims Usually Know Attacker, Says New Study." BBC News. February 28, 2018. https://www.bbc.com/news/uk-scotland-43128350.

Adler, Jonathan M. "Living into the Story: Agency and Coherence in a Longitudinal Study of Narrative Identity Development and Mental Health over the Course of Psychotherapy." *Journal of Personality and Social Psychology* 102 (2012) 367–89.

Adler, Jonathan M., and Dan P. McAdams. "Time, Culture, and Stories of the Self." *Psychological Inquiry* 18 (2007) 97–99.

Adler, Jonathan M., et al. "Narrative Meaning Making Is Associated with Sudden Gains in Psychotherapy Clients' Mental Health under Routine Clinical Conditions." *Journal of Consulting and Clinical Psychology* 81 (2013) 839–45.

Ahrens, Courtney E. "Being Silenced: The Impact of Negative Social Reactions on the Disclosure of Rape." *American Journal of Community Psychology* 38 (2006) 263–74.

Alexander, Kimberly Ervin. "Healing in the History of Christianity." Posted by Fuller Studio. March 31, 2022. YouTube video, 37:46. https://www.youtube.com/watch?v=nR2FsqEQGA0.

———. "'With Blessings They Cover the Bitterness': Persisting and Worshiping Through Brokenness—Pentecostal Women and the Pentecostal Tradition(s)." In *Grieving, Brooding, and Transforming: The Spirit, The Bible, and Gender*, edited by Cheryl Bridges Johns and Lisa P. Stephenson, 135–58. Leiden: Brill, 2021.

Alexander, Kimberly Ervin, et al., eds. *Sisters, Mothers, Daughters: Pentecostal Perspectives on Violence against Women*. Leiden: Brill, 2022.

Alpert, Judith. "Enduring Mothers, Enduring Knowledge: On Rape and History." *Contemporary Psychoanalysis* 51 (2015) 296–311.

Althouse, Peter. "Emotional Regimes in the Embodiment of Charismatic Prayer." In *Annual Review of the Sociology of Religion: Pentecostals and the Body*, edited by Michael Wilkinson and Peter Althouse, 36–54. Leiden: Brill, 2017.

Ambrose, Linda M., and Kimberly Alexander. "Pentecostal Studies Face the #MeToo Movement: Introduction." *Pneuma* 41 (2019) 1–7.

Baldwin, Jennifer. "Akroatic, Embodied Hearing and Presence as Spiritual Practice." In *Sensing Sacred: Exploring the Human Senses in Practical Theology and Pastoral Care*, edited by Jennifer Baldwin, loc. 1758–2111. Lanham, MD: Lexington, 2016.

———. *Trauma Sensitive Theology: Thinking Theologically in the Era of Trauma*. Eugene, OR: Cascade, 2018.

Bamidele, 'Seun. "'There's No Thing as a Whole Story': Storytelling and the Healing of Sexual Violence Survivors among Women and Girls in Acholiland, Northern Uganda." *African Journal on Conflict Resolution* 16 (2016) 35–56. https://www.accord.org.za/ajcr-issues/theres-no-thing-whole-story/.

Beavers, Anthony. "Introducing Levinas to Undergraduate Philosophers." Paper presented at the colloquy of the Undergraduate Philosophy Association, University of Texas, Austin, TX, 1990. https://www.academia.edu/281338/Introducing_Levinas_to_Undergraduate_Philosopher.

Belsky, Jay. "Developmental Origins of Attachment Styles." *Attachment and Human Development* 4 (2002) 166–70.

Bergo, Bettina. "Emmanuel Levinas." In *The Stanford Encyclopedia of Philosophy*, edited by Edward N. Zalta. Fall 2019 ed. Stanford: The Metaphysics Research Lab of Stanford University, 2019. https://plato.stanford.edu/archives/fall2019/entries/levinas/.

Beste, Jennifer Erin. *God and the Victim: Traumatic Intrusions on Grace, and Freedom.* Online ed. New York: Oxford Academic, 2008.

Blomberg, Craig. *The NIV Application Commentary: 1 Corinthians.* The NIV Application Commentary series, edited by Terry Muck. Grand Rapids: Zondervan, 1994.

Bowler, Catherine. "Blessed Bodies: Healing within the African American Faith Movement." In *Global Pentecostal and Charismatic Healing*, edited by Candy Gunther Brown, 81–106. New York: Oxford University Press, 2011.

Brewster, Annie. *The Healing Power of Storytelling: Using Personal Narrative to Navigate Illness, Trauma, and Loss.* Berkeley: North Atlantic, 2022.

Brockington, Guilherme, et al. "Storytelling Increases Oxytocin and Positive Emotions and Decreases Cortisol and Pain in Hospitalized Children." *Proceedings of the National Academy of Sciences* 118 (2021) 1–7.

Brown, Anna. "More Than Twice as Many Americans Support Than Oppose the #MeToo Movement." Pew Research Center. September 29, 2022. https://www.pewresearch.org/social-trends/2022/09/29/more-than-twice-as-many-americans-support-than-oppose-the-metoo-movement/.

Brown, Candy Gunther, ed. *Global Pentecostal and Charismatic Healing.* New York: Oxford University Press, 2011.

Castelo, Daniel. *Pentecostalism as a Christian Mystical Tradition.* Grand Rapids: Eerdmans, 2017. EBSCOhost. https://search-ebscohost-com.

———. "Tarrying on the Lord: Affections, Virtues, and Theological Ethics in Pentecostal Perspective." *Journal of Pentecostal Theology* 13 (2004) 31–56.

Centers for Disease Control and Prevention. "Fast Facts: Preventing Sexual Violence." CDC. https://www.cdc.gov/violenceprevention/sexualviolence/fastfact.html.

Chan, Adrienne S. "Chapter 11: Storytelling, Culture, and Indigenous Methodology." In *Discourses, Dialogue and Diversity in Biographical Research*, edited by Alan Bainbridge et al., 170–85. Leiden: Brill, 2021.

Chan, Sewell. "Recy Taylor, Who Fought for Justice after a 1944 Rape, Dies at 97." *New York Times.* December 29, 2017. https://www.nytimes.com/2017/12/29/obituaries/recy-taylor-alabama-rape-victim-dead.html.

Ciampa, Roy E., and Brian S. Rosner. *The First Letter to the Corinthians.* The Pillar New Testament Commentary. Grand Rapids: Eerdmans, 2010.

Colwell, Kelly, and Sheryl Johnson. "#MeToo and #ChurchToo: Putting the Movements in Context." *Review and Expositor* 117 (2020) 183–98.

Connors, Diane, and Kathleen Stein. "Michael Gazzaniga." *Omni* 16 (1993) 99. https://search-ebscohost-com/.
Cooper, Travis Warren. "Worship Rituals, Discipline, and Pentecostal-Charismatic 'Techniques du Corps' in the American Midwest." In *Annual Review of the Sociology of Religion: Pentecostals and the Body*, edited by Michael Wilkinson and Peter Althouse, 77–101. Leiden: Brill, 2017.
Coulter, Dale M. "The Spirit and the Bride Revisited: Pentecostalism, Renewal, and the Sense of History." *Journal of Pentecostal Theology* 21 (2012) 298–319.
Cranton, Patricia. *Understanding and Promoting Transformative Learning: A Guide to Theory and Practice*. 3rd ed. New York: Routledge, 2023. EBSCOhost. https://search-ebscohost-com/.
Daniels, David D., III. "'Until the Power of the Lord Comes Down' African American Pentecostal Spirituality and Tarrying." In *Contemporary Spiritualities: Social and Religious Contexts*, edited by Clive Erricker and Jane Erricker, 173–91. New York: Continuum, 2001. EBSCOhost. https://search-ebscohost-com/.
Davis, Edward B., et al. "God Images and God Concepts: Definitions, Development, and Dynamics." *Psychology of Religion and Spirituality* 5 (2013) 51–60.
de Haan, Edward H. F., et al. "Split Brain: What We Know Now and Why This Is Important for Understanding Consciousness." *Neuropsychology Review* 30 (2020) 224–33.
DeYoung, Patricia A. *Understanding and Treating Chronic Shame: A Relational/Neurobiological Approach*. New York: Routledge, 2015.
Dictionary, s.v. "cure." v. 2.3.0. Apple Inc. Mac OS. 2005–2022.
Dube, Musa W. "Introduction." In *Other Ways of Reading: African Women and the Bible*, edited by Musa W. Dube, 1–19. Atlanta: Society of Biblical Literature, 2001.
Earle, Mary C. *The Desert Mothers: Spiritual Practices from the Wilderness*. Harrisburg, PA: Morehouse, 2007.
Earls, Aaron. "Churchgoers Split on Existence of More Sexual Abuse by Pastors." LifeWay Research. May 21, 2019. https://lifewayresearch.com/2019/05/21/churchgoers-split-on-existence-of-more-sexual-abuse-by-pastors/.
Ellington, Scott A. "Locating Pentecostals at the Hermeneutical Round Table." *Journal of Pentecostal Theology* 22 (2013) 206–25.
EMDR Institute Inc. "What Is EMDR?" EMDR Institute. https://www.emdr.com/what-is-emdr/.
Engelbert, Pamela F. "If I Had Known Then What I Know Now: Pastoring and #MeToo." *Pam Engelbert: Embracing Absence Encountering Presence* (blog). June 12, 2021. https://pamengelbert.com/2021/06/12/if-i-had-known-then-what-i-know-now-pastoring-and-metoo/.
———. "#MeToo #ShameToo #HealingToo." *Pam Engelbert: Embracing Absence Encountering Presence* (blog). April 17, 2021. https://pamengelbert.com/?s=%23metoo+%23shametoo+%23healingtoo.
———. "Not Tongues but Listening: Moving towards a Pentecostal Embodied Praxis of Suffering." Paper presented at the 51st annual meeting of the Society for Pentecostal Studies, Costa Mesa, CA, March 24–26, 2022.
———. "The Powerful Reality of a System." *Pam Engelbert: Embracing Absence Encountering Presence* (blog). September 7, 2018. https://pamengelbert.com/2018/09/07/the-powerful-reality-of-a-system/.

———. "Tell Me the Story of Trauma: In the Body's Memory, through the Lord's Supper, and from Embodied Members." Paper virtually presented at the 50th annual meeting of the Society for Pentecostal Studies, Dallas, Texas, March 18–20, 2021.

———. *Who Is Present in Absence?: A Pentecostal Theological Praxis of Suffering and Healing*. Eugene, OR: Wipf & Stock, 2019.

———. "The Wounds that Instantaneity Forgot: 'Waiting' as a Pentecostal Praxis of Healing from Sexual Violence." Paper presented at the 52nd annual meeting of Society for Pentecostal Studies, Tulsa, Oklahoma, March 16–18, 2023.

Fee, Gordon. *The First Epistle to the Corinthians*. The New International Commentary of the New Testament, edited by F. F. Bruce. Grand Rapids: Eerdmans, 1987.

———. *God's Empowering Presence: The Holy Spirit in the Letters of Paul*. Grand Rapids: Baker Academic, 2011.

———. *Listening to the Spirit in the Text*. Grand Rapids: Eerdmans, 2000.

Frank, Arthur W. "Enacting Illness Stories: When, What, and Why." In *Stories and Their Limits: Narrative Approaches to Bioethics*, edited by Hilde Lindemann Nelson, 31–49. New York: Routledge, 1997.

French, Haley. "Marginalization at the Altar." Paper presented at the 52nd annual meeting of Society for Pentecostal Studies, Tulsa, Oklahoma, March 16–18, 2023.

Fuller, Melissa L. "Female Sexual Assault Survivors' Perceived God-Image and Identified Psychological Distress." PhD diss., Capella University, 2017. https://www.proquest.com/dissertations-theses/female-sexual-assault-survivors-perceived-god/docview/1883356364/se-2.

Garland, David. *1 Corinthians*. Baker Exegetical Commentary on the New Testament, edited by Robert W. Yarbrough and Joshua W. Jipp. Grand Rapids: Baker Academic, 2003.

Glennie, Evelyn. "Feeling Sound with Evelyn Glennie." Posted by Evelyn Glennie. July 12, 2019. YouTube video, 5:51. https://www.youtube.com/watch?v=Gl2a6w6sTAs.

———. "How to Truly Listen." TED2003. Video, 31:56. https://www.ted.com/talks/evelyn_glennie_how_to_truly_listen.

———. "Listening Is About Looking at a Person." Posted by Skavlan. November 6, 2015. YouTube video, 9:55. https://www.youtube.com/watch?v=VIlfxNHBGE8.

Gorman, Michael J. *Apostle of the Crucified Lord: A Theological Introduction to Paul and His Letter*. 2nd ed. Grand Rapids: Eerdmans, 2017.

———. *Cruciformity: Paul's Narrative Spirituality of the Cross*. Grand Rapids: Eerdmans, 2001.

Gottschall, Jonathan. *The Storytelling Animal: How Stories Make Us Human*. New York: HarperCollins, 2012.

Green, Chris E. W. *Toward a Pentecostal Theology of the Lord's Supper: Foretasting the Kingdom*. Cleveland, TN: CPT, 2012.

Green, Joel B. "Death of Jesus." In *Dictionary of Jesus and the Gospels*, edited by Joel B. Green and Scot McKnight, 146–63. Downers Grove, IL: InterVarsity, 1992.

———. *The Gospel of Luke*. The New International Commentary on the New Testament, edited by Gordon Fee. Grand Rapids: Eerdmans, 1997.

Green, Joel B., and Mark D. Baker. *Recovering the Scandal of the Cross: Atonement in New Testament and Contemporary Contexts*. Downers Grove, IL: InterVarsity, 2000.

Hafemann, S. J. "Corinthians, Letters to the." *Dictionary of Paul and His Letters*, edited by Gerald Hawthorne and Ralph Martin, 164–79. Downers Grove, IL: InterVarsity, 1993. Accordance ed.

Hardesty, Nancy. *Faith Cure: Divine Healing in the Holiness and Pentecostal Movements.* Peabody, MA: Hendrickson, 2003.

Harris, Aisha. "She Founded Me Too. Now She Wants to Move Past the Trauma." *New York Times*. October 15, 2018. https://www.nytimes.com/2018/10/15/arts/tarana-burke-metoo-anniversary.html.

Harris, Tania. *God Conversations: Stories of How God Speaks and What Happens When We Listen.* Bletchley, Milton Keynes: Authentic Media, 2017.

———. "Where Pentecostalism and Evangelicalism Part Ways: Towards a Theology of Revelatory Experience, Part 1." *Asian Journal of Pentecostal Studies* 23 (2020) 31–40. https://www.aptspress.org/wp-content/uploads/2020/02/AJPS-23.1-Full-interior-FEB-21-2020.pdf.

Hays, Richard B. *First Corinthians*. Interpretation: A Bible Commentary for Teaching and Preaching. Louisville, KY: Westminster John Knox, 2011.

Heggen, Carolyn Holderread. *Sexual Abuse in Christian Homes and Churches.* Eugene, OR: Wipf & Stock, 1993.

Heider, Fritz, and Marianne Simmel. "The Heider and Simmel Movie." Published in 1944. Posted by TheIronMagus, on January 28, 2009. YouTube video, 00:1:24. https://www.youtube.com/watch?v=76p64j3H1Ng.

Herman, Judith. *Trauma and Recovery: The Aftermath of Violence—From Domestic Abuse to Political Terror.* New York: Basic, 2022.

Hoffman, Louis. "Cultural Constructs of the God Image and God Concept: Implications for Culture, Psychology, and Religion." Paper presented at annual meeting of the Society for the Scientific Study of Religion, Costa Mesa, California, October 2005.

Houston-Kolnik, Jaclyn D., et al. "Overcoming the 'Holy Hush': A Qualitative Examination of Protestant Christian Leaders' Responses to Intimate Partner Violence." *American Journal of Community Psychology* 63 (2019) 135–52.

Houston-Kolnik, Jaclyn D., and Nathan R. Todd. "Examining the Presence of Congregational Programs Focused on Violence against Women." *American Journal of Community Psychology* 57 (2016) 459–72.

Isgrigg, Daniel D. "How Long Shall We Tarry?: A Reception History of Luke 24.49 in Early Pentecostal Testimonies." In *Receiving Scripture in the Pentecostal Tradition: A Reception History*, edited by Daniel D. Isgrigg et al., 177–93. Cleveland, TN: CPT, 2021.

Johns, Cheryl Bridges. "Grieving, Brooding, and Transforming: The Spirit, the Bible, and Gender." In *Grieving, Brooding, and Transforming: The Spirit, the Bible, and Gender*, edited by Cheryl Bridges Johns and Lisa Stephenson, 7–19. Leiden: Brill, 2021.

Jordan, Merle R. *Taking on the Gods: The Task of the Pastoral Counselor.* Eugene, OR: Wipf & Stock, 2001.

Joy, Emily. "#ChurchToo." *Emily Joy Poetry* (blog). http://emilyjoypoetry.com/churchtoo.

Kearl, Holly. *The Facts behind the #MeToo Movement: A National Study on Sexual Harassment and Assault.* Reston, VA: Stop Street Harassment, 2018. https://www.nsvrc.org/sites/default/files/2021-04/full-report-2018-national-study-on-sexual-harassment-and-assault.pdf.

Keener, Craig S. *1–2 Corinthians*. The New Cambridge Bible Commentary, edited by Ben Witherington III. New York: Cambridge University Press, 2005.

———. *Gift Giver: The Holy Spirit for Today*. Grand Rapids: Baker Academic, 2001.

———. *The IVP Bible Background Commentary: New Testament*. 2nd ed. Downers Grove, IL: InterVarsity Academic, 2014.

———. "Overrealized Eschatology or Lack of Eschatology in Corinth?" In *Scripture, Texts, and Tracings in 1 Corinthians*, edited by Linda L. Belleville and B. J. Oropeza, 43–66. Lanham, MD: Lexington/Fortress Academic, 2019.

Kennedy, James, et al. "Changes in Spirituality and Well-Being among Victims of Sexual Assault." *Journal for the Scientific Study of Religion* 37 (1998) 322–28.

Kennedy, John W. "SAGU Alumna Receives AG Young Influencer Award." SAGU News. August 1, 2019. https://www.sagu.edu/news/sagu-alumna-receives-ag-young-influencer-award/.

Kosarkova, Alice, et al. "Childhood Trauma and Experience in Close Relationships Are Associated with the God Image: Does Religiosity Make a Difference?" *International Journal of Environmental Research and Public Health* 17 (2020) 1–13.

Koyama, Kosuke. *Three Mile an Hour God*. London: SCM, 2021.

Kraus, C. Norman. *Jesus Christ Our Lord: Christology from a Disciple's Perspective*. Rev. ed. Eugene, OR: Wipf & Stock, 2004.

Lartey, Emmanuel Y. "Pastoral Counseling in Multi-Cultural Contexts." *International Perspectives on Pastoral Counseling*, edited by James Reaves Farris, 317–29. Binghamton: Haworth, 2002.

Lee, Morgan. "Max Lucado Reveals Past Sexual Abuse at Evangelical #MeToo Summit." *Christianity Today*. December 13, 2018. https://www.christianitytoday.com/news/2018/december/metoo-evangelicals-abuse-beth-moore-caine-lucado-gc2-summit.html.

Levinas, Emmanuel. "Responsibility in the Face of the Other." My Jewish Learning. https://www.myjewishlearning.com/article/responsibility-in-the-face-of-the-other/.

———. "The Strong and the Weak (English subtitles)." Translated by Salmon Philippe. Posted by Eidos84. June 26, 2011. YouTube video, 7:44. http://www.youtube.com/watch?v=8AGDjpg72ng.

Levine, Peter. *Trauma and Memory: Brain and Body in a Search for the Living Past*. Berkeley: North Atlantic, 2015.

Lipari, Lisbeth. *Listening, Thinking, Being: Toward an Ethics of Attunement*. University Park, PA: The Pennsylvania State University Press, 2014.

Lugo, Luis, et al. *Spirit and Power: A 10-Country Survey of Pentecostals*. Washington, DC: The Pew Research Center, 2006. http://www.pewforum.org/2006/10/05/spirit-and-power/.

Luhrmann, T. M. *When God Talks Back: Understanding the American Evangelical Relationship with God*. New York: Alfred A. Knopf, 2012.

Macchia, Frank D. "Waiting and Hurrying for Cosmic Healing: Implications in the Message of the Blumhardts for a Pentecostal Theology of Divine Healing." *European Pentecostal/Charismatic Research Association*, Mattersey, England, August 1995.

MacNeill, Don, et al. *Compassion: A Reflection on the Christian Life*. Rev. New York: Image-Doubleday, 2005. https://archive.org/details/compassionreflecoooomcne_g4j5/page/n1/mode/2up.

Maros, Susan L. *Calling in Context: Social Location and Vocational Formation.* Downers Grove, IL: InterVarsity Academic, 2022.

McAdams, Dan P. "Narrative Identity: What Is It? What Does It Do? How Do You Measure It?" *Imagination, Cognition and Personality: Consciousness in Theory, Research, and Clinical Practice* 37 (2018) 359–72.

———. "The Psychology of Life Stories," *Review of General Psychology* 5 (2001) 100–122.

McFarlane, Alexander C., and Bessel A. van der Kolk. "Trauma and Its Challenge to Society." In *Traumatic Stress: The Effects of Overwhelming Experience on Mind, Body, and Society,* edited by Bessel A. van der Kolk et al., 24–46. New York: Guilford, 2007.

McKnight, Scot, and Laura Barringer. *A Church Called Tov: Forming a Goodness Culture That Resists Abuses of Power and Promotes Healing.* Carol Stream, IL: Tyndale, 2020.

Menzies, Robert P. *Pentecost: This Story is Our Story.* Springfield: Gospel Publishing House, 2013.

Mezirow, Jack. "Conversation at Home with Jack Mezirow." Mezirow's NYC apartment. Posted by Nancee Bloom, on July 6, 2015. YouTube video, 56:46. https://www.youtube.com/watch?v=iEuctPHsre4.

———. "Learning to Think Like an Adult: Core Concepts of Transformation Theory." In *Learning as Transformation: Critical Perspectives on a Theory in Progress,* edited by Jack Mezirow and Associates, 3–33. San Francisco: Jossey-Bass, 2000. https://espace.cdu.edu.au/eserv/cdu:22788/doc.pdf.

———. "Transformative Learning: Theory to Practice." *New Directions for Adult & Continuing Education,* no. 74 (Summer 1997) 5–12.

———. "Transformative Learning Theory." In *Transformative Learning in Practice Insights from Community, Workplace, and Higher Education,* edited by Jack Mezirow, Edward W. Taylor, and Associates, 18–31. San Francisco: John Wiley and Sons, 2009.

Miller, Donald E., and Tetsunao Yamamori. *Global Pentecostalism: The New Face of Christian Social Engagement.* Berkley: University of California Press, 2007.

Moriarty, Glendon. *Pastoral Care of Depression: Helping Clients Heal Their Relationship with God.* New York: Haworth Pastoral, 2006.

Moriarty, Glendon L., et al. "Understanding the God Image through Attachment Theory: Theory, Research, and Practice." *Journal of Spirituality in Mental Health* 9 (2006) 43–56.

Morton, Nelle. *The Journey Is Home.* Boston: Beacon, 1985.

Murray, Christine, et al. "How Can We End the Stigma Surrounding Domestic and Sexual Violence? A Modified Delphi Study with National Advocacy Leaders." *Journal of Family Violence* 31 (2016) 271–87.

Nadar, Sarojini, and Johnathan Jodamus. "'Sanctifying Sex': Exploring 'Indecent' Sexual Imagery in Pentecostal Liturgical Practices." *Journal for the Study of Religion* 32 (2019) 1–20.

National Alliance of Mental Illness. "Dissociative Disorders." NAMI. https://www.nami.org/About-Mental-Illness/Mental-Health-Conditions/Dissociative-Disorders.

National Sexual Violence Resource Center. "What Is Sexual Violence?: Fact Sheet." NSVRC. https://www.nsvrc.org/sites/default/files/Publications_NSVRC_Factsheet_What-is-sexual-violence_1.pdf.

Nel, Marius. "African Pentecostal Spirituality as a Mystical Tradition: How Regaining Its Roots Could Benefit Pentecostals." *HTS Teologiese Studies/Theological Studies* 76 (2020) 1–10.

Neyrey, Jerome H. *Honor and Shame in the Gospel of Matthew*. Louisville, KY: Westminster John Knox, 1998.

Ngong, David. "No Condition Is Permanent: Time as a Method in Contemporary African Christian Theology." *Journal of Africana Religions* 9 (2021) 21–41.

Osmer, Richard Robert. *Practical Theology: An Introduction*. Grand Rapids: Eerdmans, 2008.

Oropeza, B. J. *1 Corinthians*. New Covenant Commentary. Eugene, OR: Cascade, 2017.

Pattison, Stephen. "Shame and the Unwanted Self." In *The Shame Factor: How Shame Shapes Society*, edited by Robert Jewett with Wayne L. Alloway Jr. and John G. Lacey, 9–29. Eugene, OR: Cascade, 2011.

Pease, Joshua. "The Sin of Silence: The Epidemic of Denial about Sexual Abuse in the Evangelical Church." *Washington Post*. May 31, 2018. https://www.washingtonpost.com/news/posteverything/wp/2018/05/31/feature/the-epidemic-of-denial-about-sexual-abuse-in-the-evangelical-church/.

Pennebaker, James W. "James Pennebaker: Using Expressive Writing to Heal Trauma." Posted by The Weekend University. January 10, 2021. YouTube video, 51:59. https://www.youtube.com/watch?v=CjEroxiXqio.

Pennebaker, James W., et al. "Disclosure of Traumas and Immune Function: Health Implications for Psychotherapy." *Journal of Consulting and Clinical Psychology* 56 (1988) 239–45.

Pennebaker, James W., and Sandra Klihr Beall. "Confronting a Traumatic Event: Toward an Understanding of Inhibition and Disease." *Journal of Abnormal Psychology* 95 (1986) 274–81.

Pentecostal Sisters Too. "A Call to Redeem Our Bodies: Weeping in Sexual Brokenness, Walking in Sexual Holiness." *Everyday Theology* (blog). https://everydaytheology.online/pentecostal-sisters-too/.

Peperzak, Adriaan. *To the Other: An Introduction to the Philosophy of Emmanuel Levinas*. West Lafayette, IN: Purdue University Press, 1993.

Peterson, Cheryl. "Pneumatology in the Time of #MeToo: An Exploration of the Spirit's Role in Suffering." In *Sisters, Mothers, Daughters: Pentecostal Perspectives on Violence against Women*, edited by Kimberly Ervin Alexander et al., 13–32. Leiden: Brill, 2022.

Pierre, Elizabeth Odette. "Black Christian Women and Sexual Violence: Caring for the Souls of Survivors." PhD diss., Garrett Evangelical Theological Seminary, 2016.

———. "Sexual Violence: The Sacred Witness of the Church." *Review and Expositor* 115 (2018) 362–71.

Poloma, Margaret. *Mainstreet Mystics: The Toronto Blessing and Reviving Pentecostalism*. Walnut Creek, CA: Altamira, 2003.

Poloma, Margaret M., and John C. Green. *The Assemblies of God: Godly Love and the Revitalization of American Pentecostalism*. New York: New York University Press, 2010.

Raine, Susan, and Stephen A. Kent. "The Grooming of Children for Sexual Abuse in Religious Settings: Unique Characteristics and Select Case Studies." *Aggression and Violent Behavior* 48 (2019) 180–89.

The Rape, Abuse & Incest National Network. "The Criminal Justice System: Statistics." RAINN. https://www.rainn.org/statistics/criminal-justice-system.

———. "Perpetrators of Sexual Violence: Statistics." https://www.rainn.org/statistics/perpetrators-sexual-violence.

———. "Types of Sexual Violence." https://www.rainn.org/types-sexual-violence.

Raley, Lauren J. "Toward a Pentecostal Ecclesiology: Making Room for Survivors of Gender-Based Violence." In *Sisters, Mothers, Daughters: Pentecostal Perspectives on Violence against Women*, edited by Kimberly Ervin Alexander et al., 207–22. Leiden: Brill, 2022.

Rambo, Shelly. *Spirit and Trauma: A Theology of Remaining*. Louisville: Westminster John Knox, 2010.

———. "Trauma and Faith: Reading the Narrative of the Hemorrhaging Woman." *International Journal of Practical Theology* 13 (2010) 233–57.

Rasar, Jacqueline, et al. "The Efficacy of a Manualized Group Treatment Protocol for Changing God Image, Attachment to God, Religious Coping, and Love of God, Others, and Self." *Journal of Psychology and Theology* 41 (2013) 267–80.

Reed, Teresa L. "Shared Possessions: Black Pentecostals, Afro-Caribbeans, and Sacred Music." *Black Music Research Journal* 32 (2012) 5–25.

Richardson, Ronald W. *Family Ties That Bind: A Self-Help Guide to Change through Family of Origin Therapy*. Vancouver: Self-Counsel, 2012.

Riches, Tanya. "Nevertheless, She Persisted: Freeing Women's Bodies from Silent Theological Sacrifice Zones." In *Sisters, Mothers, Daughters: Pentecostal Perspectives on Violence against Women*, edited by Kimberly Ervin Alexander et al., 49–68. Leiden: Brill, 2022.

Riemersma, Jenna. *Altogether You: Experiencing Personal and Spiritual Transformation with Internal Family Systems Therapy*. Marietta, GA: Pivotal, 2020.

Rimé, Bernard. "Mental Rumination, Social Sharing, and the Recovery from Emotional Exposure." In *Emotion, Disclosure, and Health*, edited by J. W. Pennebaker, 271–91. Washington, DC: American Psychological Association, 1995.

Robeck, Cecil M., Jr. *The Azusa Street Mission and Revival: The Birth of the Global Pentecostal Movement*. Nashville: Thomas Nelson, 2006.

Root, Andrew. *The Church after Innovation: Questioning Our Obsession with Work, Creativity, and Entrepreneurship*. Grand Rapids: Baker Academic, 2022.

———. *Churches and the Crisis of Decline: A Hopeful Practical Ecclesiology for a Secular Age*. Grand Rapids: Baker Academic, 2022.

———. *The Pastor in a Secular Age: Ministry to People Who No Longer Need a God*. Grand Rapids: Baker Academic, 2019.

Rosenthal, Gabriele. "The Healing Effects of Storytelling: On the Conditions of Curative Storytelling in the Context of Research and Counseling." *Qualitative Inquiry* 9 (2003) 915–33.

Rothschild, Babette. *The Body Remembers: The Psychophysiology of Trauma and Trauma Treatment*. New York: W. W. Norton, 2000.

Ryden, Wendy. "Stories of Illness and Bereavement: Audience and Subjectivity in the Therapeutic Narrative." *Storytelling, Self, Society* 1 (2005) 53–75.

Scaer, Robert. *8 Keys to Brain-Body Balance*. New York: W. W. Norton, 2012.

Siegel, Daniel J. *The Developing Mind: How Relationships and the Brain Interact to Shape Who We Are*. 2nd ed. New York: Guilford, 2012.

Smietana, Bob. "Pastors More Likely to Address Domestic Violence, Still Lack Training." LifeWay Research. September 18, 2018. https://lifewayresearch.com/2018/09/18/pastors-more-likely-to-address-domestic-violence-still-lack-training/.

Smith, Ed. "Transformation Prayer Ministry." Sermon preached on Sunday morning. Buffalo, NY. October 2019. Vimeo video, 34:25. https://vimeo.com/371453317.

Smith, James K. A. *How (Not) to Be Secular: Reading Charles Taylor*. Grand Rapids: Eerdmans, 2014.

———. *How to Inhabit Time: Understanding the Past, Facing the Future, Living Faithfully Now*. Grand Rapids: Brazos, 2022.

Smith, Joyce. *Breakthrough: The Miraculous True Story of a Mother's Faith and Her Son's Resurrection*. New York: FaithWords, 2019.

Starks, Sandra, et al. "Gathering, Telling, Preparing the Stories: A Vehicle for Healing." *Journal of Indigenous Voices in Social Work* 1 (2010) 1–18. https://scholarspace.manoa.hawaii.edu/server/api/core/bitstreams/21462fae-d38a-4a9a-a705-90b4da1d7ac1/content.

Stephenson, Lisa P. "Toxic Spirituality: Reexamining the Ways in which Spiritual Virtues Can Reinforce Violence against Women." In *Sisters, Mothers, Daughters: Pentecostal Perspectives on Violence against Women*, edited by Kimberly Ervin Alexander et al., 33–48. Leiden: Brill, 2022.

Sunwolf. "R× Storysharing, prn: Stories as Medicine Prologue to the Special Healing Issue." *Storytelling, Self, Society* 1 (2005) 1–10.

Swinton, John. *Becoming Friends of Time: Disability, Timefullness, and Gentle Discipleship*. Waco: TX: Baylor University Press, 2016.

Talbert, Charles. *Reading Corinthians: A Literary and Theological Commentary*. Macon, GA: Smyth & Helwys, 2002.

Taylor, Edward W. "Fostering Transformative Learning." In *Transformative Learning in Practice Insights from Community, Workplace, and Higher Education*, edited by Jack Mezirow Edward W. Taylor and Associates, 3–17. San Francisco: John Wiley and Sons, 2009.

Thiselton, Anthony C. *The First Epistle to the Corinthians*. The International Greek Testament Commentary, edited by I. Howard Marshall and Donald A. Hagner. Grand Rapids: Eerdmans, 2000.

———. "Realized Eschatology at Corinth." *New Testament Studies* 24 (1978) 510–26.

Torrance, Thomas F. *Atonement: The Person and Work of Christ*. Edited by Robert T. Walker. Downers Grove, IL: InterVarsity Academic, 2009.

van der Kolk, Bessel A. *The Body Keeps the Score: Brain, Mind, and Body in the Healing of Trauma*. New York: Viking, 2014.

———. "The Body Keeps the Score: Brain, Mind, and Body in the Healing of Trauma." Posted by CenterScene, Center for Healthy Communities. May 22, 2015. YouTube video, 1:40:27. https://www.youtube.com/watch?v=53RX2ESIqsM.

van Horne, Faith. "Atonement for Sexual Abuse Survivors: A Pentecostal-Feminist Somatology." Paper presented at the 51st annual meeting of the Society for Pentecostal Studies, Costa Mesa, California, March 24–26, 2022.

van Horne, Faith, and Shane Claiborne. "Trauma, Atonement + Healing." *Red Letter Christians*. September 12, 2022. Podcast, MP3 audio, 28:10. https://redletterchristians.podbean.com/e/faith-van-horne-trauma-atonement-healing/.

Vondey, Wolfgang. *Pentecostal Theology: Living the Full Gospel*. London: Bloomsbury T. & T. Clark, 2017.

Wallace, Daniel B. *Greek Grammar: Beyond the Basics*. Grand Rapids: Zondervan, 1996.
Warrington, Keith. *Pentecostal Theology: A Theology of Encounter*. London: T. & T. Clark, 2008.
Wieskamp, Valerie N. "'I'm Going Out There and I'm Telling This Story': Victimhood and Empowerment in Narratives of Military Sexual Violence." *Western Journal of Communication* 83 (2019) 133–50.
Wigger, John. "Jessica Hahn and Pentecostal Silence on Sexual Abuse." *Pneuma* 41 (2019) 26–30.
Wilkinson, Michael. "Pentecostalism, the Body, and Embodiment." In *Annual Review of the Sociology of Religion: Pentecostals and the Body*, edited by Michael Wilkinson and Peter Althouse, 17–35. Leiden: Brill, 2017.
Wilkinson, Michael, and Peter Althouse. *Catch the Fire: Soaking Prayer and Charismatic Renewal*. DeKalb: Northern Illinois University Press, 2014. Ebook.
Wilkinson, Michael, and Steven M. Studebaker, eds. *A Liberating Spirit: Pentecostals and Social Action in North America*. Eugene, OR: Pickwick, 2010.
Winter, Bruce. *After Paul Left Corinth: The Influence of Secular Ethics and Social Change*. Grand Rapids: Eerdmans, 2001.
Wolfelt, Alan. *Companioning the Bereaved: A Soulful Guide for Caregivers*. Fort Collins, CO: Companion, 2006.
———. *Understanding Your Grief: Ten Essential Touchstones for Finding Hope and Healing Your Heart*. 2nd ed. Fort Collins, CO: Companion, 2021.
World Health Organization. "Violence against Women." WHO. March 9, 2021. https://www.who.int/news-room/fact-sheets/detail/violence-against-women.
Wright, N. T. *The Resurrection of the Son of God*. Christian Origins and the Question of God 3. Minneapolis: Fortress, 2003.
Yonack, Lyn. "Sexual Assault Is about Power: How the #MeToo Campaign Is Restoring Power to Victims." *Psychology Today*. November 14, 2017. https://www.psychologytoday.com/us/blog/psychoanalysis-unplugged/201711/sexual-assault-is-about-power.
Yuvarajan, Elil, and Matthew S. Stanford. "Clergy Perceptions of Sexual Assault Victimization." *Violence against Women* 22 (2016) 588–608.

www.ingramcontent.com/pod-product-compliance
Lightning Source LLC
Chambersburg PA
CBHW050347230426
43663CB00010B/2019